Caring for Family Pets

Caring for Family Pets

Choosing and Keeping Our Companion Animals Healthy

Radford G. Davis, DVM, MPH, DACVPM, Editor

 PRAEGER

AN IMPRINT OF ABC-CLIO, LLC
Santa Barbara, California • Denver, Colorado • Oxford, England

Copyright 2011 by ABC-CLIO, LLC

All rights reserved. No part of this publication may be reproduced, stored in a retrieval system, or transmitted, in any form or by any means, electronic, mechanical, photocopying, recording, or otherwise, except for the inclusion of brief quotations in a review, without prior permission in writing from the publisher.

Library of Congress Cataloging-in-Publication Data

Caring for family pets : choosing and keeping our companion animals healthy / Radford G. Davis, editor.
   p. cm.
   Includes bibliographical references and index.
   ISBN 978–0–313–38527–8 (hard copy : alk. paper) — ISBN 978–0–313–38528–5 (ebook)
   1. Pets—Health. 2. Pets—Diseases. I. Davis, Radford G.
SF413.C375   2011
636.088′7—dc23   2011023361

ISBN: 978–0–313–38527–8
EISBN: 978–0–313–38528–5

15 14 13 12 11   1 2 3 4 5

This book is also available on the World Wide Web as an eBook.
Visit www.abc-clio.com for details.

Praeger
An Imprint of ABC-CLIO, LLC

ABC-CLIO, LLC
130 Cremona Drive, P.O. Box 1911
Santa Barbara, California 93116-1911

This book is printed on acid-free paper ∞

Manufactured in the United States of America

Contents

Introduction

Radford G. Davis, DVM, MPH, DACVPM

If we were to stop for a moment to consider how animals have touched our lives, and perhaps shaped our childhoods and our adult views of the world, we would only just begin to reveal the connection we humans have with pets. Of course, humans and animals have had some form of relationship for millennia, with animals kept as companions or raised for food since humankind walked the earth. Intuitively, we know that pets add something to our lives, improve our lives, even shape our lives. Many an adult can recall with fondness his or her favorite pet companion growing up, the antics of the pet, the animal's patience with human emotion, forgiveness, and the sad parting. Many people consider their pet to be part of the family: they name their pet, have photos of their pet ready to whip out from their wallet or set as wallpaper on their computer desktop, and sign holiday cards with their pet's name. Pets are part of who we have become. As part of the family, then, it is natural to want to provide for your pet in the best possible manner—and that is the thrust of this volume.

Within the pages of this book, you will find expert information on how to choose the best pet for you, what your responsibilities as a pet guardian are, why pets behave the way they do, and, of course, how to care for them both in an everyday manner and in times of emergencies. To fulfill your obligation to your animal companion, and to maintain your wonderful friendship as long as possible, it is important that you find a veterinarian who understands your needs and the needs of your pet. This quest may require you to visit a handful of veterinarians to find the one who truly "gets you" and your pet. And once you find that veterinarian, don't let go; use her or him to the fullest extent.

This book, which features the contributions of expert veterinarians in their field, is a wonderful start to helping you care for your companion animals and keeping them healthy—think of it as an introductory owner's manual. But the learning and the responsibility, and the fun, do not end with the last chapter. Continue to build on the content in this book by seeking out that veterinarian, that behaviorist, that trainer, that DVD or library book to extend your reach into the wonderful world of companion animals and to better understand that lifelong friend. For even if we are adults now, our childhood pet is still our lifelong friend, and always will be.

1

Choosing a Pet

MeLissa Ciprich, DVM

The human-animal bond is something that continues to evolve as the role of companion animals plays a more integral part of human life. Human perceptions of just what role these animals play are extremely diverse, yet it is very apparent that many people in our society have shifted from a "backyard dog or wandering tom-cat" mentality regarding pets to one of family member status. Studies have shown significant health benefits from people who have positive interactions with animals, such as petting a dog or even watching fish in an aquarium.[1, 2] Rehabilitation therapy using animals for physical, emotional, and addictive health problems is becoming more widely accepted as it becomes more successful and as the bond between humans and companion animals strengthens. By choosing the appropriate companion animal, you can greatly influence how strong this bond becomes and what role the animal will serve in your life.

For many people, a family pet has been part of everyday life from early childhood. For others, owning a pet be a completely novel experience, one that comes with many questions and concerns. Many times, a companion animal is acquired with little or no planning, just happening by circumstance. An example would be taking in a "stray" dog or cat, or receiving an animal from a family member or friend. Animal guardianship should include the understanding that this is a lifelong commitment, which may not be the first thing you consider in this situation. Common considerations in acquiring an appropriate companion animal are discussed in this chapter, including how to choose a pet that is right for your lifestyle, which species is appropriate, and how and where to acquire a pet.

WHICH COMPANION ANIMAL FITS WITH MY LIFESTYLE?

It is important to recognize the kind of lifestyle you lead before bringing a companion animal into your home. The amount of time you can devote to your pet and space are two components of your lifestyle that greatly affect the livelihood and well-being of animals in your home.

How much time you have to provide for the basic needs and enrichment requirements of the animal on a daily basis is an essential consideration. This issue can vary depending on where you live, which type of job you have, how often you travel, and which household responsibilities you have. For instance, someone with a commute and long workdays or someone who travels often may find that meeting the needs of one species may be easier than another. For example, cats have daily requirements that are less demanding than those for dogs, because cats do not need to be walked outside on a scheduled basis. Fish have minimal daily requirements but do need maintenance for tank cleaning, which may take a larger portion of time at once. A person who spends most of his or her time at home may have more time to invest in meeting the demands of raising a young pet such as a puppy or kitten.

The home environment will have a profound influence on your choice of animal. Those persons living in an urban area in an apartment setting will have different challenges and considerations for their pet than those individuals who own a home with a yard in a suburban or rural area.

Simple questions to ask yourself about whether your lifestyle and your home environment are a good match for your hoped-for new companion animal may include the following:

- Do I have the time it takes to meet the basic needs of this kind of animal?
- Do I have enough space for my animal to be comfortable and get enough exercise?
- Will my animal need to go outside and if so, how often?
- Do I have an appropriate place to walk the dog?
- If I rent or lease my home, does my housing authority place special restrictions on having pets?
- Am I ready to make a lifelong commitment to this animal?
- Can I afford to care for this animal, including veterinary care?

There is certainly some degree of flexibility in considering your home environment. Even though you may live in a city, that fact does not mean that a larger-sized dog is not the right companion for you, provided you have taken the animal's needs into consideration. There are five accepted basic needs that animals should be afforded by their caretakers, often referred to as the "Five Freedoms," which are discussed in Chapter 2 on the responsibilities of pet owners. As an owner, you should be able to meet all five of these basic needs.

KNOW YOUR SPECIES

An important first step in identifying the type of animal that appeals to you is learning about the characteristics of that species. This simple, yet fundamental approach is extremely important in matching your expectations to an animal's physical and personality traits. Consider more than just the animal's appearance when deciding if he or she is right for you. Taking such a narrow view tends to be a common mistake that both new and experienced pet owners make. The result can be an unfulfilling relationship, or a relationship that comes with inconveniences that may result in your giving up the animal.

Although most people with pets report that the benefits of companion animals greatly outweigh the drawbacks of such ownership, it is important to consider some of the animals' traits that are not typically viewed as positive. Some examples may be hair shedding, "bathroom habits," jumping up or scratching on furniture, certain odors, feeding requirements, grooming needs, medical care expenses, and ease or difficulty of caretaking arrangements while you are away from home. For many animals, the cost of upkeep can be considerable. Remember that even an animal that comes to you at no cost will require some financial obligation to provide proper nutrition and healthy maintenance through routine visits with your veterinarian.

As a general consideration, think about what you hope to gain by having a companion animal. A good suggestion is to keep in mind the mutual benefits for both you and your potential pet. Some people are tactile, or physical, in their desire for companionship and want an animal that they can pet, hold, or perhaps even snuggle. Others may enjoy having an animal that is fun and relaxing to watch, but is more independent and does not require much hands-on activity. You may enjoy relaxing in a quiet setting and prefer an animal that might not make a lot of noise. There is a diversity of animal species that can accommodate many of these desired traits.

Your interests or hobbies may also factor into which species fits you best. For instance, many runners might enjoy a dog that can accompany them on their daily jog. Not only is this time spent together rewarding for both dog and human, but it also encourages a healthy lifestyle.

FAMILIES AND COMPANION ANIMALS

The majority of U.S. pet households are families, because both parents and their children can truly benefit from having companion animals. Many parents believe that having an animal as part of the family promotes responsibility in being safe around animals, encourages nurturing relationships, and strengthens emotional stability. Choosing the appropriate pet for your family should be based on a variety of factors and considerations, such as the ages of the children, their basic animal handling competence, and your expectations of the interaction between child and animal.

Bringing an animal into the family home means adult supervision should always be in place, for the health and safety of both child and animal. Family households can often be filled with different sounds and commotion that may be stressful to particular animals. Having a "safe" place for the animal to escape from these events should be a special consideration in this type of home environment. Any animal can defensively bite in a stressful situation and potentially inflict an injury. Animals that show signs of aggression toward children are not appropriate for such a home environment. Proper education on appropriate behavior around animals is a must and should be routinely emphasized. Key points include a gentle approach for touching as well as proper hygiene following animal handling.

Parents should also understand any health risks that may exist for certain species. The Centers for Disease Control and Prevention (CDC) recommends that families with small children, typically younger than the age of five years, should avoid animals such as snakes, lizards, and turtles, as well as baby chicks or ducklings, due to the health risks associated with these animals—particularly the risk of infection with the *Salmonella* pathogen.[3] This factor should also be a consideration for senior or elderly populations and for people with illnesses that compromise their immune system. Before bringing one of these animal species to your home, you may want to refer to the CDC's information pages on owning healthy pets. An Internet link for this site has been included in the Further Reading list.

Your veterinarian is another helpful resource when you are deciding which kind of animal is best for you and your family. If you or a family member suffers from allergies, you may also want to consult with the family physician on ways to manage these sensitivities in conjunction with having animals in the home. Depending on the severity of the allergies, it may not be necessary to avoid having animals altogether, but you may need to follow special grooming habits to control allergen sources such as pet dander.

A LIFETIME OF COMPANIONSHIP

Awareness of the pet's average life span is an important issue when considering which type of pet you should get. Many individual animals may live well beyond the expected average age for their species or their breed; others may suffer an unexpected injury or illness that cuts short their life. You will also want to consider the possible expenses that are associated with these situations. An animal that is sometimes kept outside may be at higher risk of escaping from the yard and being injured by a vehicle, or may be at increased risk for exposure to various toxins. The loss of a pet can be a traumatic experience for anyone, but may be especially difficult for children. Emotional preparation for the loss of a beloved pet may not always be a forethought, but is equally important in choosing whether to have a companion animal.

WHERE TO GET YOUR NEW COMPANION ANIMAL

People acquire their pets from a variety of places and under many different circumstances. The type of animal you are interested in bringing into your home may greatly influence where you acquire your pet. For example, if you are interested in having a saltwater fish tank or a specific type of tree frog, you may be limited to specialty pet retail stores. For more common companion animal species, the choices may be overwhelming. Some of the most frequently used sources of pets include friends or relatives, animal breeders, animal shelters, newspapers, online sources, and pet stores and superstores, as well as taking in a neighborhood "stray." All resources for finding the right animal are not created equal, however, and there can be both positive and negative aspects to nearly all of these options. Being informed of the general pros and cons for the most commonly used sources of finding a pet can be valuable to you and your family in making this decision. The following subsections provide an introductory overview of some of these animal sources.

Breeders

"Breeders" are people who purposefully reproduce animals of a specific breed or type to raise and sell for profit. Dogs and cats are the most common animals raised by breeders. Many dog and cat lovers are drawn to specific breeds because of their appearance or their general personality traits and behaviors. For dogs, this is the most common way people acquire their canine companions, especially for smaller purebreds.

Becoming familiar with the specifics of a given breed before purchasing an animal is extremely important. Although almost all breeds of dogs possess positive qualities and traits, many popular breeds are known to have a genetic predisposition to certain physical limitations or problems. For example, some of the smaller breeds with short, "pushed-in" faces, such as pugs, Pekingese, Shih Tzus, and English bulldogs, are prone to having respiratory problems due to their facial structure. This structure is a direct result of genetic manipulation via breeding to produce their highly popular, appealing appearance. Because of this physical condition, however, these dogs have higher incidence rates of tracheal collapse, which limits their ability to breathe. The severity of this problem can range from simple annoyances, such as loud breathing when awake and snoring when the animal is sleeping, to a medical emergency caused by lack of oxygen. Other breeds may have heritable biological problems: Labrador retrievers, Rottweilers, and several other large breed dogs are genetically prone to hip dysplasia; golden retrievers are at a higher risk for diagnosis of lymphosarcoma; boxers have an increased risk of developing mast cell tumors; and Doberman pinschers are vulnerable to a serious genetically inherited bleeding disorder known as Von Willebrand's disease. Learning about these genetic conditions of purebreds before approaching a breeder will help you make a more informed decision about the dog you want to buy.

The quality and integrity of breeders are as important as the quality of animals they sell. Breeders range from very responsible individuals or businesses to those who run a factory-type business for reproducing dogs (often referred to as "puppy mills"), which

---

DID YOU KNOW?

- Of pet owning households, most view their animals as a family member, while fewer than 2 percent of households refer to the animals in the home as "property."
- The dog is the most common household pet in the United States.[4]

---

often raise animals in less than ideal conditions in an attempt to save money. It is important to appreciate the difference between such types of breeders. Most states require those who breed animals to have a license and to submit to having their operations inspected annually. A license will not guarantee that a breeder is truly responsible, but it should be one of the first credentials you inquire about when you contact the breeder.

Responsible breeders invest a great deal of time in caring for their breeding animals and take many precautions in deciding to whom they sell their puppies (or kittens). Typically, these breed advocates are extremely familiar with the physical and behavioral traits of the animal and may have strong opinions about which environments are right for the animal. When interacting with such breeders, be prepared to supply plenty of information about yourself: they may have as many questions about your lifestyle and provisional living environment as you have about the quality of their animals. Responsible breeders will have thorough knowledge about the pedigree, or family history, of each of the parents of their litters, and they should inform you of any known genetic problems that this history may have shown.

Often, responsible breeders will have taken initial steps to ensure the health of their puppies or kittens for sale. This may include the first veterinary check-up with preventive deworming as well as the animal's first vaccinations. The breeder should be able to provide you with written proof, such as a veterinary record or health certificate, that these procedures have been completed. Some breeders may ask you to sign a contract that indicates the purchase price and your intention to care for the animal; some may also require you to have the dog or cat spayed or neutered so that you cannot breed the animal and sell the offspring. The contract may also state the conditions upon which the breeder will refund either all or a portion of the selling price. An example may be if certain inherited physical problems are likely to cause you to incur future medical care expenses. Breeders may also request that you return the pet to them if you decide within a reasonable amount of time that your home is not the best environment for this animal.

One excellent resource for researching breeds of dogs and breeders is the official American Kennel Club website (its address can be found in the Further Reading list at the end of the chapter). Usually, each breed has a club representative who knows responsible breeders and can provide you with contact information. Be cautious when dealing with any breeders who refuse your request to visit and tour their facilities. In fact, you should make such a visit a requirement for any purchase consideration. If a breeder refuses the request for a visit, it may be a red flag that you are dealing with someone who is not providing proper care for his or her animals and does not want you to see how the animals are being raised. If the breeder wants to meet you at a separate location to complete the purchase, this request may be an indication that you are dealing with a puppy mill breeder rather than a responsible breeder. Another indication that you are dealing with a high-volume breeder or puppy mill is if the breeder tends to have puppies available for sale at any time during the year, which requires a significant number of animals. Dogs are seasonal breeders, so it is unlikely that a respectable breeder with a few well-cared-for parent dogs would be able to offer puppies at this rate.

Because of their less than ideal practices, puppy mills and high-volume catteries can affect the pet population negatively. Very often their animals are kept confined in small wire cages most of their lives and are continually bred. It is not uncommon for the offspring of such parent animals to have a higher prevalence of genetic problems due to inbreeding and unhealthy living conditions. The housing tends to be crowded and poorly ventilated, which can cause physical deformities because the animals are unable to stand comfortably or exercise. Proper veterinary care is often lacking or nonexistent, and the animals suffer as a result. Such crowded conditions also increase the likelihood of infectious diseases within the animals and throughout the facilities, including diseases that may be transmissible to humans, such as ringworm.

You may be aware of some of these issues because of the increasing amount of media attention puppy mills have received recently. Much of this attention is largely due to legislative campaigns directed at limiting the number of animals that these businesses can have in hopes of improving the animal welfare within the industry. Many states have already made it illegal for these operations to exist. Often, if these facilities do not pass inspection or shut down due to financial reasons, the unsocialized and often physically disabled animals are abandoned, which can overwhelm local animal shelters and rescues. Many of these animals are in need of significant medical care, training, and socialization. By choosing not to purchase your animal from such a facility, you are being an advocate for responsible animal care.

But how do you know whether you are supporting such a business? In addition to the signs mentioned earlier, places where these animals are typically sold include market pet stores (pet stores that primarily sell purebred or exotic animals), parking lots, large events such as flea markets, and newspaper or online advertisements. Asking to visit the breeder's facility, meet the parents of the animal, and see an official health certificate and veterinary record of examination are all ways to help ensure that you are not supporting this cruel industry. Price will never be an indication that you are receiving a healthy animal from a responsible breeder.

If your interest in a companion animal is breed related, there may be other options for you to consider when acquiring a pet, such as a breed rescue. Many of these rescue operations are associated with people who have a strong interest in a particular breed and give temporary care for animals, such as fostering animals from a shelter or taking in animals that have been given up by an owner until a permanent home can be found. Because of their familiarity with the breed, rescue groups can be a good resource for understanding how to cope with animals that suffer from particular genetic problems or that have inherent behavioral issues related to the breed. Many of the individuals involved in rescue are either current or former responsible breeders who truly have a passion for the animals and will invest a great deal of time and travel great distances to locate new homes for the rescued pets. These individuals are also key players when a puppy mill has been closed or condemned, leaving hundreds of purebred or "hybrid" dogs or cats in need of homes.

Animal Shelters

The number of animals that enter the more than 5,000 shelters found in the United States is estimated to be somewhere between 5 million and 7 million per year. Although this number represents a sharp decline from the volume years ago, approximately 75 percent of these companion animals will never find a permanent home and will be euthanized.

The concept of animal shelters has truly evolved over the last several decades. Due to the large number of homeless animals in the United States, these facilities are desperately needed to help provide for the basic needs of animals in the community. Previously, these places were more commonly referred to as "the pound"—a place where stray, lost, or unwanted animals were taken with little chance of being rehomed. A great deal of effort has been invested into changing that image by providing education to the community about responsible animal ownership and promoting spaying and neutering to keep the pet population from producing more homeless animals. Shelters today can be significantly different from one location to another. They may be municipally run (i.e., run by the town, city, or county), or they may be established as private nonprofit organizations. What the local shelter offers in terms of animal services depends on both its mission and its financial capabilities. Many city or township shelters have a dual role in serving the community and providing animal sheltering.

Animals found in shelters are not limited to just dogs and cats. Many shelters care for a variety of animals, including small mammals such as rabbits, ferrets, and rats, but you may also find birds, reptiles, and amphibians, and possibly even farm animals such as goats and horses.

Animals being cared for in shelters come from many different sources. Approximately half of shelter intakes are picked up "at large" or while running loose by animal field service officers; the other half are animals relinquished by their owners for a variety of reasons. Very few lost companion animals that end up in a shelter are returned to their original homes. In fact, the average rate at which dogs are returned to their original homes is approximately 25 percent; for cats, it is less than 2 percent. The low rehoming rates reflect the fact that most animals lack a form of identification such as collars and microchips.

The reasons for relinquishing or giving up a companion animal to a shelter are diverse and vary with the species. A common misconception about animals in shelters is that something must be wrong with these animals and, therefore, they would not make good pets. Most often this is not the case, or else the perceived problem with the animal is one that can be corrected through medical treatment, behavioral training, or education for potential adopters. Research on relinquishment shows that the top reason for a person giving up a dog or cat is because the individual is moving and cannot take the animal to the new home.[5] The second most common reason for relinquishment of dogs is that the landlord does not allow pets, and for cats it is that the person already has too many animals. In other words, the top two reasons are neither medical nor behavioral in nature.

Approximately 25 to 30 percent of dogs taken in by shelters are purebred animals. Thus, if you have a particular interest in a specific breed, you can still consider adopting from a shelter. Often, shelters will keep a list of people interested in specific breeds; when a member of that breed arrives, they will call people on the list to visit with the animal.

As previously mentioned, some of the dogs and cats being cared for at shelters may come from breeding facilities that have been closed or be animals rescued from neglect or hoarding cases. Animals with this history may have an increased risk of medical or social issues, and potential adopters will often receive special counseling on how to manage these issues.

An animal's medical and home environment history may or may not be known in a shelter environment, and for some potential pet owners this issue can be somewhat of a negative component in considering adoption of a companion animal. Often, a brief survey might be taken on an animal that is being signed over to the shelter, which can give some information about the animal's temperament, vaccination history, and spayed/neutered status. This information can be valuable because it will allow the potential shelter to know if this particular animal has been around other animals or children. To prevent the spread of infectious diseases from one animal to another, many shelters that have the personnel and funding will give basic preventive medical treatments to their incoming animals. This care may include vaccinations, treatments for intestinal parasites or worms, and flea and tick treatments. Facilities that have access to a veterinarian may also spay or neuter the animal prior to the pet's adoption, which is a very important part of preventing more unwanted animals and the unnecessary loss of life through euthanasia.

When describing the adoption fees for a particular animal, the shelter staff will be able to inform you about which treatments the adoptee has had and provide you with a written record to take home. To ensure that you establish a relationship with a veterinarian for future medical services, many adopted animals will come with a voucher for a free or discounted examination by a local veterinarian. Also, the shelter may require you to take your new pet to a veterinarian within a set time period.

Because many shelters often do not have adequate space, the crowded and stressful conditions can make it likely that animal residents are exposed to different types of bacteria and viruses. Awareness of some of the more common infections of shelter animals and the impact they may have on a potential adoption is important. With proper treatment and improved stress management, most of these animals will recover without complications, so adoption should still be encouraged. Cats can be more prone to this type of event in a shelter, often acquiring upper respiratory infections or "kitty colds." Depending on the severity of the illness and the need for medication, they often recover better in a new home environment than they would with a prolonged stay in the shelter. Dogs being housed in some shelters may become infected with the respiratory infection complex known as "kennel cough," which can sometimes produce a loud honking-type cough. This infection, although quite contagious from dogs that come in close contact with one another, is usually self-limiting and most cases resolves with minimal medical treatment.

Many sheltering organizations are beginning to recognize the importance of understanding each shelter animal's general behavior so as to match the pet with the right adopter. Behavioral or adoption assessments are performed primarily with dogs, although some shelters and rescue operations may also do feline behavioral assessments. There are many different ways to make these observations, and none of them can truly tell how animals might react when they are not in the shelter setting. Shelters are full of smells and sounds that may affect how an animal reacts to these tests, so they are not fool-proof. There are now great programs in many shelters that successfully match personality and appearance traits of an animal with the desired qualities and interests that an adopter may have when searching for the right companion. The benefit for the shelter in having a profile matching program takes the form of a decrease in the number of animals that are returned for incompatibility. Some people may go to a shelter and feel they must "save a life" by adopting, so they take the animal home without considering what the traits of that animal are and how the pet will integrate with the home they can provide. The resulting mismatch can be detrimental to the animal and the family, in addition to being costly for the shelter. Some shelters have very limited number of staff, which may prevent a thorough assessment of each animal because of the amount of time it takes to do the daily cleaning and care of their animal population as well as serve the public needs. These facilities, however, often have "meet and greet"–type rooms where you can spend time with an adoptee and even bring your other animals in to meet your proposed new pet and observe the interactions between them.

It is common for shelters to use an application process in adopting an animal. This process is intended to prevent the incompatible matches mentioned previously. For example, very large breed or excitable dogs, or extremely fragile and shy animals, may come with an age restriction for children in the family. Such a constraint may be an effort to avoid a child being injured from being knocked over by the large animal, or to limit the noise and stress level for animals that are timid around little ones. Questions by the shelter personnel are often meant to give them a better understanding of how well you can provide a safe environment for your companion animal. For example, questions may focus on how much time the animal will spend indoors versus outdoors, and whether you have a yard with a fence to keep your animal confined and safe. It is important to keep in mind that this application process seeks to promote the best possible care for the animal while protecting the best interest of the community members.

If you are still unsure whether your household is ready for a lifelong commitment to an animal, another option you may want to consider is fostering. Often shelters and rescues will have animal residents that are very young, such as new litters of puppies or kittens, which are much more susceptible to infections, or perhaps an animal that behaviorally needs more attention or a lower-stress environment. These animals are great candidates for temporary fostering. People who have lifestyles that may change due to work commitments or travel may find that fostering provides a somewhat temporary way to enjoy the benefits associated with pet companionship and to help combat the overcrowding conditions in shelters. Recognizing that you must still be able to meet the needs of this animal is important, and you may find that caring for such an animal is not for you. Often, the most challenging part of fostering can be returning the animal to the organization for adoption by someone else, so it certainly takes a special kind of commitment.

You may be familiar with the terms "Humane Society," "SPCA," or even "animal control." It is important to note that the national organizations known as the Humane Society of the United States (HSUS) and the American Society for the Prevention and Cruelty of Animals (ASPCA) are different from the animal shelters found throughout the country that may share similar names. These animal advocacy groups work toward improving animal welfare and provide resources for shelters and other animal rescue groups, but do not own or operate animal care facilities. They are often associated with disaster response efforts for companion animals, or they may respond to animal cruelty cases. Just because a local sheltering organization may share similar words in its name, that does not mean it shares the same missions or position statements that these large national organizations advocate. Services whose names include the title "animal control" have a commitment to serving the safety of the community. This may entail securing and removing at-large animals that endanger traffic, removing and relocating disruptive wildlife from homes or yards, or responding to bite cases or dangerous animal field calls.

Specialty Pet Shops and Pet "Superstores"

The retail market for pets and pet supplies is an ever-growing industry. Although the once common typical feed stores still exist, people today are probably more familiar with the larger "big box" pet superstores or the local pet shop. These stores will differ in the types of animals they sell or adopt as well as the types of animal-related services and products they carry. It is important to recognize that these different types of stores do not always have the same animal-sale positions. Although they have some smaller and more exotic species for sale, many of the larger superstores recognize the homeless animal population problem and its direct relation to the sale of animals. They typically will have dogs and cats from the local shelter or rescue organization available through adoption-type services.

Some retail stores that are strictly for-profit operations carry puppies or kittens that are purebred and sell them for the market price, in addition to other species such as small mammals, reptiles, and fish. The sources of these animals may be unknown, however, and it may be difficult to obtain some of the important information discussed earlier in relation to breeders. The strictly for-profit sales of cats and dogs in these stores is strictly opposed by many in the animal industry, because some of these animals may originate from the puppy-mill facilities mentioned previously. If you choose to purchase a companion animal from one of these retail stores, you should ask specific questions about the animal, such as the place where it originated, the animal's registration status, and medical record information, as well as inquire about any policies the store has regarding returning animals. Special policies may exist for returns of animals that become severely ill or that later show signs of an inherited disease or physical deformity after purchase.

Similar to what happens in some shelter settings, owing to the large number of animals and their increased contact with one another and with caretakers, it is not uncommon that some of pet-store animals will acquire upper respiratory infections. Exposure to some infectious diseases such as parvovirus or distemper, however, can also be common in puppies and kittens in these settings, and can be life-threatening and costly to treat. It is advisable for would-be owners to be familiar with some of these diseases before purchasing any animal, but especially younger ones that have not received their full set of vaccinations.   ·

Newspaper and Online Animal Sales

Newspaper advertisements for animal sales still exist, but have been largely overtaken in popularity by the use of the Internet to present "classified ads." Both the in-print newspaper ads and the Internet ads are most heavily used by breeders for litter sales or by people who have litters of puppies or kittens as a result of not having their animals spayed or neutered. Shelters may have a spotlight ad in the community paper that highlights some of their adoptable companion animals with photos and descriptions. Likewise, a number of Internet sites, such as Petfinder.com, have been created for shelters, rescue facilities, and individuals to enable them to post information on their adoptable animals. You can typically find photos of the animal and background information, along with the animal's location. Such sites also offer tips on adoption and educational materials so that potential adopters can be better informed about meeting the needs of companion animals before acquiring them. In contrast, selling or auction sites such as online classifieds ads may not reveal that level of information or allow communication with the seller to ask questions before making a purchase.

Because both types of media sources greatly restrict the ability to visually assess animals or their environment of origin, it is imperative that you explore these options with caution—and even try to avoid them for the purpose of finding a companion animal. Because of the lack of monitoring and restrictions on animal sales via the Internet, facilities such as puppy mills, foreign animal sources, and exotic animal trade groups use this outlet frequently to sell their animals. The Internet is also used to aid in the importation and often illegal trade of animals, which can potentially cause harm to the health and well-being of domestic and wild animals, as well as people, in the animals' new homes. Visit the CDC website on Internet scams (address is provided in the Further Reading section) to become more informed about how to avoid these types of fraudulent animal sales.

MAKING A LIFELONG COMMITMENT

Reading this chapter should have enabled you to become familiar with the steps in considering whether a specific companion animal is right for you and your family. Although you may be required to make some adjustments for this mutual relationship to work, you will find that having a pet can be a truly wonderful and worthwhile experience that offers many benefits.

Recognizing that being a responsible animal guardian takes a lifelong commitment is one of the most fundamental guidelines offered here, along with the idea that bringing in or giving up a pet should not be a quick decision. A variety of resources are available to help you identify and attempt to resolve many of the issues that might otherwise result in relinquishment of an animal. If possible, you should seek counsel with your veterinarian, who may be able to provide you with knowledge and support in making the decision to relinquish your animal. The species of animal, the cost of the pet's care, and the time commitment are all important components when you are making the decision to have an animal in your home and trying to ensure that the relationship is a happy and long one. You should also think about how a life-changing situation may affect your ability to meet the needs of your companion animal. Challenges to having an animal may arise; however, there are many great resources available to assist you in overcoming most of these issues, including behavioral training, fostering programs, and animal-owner counseling services.

REFERENCES

1. Barker, S., J. Knisely, N. McCain, and A. Best. "Measuring Stress and Immune Response in Healthcare Professionals Following Interaction with a Therapy Dog: Pilot Study." *Psychological Reports* 96 (2005): 713–29.

2. DeSchriver, M. M., and C. C. Riddick. "Effects of Watching Aquariums on Elders' Stress." *Anthrozoos* 4 (1990): 44–48.

3. Centers for Disease Control and Prevention. "Healthy Pets, Healthy People." http://www.cdc.gov/healthypets/petscription_gen.htm

4. *2007–2008 APPMA National Pet Owners Survey.* Greenwich, CT: American Pet Products Manufacturers Association; 2009.

5. Salman, M. D., J. Hutchison, R. Ruch-Gallie, et al. "Behavioral Reasons for Relinquishment of Dogs and Cats to 12 Shelters." *Journal of Applied Animal Welfare Science* 3 (2000): 93–106.

FURTHER READING

Organization	URL	What You Can Find Here
American Society for the Prevention of Cruelty to Animals	www.aspca.org	Information on health, welfare, sheltering, and adoption of pets.
Centers for Disease Control and Prevention	http://www.cdc.gov/healthypets/index.htm	Keeping family and pets healthy, with outlines of risks and precautions when having a companion animal.
Centers for Disease Control and Prevention	http://www.cdc.gov/animalimportation/internetscams.html	Strategies to avoid fraudulent commercial trade of animals.

(Continued)

Organization	URL	What You Can Find Here
Animal Rescue League of Boston	http://www.centerforshelterdogs.org/Home.aspx	Information on animal welfare programs being developed for evaluating the behavior of shelter dogs to ensure they are placed into the right home environment.
Petfinder	www.petfinder.com	A wealth of information on shelters and rescues; where to find particular animals for adoption, fostering, and training resources; and posting companion animals for adoption.

2

The Responsibilities of Pet Ownership

Kristina D. August, DVM

Humans have a natural bond with animals, and we cannot seem to resist sharing our lives with them. They comfort us, make us laugh, and give us something to care for, which in turn cares for us. When you bring an animal into your home and your life, you are taking on a lifelong responsibility (at least for the life of the animal). Throughout that life, the needs of the animal will change, and your approach to your pet must adapt and change as well, from puppy training to geriatric care.

As you read through this book, you will find many details on various aspects of pet ownership, including the important responsibilities of day-to-day care, but there are other responsibilities to consider when owning a pet as well. These responsibilities can seem overwhelming at times. Of course, the best time to consider these important responsibilities and how a pet would fit into your busy life is before bringing the pet home. Even so, whatever stage of pet ownership you are in, now is a good time to think about these responsibilities you have and the best way to integrate them into your daily life. Many of the responsibilities of a pet owner are common sense and can be included in your life without much thought; others, however, might require some careful consideration to discover what works best for you and your animal companion.

RESPONSIBILITIES TO YOUR PET

Basic Care Needs

The basic needs of a pet are generally provided for in the home environment; they include the need for fresh food and water, shelter, exercise and enrichment, training, and grooming. (These topics are covered in more detail in the later chapters on pet care.) Your pet may let you know right away if her needs, such as food or water, are not met, but other items on this list may take years before the effects

Table 2.1
The Five Freedoms

---

1. Freedom from hunger and thirst—by ready access to fresh water and a diet to maintain full health and vigor.

2. Freedom from discomfort—by providing a suitable environment including shelter and a comfortable resting area.

3. Freedom from pain, injury, or disease—by prevention or rapid diagnosis and treatment.

4. Freedom to express normal behavior—by providing sufficient space, proper facilities and company of the animal's own kind.

5. Freedom from fear and distress—by ensuring conditions that avoid mental suffering.

Source: Farm Animal Welfare Council. "Five Freedoms." http://www.fawc.org.uk/freedoms.htm.

are realized, such as obesity from lack of exercise and too much food, or dental disease from lack of regular dental care. For our animal friends, and ourselves, prevention is so much easier than trying to recover health later in life.

Basic guidelines for animal care can be found in the "Five Freedoms" statement developed by the Farm Animal Welfare Council of the United Kingdom (Table 2.1). These guidelines are internationally recognized for use in farming and by animal shelter organizations; they are appropriate for animals kept as pets as well. The "Five Freedoms" are endorsed by many humane organizations and veterinary associations, including the American Animal Hospital Association (AAHA) and the American Association of Feline Practitioners (AAFP).

Health Care Needs

In addition to meeting the needs mentioned previously to give your animal a great start on a long and healthy life, your companion deserves the benefit of regular veterinary care. In their first year of life, dogs and cats require a series of vaccinations to build their immunity; spaying or neutering is also appropriate at this time. After the first year, veterinary visits should be scheduled every six months to one year for the rest of the animal's life. Animals age much more quickly than humans do—a year for us is equivalent to five to seven years for them—and these regular examinations and assessments can help to catch signs of illness early, often making treatment simpler and less costly.

The need for vaccination boosters throughout your pet's life should be discussed with your veterinarian, as these needs vary for individual animals based on their health, exposures to other animals, diseases common in the area where they live, the duration of immunity provided by the different vaccines, and other factors. Vaccination guidelines change frequently as more is discovered about the effectiveness and duration of vaccine immunity, so it is important that you consult with your veterinarian to determine which vaccines are needed for your pet.

Other essential care provided by your veterinarian may include heartworm testing and preventative medications, as well as advice on flea and tick products appropriate for your animal and your area. The products carried in veterinary offices are generally more effective, less toxic, and sometimes more environmentally friendly than many of the powders, shampoos, dips, flea collars, and chemical bombs that are sold over-the-counter for flea and tick control. However, any of these products can be toxic, especially if used incorrectly, so it is always best to consult with your veterinarian before using them. The appropriate dose should be given for the size and species of the animal—dog products should never be used on cats, and some products that are safe for dogs can pose a health risk for cats living in the same household. It is critical to read the labels on these insecticide products to ensure that you administer them properly and to have your veterinarian demonstrate their proper application.

Hazard-Free Environment

Your companion must be provided with a safe living space free of environmental hazards. The string, rubber bands, tinsel, and threaded needles that cats find so intriguing can lead to serious gastrointestinal obstruction, puncture, or other complications necessitating immediate medical or surgical intervention. Tempting foods that are left sitting out might contain ingredients toxic to animals such as xylitol (a sugar substitute that is highly toxic to dogs) or chocolate. Keeping poisonous plants in the home is not recommended, but if you must keep them, put them far out of reach of your pet. Also, rodenticides must not be used in or around your home or garage because pet animals may ingest the poison, or an affected rodent, and die (see the Resources list).

Financial Responsibilities

That free kitten or stray dog you take into your home can carry many unexpected expenses if you have not done your research ahead of time. Consider the costs of food, bedding, grooming, training, and a safe enclosure—be it a fenced yard or a hamster cage—before you bring a pet home. Veterinary care costs must be considered as well when choosing a pet. The first year of a pet's life is generally the most expensive, with additional veterinary visits being necessary to administer vaccine boosters and perform sterilization surgery (another responsibility we will spend more time on later). To get an idea of how much you will have to spend, contact your local veterinary office for an estimate of costs. Explain that you are planning ahead; most clinics are very happy to schedule a visit before you bring an animal into your life to discuss choosing the best pet for your lifestyle as well as costs and responsibilities involved in pet ownership.

To prepare ahead, it is a good idea to set aside money to pay for both expected and unexpected veterinary costs. Even pets who receive the best care can have medical emergencies, and having to worry about these costs adds extra stress to an already stressful situation. Pet insurance is available from a number of companies. Some insurance covers preventive care and vaccines, while other policies cover only emergency care. Consider the costs and your needs to decide what you are able to cover yourself and in which areas your family might need help if an emergency arises. If you decide instead to put a regular amount aside every month to create your own emergency fund for veterinary expenses, be sure this account will not be touched for other purposes. It is sad and unfortunate to be faced with a large medical bill without being prepared, and many pets are euthanized every year for this very reason. Consider how much you are willing and able to spend on your pets *before* you are faced with an emergency situation.

Types of Veterinary Services

When choosing a veterinarian and a clinic, you have a number of options that may differ based on the services they offer, their approach to care, specialty certification, and more. Search your local area to determine the availability of these services, or ask a friend or neighbor for a recommendation. Ensuring proper and adequate medical care for your animal during unexpected illnesses or injury is also the responsibility of a pet owner, so it is important to talk to your veterinarian about the availability of emergency care *before* you are faced with one of these often frightening situations.

Veterinary Hospitals

Most veterinary clinics really should be considered hospitals because they are equipped with a full complement of medical technology and services, including radiography, anesthesia and surgery, dentistry, emergency support, specialized cages and bedding, and a well-stocked pharmacy. Many of today's hospitals also offer more advanced services such as ultrasound, endoscopy, and other specialized diagnostics and treatments.

House-Call Veterinarians

House-call (mobile) veterinarians come in many varieties, from those who basically carry a hospital on wheels and can perform surgery and x-rays right inside their vehicle, to those who focus more on preventive care and services done in the home, such as routine examinations, vaccinations, blood work, and care for some chronic illnesses. This type of service can be very helpful for homebound pet owners as well as for busy professionals and families. For end-of-life care, many people appreciate the privacy of in-home euthanasia provided by house-call veterinarians.

Emergency Services

Many communities have a dedicated animal emergency clinic for evening and weekend care. Veterinarians have families and lives, too, and for their own health and well-being they cannot be available 24 hours a day, 7 days a week. In some rural communities, there are still veterinarians who are available most times of the day or night, like James Herriot, the British veterinarian in the *All Creatures Great and Small* books. If you have a James Herriot in your community, cherish him or her and be appreciative!

Veterinary Specialists

Veterinary specialty practices can be found in most larger cities in the United States. These veterinarians have undergone extensive training to become board certified in an area of expertise such as orthopedics, dermatology, ophthalmology, internal medicine, dentistry, feline medicine (cats are not small dogs!), behavior, or other fields. You may be referred to a specialist by your veterinarian from time to time, just as in human medicine when we are referred by our family physicians. Note that some general veterinary practitioners may have a special interest and skill in an area, yet not be certified specialists.

Complementary and Alternative Veterinary Medicine

Another growing area of veterinary practice specialty is the practice of complementary medicine, which uses therapies not included in "conventional" medicine—although many of these therapies are finding their way into the conventional world. These therapies include the use of neutraceuticals such as fish oil for skin and joint conditions, herbs (including milk thistle) for liver support, and different forms of massage, commonly used in physical rehabilitation therapy. Some alternative veterinarians practice only the modality that they have studied, such as traditional Chinese medicine or homeopathy. Others integrate these therapies into their regular veterinary practice, such as using acupuncture or herbal medicine to complement conventional treatments. Chapter 10 provides a window into the possibilities of alternative medicine.

With all types of veterinary practices and specialists, your best approach is to call or visit these offices to learn more about the services they provide to determine if they are right for you and your pet. Many clinics also have websites that provide information on their services.

End-of-Life Issues: Hospice Care and Euthanasia

The final stage of our animal companions' lives can be the most difficult, as we humans have a hard time saying goodbye. The death of our animals can bring up

DID YOU KNOW?

Research studies have indicated that:

- Owning a pet enhances a child's self-esteem.
- Having pets teaches children responsibility and respect toward other living beings.
- Children who own a pet are more involved in activities such as sports, hobbies, clubs, and chores.
- Having an animal during therapy sessions or other animal-assisted activities/ treatment produces significant improvements in the treatment outcomes for a child who is suffering from an ailment.

Source: Delta Society. "Health Benefits of Animals for Children." http:// www.deltasociety.org/Page.aspx?pid=359

many feelings of grief, some unexpected, and certainly it reminds us of other deaths and goodbyes we have had in our lives. We know when we bring these creatures into our lives that most likely they will die before we do, that we will have to say goodbye—but this knowledge does not seem to make the loss any easier. The best you can do for yourself and your pet is to prepare for that time. Think about how you would like to remember your friend—a scrapbook, a paw print, photos, a lock of hair. Do you have a place to bury your pet (and is it legal in your city?), or would it be better to have ashes to bury with a newly planted tree or to sprinkle in a favorite meadow? Would you want to be present for euthanasia if that step becomes necessary? How would that procedure be performed and where—would you prefer to be in a clinic or in your home? These are issues to discuss with your veterinarian and family ahead of time so everyone is prepared when the moment arrives.

We never know how that end will present itself, and we often wish our animal companion could pass peacefully at home on their favorite bed after many long and happy years. This outcome can and does happen, although there may be some intensive end-of-life care leading up to that moment. What happens more often is that pet owners decide to euthanize their pet to prevent any suffering that might occur at the end of life. These are very personal decisions, and the people closest to the animal are usually the best ones to decide whether the animal is suffering or whether it still has a "will to live." Some guidelines are available to help in these considerations, rating the animal's activity and appetite, among other things, but the final decision is still an emotional one, and your veterinarian can be helpful as the time and need approach. One thing to note is that for a dying individual (human or animal), loss of appetite and decreased activity are normal and part of the process of dying.

Hospice care is a very new development in the professional veterinary world, and there is still much to be learned about the end-of-life needs of animals. In a reverse of the usual pattern, we are learning from human hospice experiences how to better care for our animals. The primary concern must always be to relieve pain or suffering, through either medications; alternative therapies such as massage, herbs, or acupuncture (or a combination of these); or euthanasia. Many pet owners, for a variety of personal reasons, are unable to provide intensive hospice care for their pets, and hospice facilities such as those found in the human world are not generally available for animals. If you would like to provide hospice care to any degree for your pet, discuss the issue with your veterinarian and seek out the available support. Several helplines are also available to provide animal and human support during these difficult times (see the Resources list at the end of the chapter).

RESPONSIBILITIES TO YOURSELF AND YOUR FAMILY WITH YOUR COMPANION

Providing the Basics

You owe it to yourself and your family to find ways to provide the care your pet needs in a way that fits into your lifestyle and day-to-day activities. An animal companion is not meant to add stress to your life, but rather is there to live beside and with you, supporting you as much or more than you support your pet.

Together with the other individuals who are involved with the care of your pet, make a list of the daily, weekly, monthly, and yearly needs of this member of the family. Schedule time each day for feeding, providing fresh water, cleaning (including daily litter box scooping and disposal of stool), brushing of the animal's teeth and coat, walks or other exercise or enrichment activities, training (which can also count as exercise and enrichment), and any other needs you identify for your individual pet. The chapter on pet care for your specific animal species will help you to create this individual care list.

Next, decide who is responsible for each item, remembering that ultimately *the adults in the family are responsible*. Although children can be very capable of accomplishing many things on your list, they must be supported and supervised in these tasks. When these components of care are integrated into your life, they become habits that do not require much thought and planning, and are mostly quite enjoyable and the reason you wanted a pet in the first place.

Behavior and Training

Many pets are given up to animal shelters every year for behavioral problems, making behavioral training one of the most important responsibilities of pet care. Part of the reason for giving up a pet may be failure of the owner to consider the lifestyle issues related to pet care. For example, a working couple may need to leave an energetic Labrador retriever home all day with no outlet for her energy—except destroying the house. Another area where new owners can fail is not giving behavior and training enough attention during the animal's formative months. Training and consistency are much easier to instill from the beginning with a pet of any age, and it is much harder to break the habits of both owners and pets after they have been established.

Give your pet the best chance at a happy life by providing clear behavioral guidelines and training. There are countless resources and opinions on animal behavior and training, which can make training seem a daunting task. Certified veterinary behaviorists are a great source for recommendations on animal training based on the most current research. (See Chapter 9 for more on animal behavior.)

RESPONSIBILITIES AND CHILDREN

As adults, we have a responsibility to teach children to respect and interact with animals in a positive way. Children love animals; they are fascinated by them and can develop very special connections and relationships with them. At the same time, they need to be taught how to interact with animals and, most importantly, when to leave the animals alone. Children must be taught not to chase the family dog or cat, or the wild birds and rabbits at the park. Such lessons help to instill a strong love and respect for all living things—animals can play a huge role in the development of compassion and understanding for our fellow human beings. It is well known that children who mistreat animals often grow into adults who are prone to violence against people. People who never learn to treat animals with respect have a more difficult time treating people with respect.

Babies have a natural reflex to clinch their fists, which diminishes during the toddler years as they gain more body control. Hair pulling and hitting—an outgrowth of the natural reflex—can severely damage a young child's relationship with his or her pet. The animal may become frightened of the child, which can be difficult to reverse. Very young children can be taught to go slow and "pet nice" by having an adult help them to hold their hand flat while petting patient animals.

Toddlers who are just learning to walk delight in the fact that they can now take themselves where they want to go and may chase after those fascinating animal friends. Babies and children younger than 5 years of age *must* be supervised with animals at all times to protect themselves and the animals, and many children are 7 to 10 years old before they have developed the self-control and focus required to read animal language, or at least to respond to it. Learn what your cat is saying when he puts his ears back or twitches his tail, and point these things out to children. The cat may be saying, "That's enough—I'd like some time to myself now." Most animals start with very polite, subtle signs before actually biting or scratching to get their point across. When a dog licks his lips or looks away, that usually means he is nervous and may need a little extra space. A "smile" on a dog may actually be the signal that comes before a growl or bite. Take some time to learn animal language, and use that knowledge to enhance your own and your children's animal relationships.

It is critical for pet owners to learn and understand what their animal's natural behaviors are, how to use training to best channel them, and how to arrange their homes so that the pets may have a peaceful, safe retreat when they are feeling anxious. A crate for a dog that is off limits to children or a high perch for a cat may be just the thing.

RESPONSIBILITIES TO YOUR NEIGHBORS, YOUR FRIENDS, AND THE WORLD AROUND YOU

Besides the responsibilities to your pet and your family already discussed, you must also consider the people around you and their needs when you have a pet. Controlling your pet through basic behavioral training will not only benefit you and your neighbors, but also help your pet live a happy, positive life. Pets do not willfully and maliciously cause mayhem. Dogs especially are programmed to please, but it is up to you to help them understand what is acceptable behavior and what is not. Neighbors will appreciate that you keep your dog in your own yard, while your visitors and mail carrier will appreciate that you have an animal that does not jump up on them, growl, or bite.

Most cities have laws that require pets to be leashed or under control at all times. These laws are intended to protect the safety of other people and animals—even the best-trained dogs can be distracted by squirrels, other dogs, or running children. A good fence is the best way to provide this control for dogs at home. On walks, a sturdy, reliable leash is vital, along with some basic training, to make the venture safe and pleasurable. Children should not be sent out alone to walk the dog: A child may not be able to hold onto a leash if the dog becomes excited and tries to run or, worse, may not be able to avoid a confrontation between the dog and another free-roaming dog. If a dog on a leash is approached by another dog, this situation can be dangerous depending on the temperaments of the animals. A child might try to intervene, risking injury, whereas an adult might be better able to avoid conflict.

Most cities have animal control facilities, which they often maintain in conjunction with a local animal shelter. These facilities are extremely important in keeping companion animals safe from roaming—and perhaps unvaccinated—strays and in helping us to retrieve our own lost animals. Identification is important in reuniting you with a lost pet and can be accomplished through tags worn on the collar, tattoos, or microchips. Tags can fall off and tattoos can be hard to read, but microchips are a long-lasting and very reliable way to permanently identify your animal. A tiny microchip injected under the skin can be detected by microchip readers found at most animal shelters and veterinary clinics. Each microchip carries a unique ID that should be registered with a tracking company.

If your pet is found wandering and is taken to a shelter or a veterinary clinic, the first thing technicians will do is scan for a microchip; if your contact information is on record, then you and your pet will soon be reunited.

Keeping cats under control can be more challenging. Many people believe that a cat should be allowed to live naturally, exercising his hunting instincts and experiencing the outside world. The risks of this lifestyle must be weighed with the benefits, especially taking into consideration the local environment and hazards. Aside from being illegal in many cities, outdoor cats are at higher risk than indoor cats for exposure to infectious diseases, attacks from other animals, poisons, injury due to cat-fights, collisions with cars, or other accidents. Outdoor cats can also affect fragile populations of birds and other wildlife with their hunting.

Indoor cats generally have longer, healthier life spans, and their lives can be enriched with high perches, window views, and hunting toys. Cats can also be trained to walk on a leash, or at least to tolerate the leash while they do their own meandering. Covered outdoor yards are also a good option for cats that need some outdoor time. Some good resources on keeping an indoor pet happy and healthy are listed at the end of this chapter.

Population Control

A discussion of pet overpopulation could fill an entire book, but the space considerations here allow for only a cursory treatment. Pet overpopulation is a huge issue that forces shelters across the United States (and across the world) to euthanize millions of animals every year to control populations and protect animal and human health. Unless your pet is a breeding animal, it is best to have the pet spayed or neutered before six months of age (for dogs and cats). Spaying and neutering also provide health benefits to the animal, in addition to keeping populations in check.

PET RESPONSIBILITIES AND THE ENVIRONMENT

As in many aspects of our lives these days, the choices we make regarding our pets impact upon the environment. Naturally, there are things that you can do for your animals that are helpful to the environment. Picking up your dog's feces not only keeps parks, sidewalks, and lawns cleaner and more beautiful, but also protects public health. Certainly, wild animals poop outside all the time, but it is not concentrated in such visible, high-traffic areas or in such large amounts as it is when our pets do it. Yards, gardens, and parks can become contaminated with parasite eggs found in dog and cat feces, and some of these parasites can cause severe illness or blindness in children. Animal feces should be flushed down the toilet or bagged and thrown in the garbage as soon as possible. Although fecal composters are available, these small bins—which are usually set into the ground outside—are not recommended because certain parasite eggs, including round-worm eggs, which can cause serious disease in people, may survive composting.

For cats, flushable litters make clean-up and disposal much easier, and litter types such as recycled newspaper, corn, or wheat products are biodegradable. If you decide to use newspaper-based litter, make sure it is soy based, as the chemical found in ordinary newspapers can be toxic to cats. Interestingly, there have been reports of flushed cat feces contaminating the environment, including oceans, with *Toxoplasma* eggs (a protozoan parasite of public health importance). For this rea-son, some municipalities discourage owners from flushing cat litter. Indoor cats that do not eat raw meat or animals (such as wild birds or mice) are less likely to carry parasites like *Toxoplasma*, so their feces is less likely to harbor such parasites.

A final comment on cat litter: Cats can be very picky about their litter, so make any changes in the type or brand of litter gradually, or offer a choice of boxes with different litter to determine your cat's preferences. You do not want to discourage your cat from using the litter box!

FINAL THOUGHTS

Sometimes, despite the best planning (or due to poor planning), the best option for all parties is rehoming an animal. Situations in which this might become neces-sary include changes in the home, such as the addition of children or other individ-uals who may be harmed by the animal, or vice versa. Medical or behavioral issues, in the humans or in the animal, can arise and complicate the home environment. There is also a limit to the number of pets that a person can care for well—know these limits for yourself and stay within them.

The first priority must always be to provide the best possible care for the humans and the animals in our lives. Even though pet ownership is a lifelong commitment, we also have the responsibility to acknowledge that an animal might be better off living in a different home if we are not providing the best possible care. Obviously, in our "disposable" society, we do not want animals to be seen as disposable; they deserve to be treated kindly and have happiness. If you find yourself facing the pos-sibility of having to rehome a pet, seek out the assistance of animal care profes-sionals, veterinarians, and behavior specialists; perhaps any medical or behavioral issues can be resolved in a ways that will allow you to keep your pet. Also, informa-tion is available to help keep owners and animals together when the owner is elderly or disabled or living with an immune deficiency disorder (see the Resources list).

It is my hope that this book will help you find the information and resources you need to care for your pet to the best of your ability. Pet ownership is not just a great responsibility, but also a great joy. The more consideration you put into lifestyle decisions and developing healthy habits with your pet, the more relaxation and companionship you will receive from the relationship.

FURTHER READING

Books

Donaldson J. *The Culture Clash*, 2nd ed. Berkley, CA: James & Kenneth Publishers; 2005.
Pryor K. *Don't Shoot the Dog! The New Art of Teaching and Training*. New York: Bantam Books; 1999.

Websites

Veterinary Partner: www.veterinarypartner.com. Offers a wealth of articles on many animal care topics provided by the Veterinary Information Network (VIN).

RESOURCES

Resources for Finding Veterinary Specialists

American College of Veterinary Behaviorists: www.dacvb.org. Provides information on behavioral issues as well as the ability to search for veterinary behaviorists in your area.
American Holistic Veterinary Medical Association: www.ahvma.org. Enables you to locate a veterinarian who practices various modalities of complementary and alternative medicine.
American Association of Housecall Veterinarians (AAHV): www.homevets.org. Enables you to locate a house-call veterinarian in your area.
American Veterinary Medical Association: www.avma.org: The general veterinary medical association in the United States.
There are many veterinary specialties. Asking your veterinarian or conducting an Internet search can lead you to specific organizations.

Pet Care Resources

American Society for the Prevention of Cruelty to Animals (ASPCA): http://www.aspca.org/pet-care/poison-control/. An extensive list of plants and other substances poisonous to animals. (Keep in mind that some plants may be used at therapeutic doses by veterinary herbalists, but can be toxic at higher doses. These treatments should be used only under supervision.)
Healthy Pets, Healthy People: www.cdc.gov/healthypets. Articles on diseases that can be shared between humans and animals and resources for immune-suppressed individuals.
Indoor Pet Initiative: http://indoorpet.osu.edu/. Information on basic care for dogs and cats, including tips on enriching their home environment.
Open Paw: http://www.openpaw.org/. Tips for choosing a pet and living with the one you already have. The "pet basics" section has many training tips.

Hospice and Grief Support

Argus Institute: http://www.argusinstitute.colostate.edu/. Useful resources especially for grief support; links to support hotlines.
Spirits in Transition: www.spiritsintransition.org. Hospice care resources for animals, including integrative holistic care; also has a support hotline.

3

The Human-Animal Bond and Animal-Assisted Therapy

Rebecca A. Johnson, PhD, RN, FAAN

The wish to keep an animal usually arises out of general longing for a bond with nature . . . analogous with those human functions that go hand in hand with love and friendship in the purest and noblest forms.
—Nobel Laureate Konrad Lorenz[1]

DEFINING "THE BOND" AND HUMAN-ANIMAL INTERACTION

The human-animal bond has been defined by the American Veterinary Medical Association as "a mutually beneficial and dynamic relationship between people and animals that is influenced by behaviors that are essential to the health and well-being of both."[2] This definition implies that when bonded, people and animals can depend on each other for their well-being. Such dependence means that both giving and receiving occur between people and their pets. The fact that it is even possible to create a book dedicated to helping keep family pets healthy suggests that pet owners are highly tuned into what they give and receive from their relationship with their pets. The human-animal bond has been called immeasurable, indefinable, and even mystical. Of course, it may actually be more practical than any of these descriptors, relating to the reciprocity that occurs when people and animals co-reside, and the love that develops between them.

The broader phrase of "human-animal interaction" (HAI) is used to encompass the wide spectrum of relationships that people and animals share. It can range from the strong bond that people feel with their pets, to a glance at a flock of wild geese flying overhead, to fulfilling responsibilities for care of animals in a variety of settings such as a farm, laboratory, or animal shelter. HAI also includes more structured activities in which companion animals serve as a medium through which people in therapeutic situations are helped to feel less frightened, more relaxed, and in less pain. During the past three decades, HAI has received growing attention as something that is beneficial for people. Research has been conducted worldwide to investigate these benefits in a variety of situations. Generally, people who do not like animals do not benefit from HAI. However, for people who are at least not averse to interacting with animals, several physical and mental health benefits have been identified from this interaction. This chapter discusses the health benefits of HAI through pet ownership and special kinds of HAI aimed at therapeutic outcomes for people. The neurochemical response to HAI forms the foundation of this discussion.

WHY OWN A PET?

Pet ownership has been defined as "pet-keeping," or the practice of taking care of and living with companion animals. The patterns of this ownership have evolved over time from a period when animals were expected to "earn their keep" by protecting livestock and material possessions, to "watch" their owner's property and alert their owner to the presence of intruders or danger, through what is commonly observed today whereby pets may even serve as surrogate children or grandchildren. This movement of pets from the yard, to the porch, to the kitchen, to sleeping on our beds shows a steady increase in the participation of pets in our lives and our reciprocal participation with them. When we own pets, we commit to taking care of their basic needs for the duration of their lives. This essentially involves the work of providing for their shelter, safety, health care, nutrition, exercise, play, and companionship. So why are people willing to take on the extra work of tending to a pet at all, let alone for a period of several years?

Taking care of our pets' needs means that we are likely to be very closely involved with them on a daily basis, and they with us. Enter the human-animal bond. The bond that develops during this process may be a very intense one, to the point that we know the animal so well that we can predict her behavior, tell others about her likes and dislikes, and even brag about our pet's smart or cute behavior. When we are bonded with our pet, in fulfilling our commitment to meeting our pet's needs, we receive positive reinforcement for our actions and can feel rewarded for being a "good" pet owner. But Konrad Lorenz's statement at the beginning of this chapter implies that we actually *need* this bond, and that perhaps people can thrive in a situation when this type of love and friendship comes without hidden agendas or ulterior motives. The whole process sounds incredibly "warm and fuzzy." Scientists like to discount what is "warm and fuzzy," to explain things numerically or in ways that can be measured "objectively." It turns out that the human-animal bond is not just "warm and fuzzy," but has actually been measured "objectively" by scientists.

Here is how it seems that HAI and the human-animal bond actually "work." Groundbreaking research has found that when we interact with our pets, powerful chemicals that affect our brain are released. Dr. Johannes Odendaal at the Technikon Pretoria in South Africa studied the effects of quiet interaction among 18 people, their own dogs, and an unfamiliar dog.[3] He found that blood levels of the stress hormone (cortisol) decreased significantly in both the people and the dogs during their interaction. He also found significant increases in helpful hormones in the blood, such as oxytocin (helps us to feel happy and trusting), prolactin (helps us to feel nurtured and nurturing), endorphin (gives us a "runner's high"), dopamine (helps us feel energized), and phenylethylamine (helps us feel elated). These changes took place after only a 30-minute quiet petting interaction. Probably the most interesting finding was that the changes were strongest when people interacted with their own dogs and when dogs interacted with their own people.

These research findings usually surprise people who think that what they and their pet feel for each other is magical and spiritual. Actually it is chemical, just as in any number of other situations in which beneficial chemical changes occur in our bodies. Knowing that the human-animal bond is actually a chemically based phenomenon, we can imagine all kinds of situations in which it might help both people and animals. But what about owning a pet? Can there be long-term benefits of the chemical response that help us be healthier through our lives?

CAN OWNING PETS HELP US BE HEALTHY?

The nice thing about the human-animal bond is that it really does "work." A wide range of research evidence supports the healthy outcomes of pet ownership. For example, one benefit of dog ownership is that because dogs need exercise and pet owners commit to meeting this need, the people themselves get exercise. People are more likely to commit to exercise to help their dog get some exercise than to walk or run on a treadmill in the basement. The treadmill does not give us any positive feedback except number of minutes or miles walked or run. If treadmills were the answer to exercise, there would not be a 70 percent adult incidence rate of overweight and obesity in the United States. In fact, many treadmills become expensive "clothing racks" within a few months of their purchase.

By comparison, our dogs give us multiple levels of positive feedback when we take them for a walk. Dog walking as a beneficial physical activity is being recognized and studied worldwide. In fact, in the United States, one study showed that adults who walked dogs accumulated at least 30 minutes of walking in bouts of at least 10 minutes—a regimen that meets the Centers for Disease Control and Prevention's (CDC's) exercise guidelines for a healthy lifestyle.[4] Similar results have been found in Australia. In Japan, researchers found that when older adults walked a dog, they had beneficial changes in their heart function, which not only continued during the walk but also lasted afterward, and accumulated over time.[5] In regard to weight loss, scientists found that sedentary, overweight dog walkers lost an average of 14.4 pounds by walking loaner dogs for 20 minutes, 4 days per week, for 50 weeks, and achieved a 72 percent rate of adherence to the walking program.[6]

Thus dog walking may be beneficial by helping us to get needed exercise, be less sedentary, lose some weight, have positive interaction with dogs, and spend time outdoors. It has also been found to help older people keep functioning at higher levels so that they can remain independent even later in life. In fact, this activity has been found to be related to improved and maintained walking speed among older adults—a consideration that is especially important because walking speed predicts an older adult's ability to remain independent.

Dog walking is, of course, good for dogs as well. Like the human population, a large percentage of dogs are overweight or obese. This excess weight means that they probably are not being walked enough by their owners. A commitment of dog owners to walking their dogs will facilitate health for the individuals on both ends of the leash.

Dog walking may also improve neighborhoods by making them seem friendlier. Dog walkers may serve as watchful eyes for preventing potential criminal activities and in looking out for neighbors who may need help. When neighbors are outside more, they may be more likely to interact, thereby contributing to the quality of life for residents of the neighborhood. In other words, in the case of dog walking, the human-animal bond may extend outside of the owner-dog dyad to provide benefits to the overall community.

Dog walking is one outward way that pet ownership and the human-animal bond facilitate health. But simply owning and caring for a dog have been found by many researchers to be beneficial to human health. For example, dog ownership has been associated with lower blood pressure, cholesterol, and triglyceride levels, and owning a dog seems to help people with high blood pressure respond better to stress. Older dog owners have been found to make fewer nonroutine appointments to see their physicians, which can save millions of dollars in health care expenditures. In one of the most cited studies, dog and cat owners were found to have better one-year survival after a heart attack than non-pet owners.[7] The researchers were able to rule out the effects of severity of the heart attack, length of time that the participants had heart disease, other health problems, and age as influencing the participants' outcomes; pet ownership still held as the strongest predictor of survival. In another study, people who had never owned a cat were found to have a much greater risk of dying from a heart attack.

These research findings are easy to understand if we remember the mechanism through with the human-animal bond "works." Because stress is a major factor in heart disease, along with blood pressure, cholesterol, and triglyceride levels, it is understandable that the beneficial decreases in the cortisol stress hormone that occur when pet owners interact with their pets might contribute to better heart-related outcomes. Considered together with the increase in exercise (for people who regularly walk their dogs), it is easy to see how pet ownership can facilitate human health.

CAN OWNING PETS HELP US FEEL HAPPIER?

When the human-animal bond is considered in relation to emotions, it is clear how both people and pets can benefit from this interaction. Most of our pets provide us with unconditional love (some people argue that cats do not do this, or do it only on their own terms). A wagging tail and other greeting responses when we return home can do much to help us begin to forget a stressful day and to live in the moment of the greeting. By expressing their pure joy at seeing us, our pets teach us that living in the moment is not only a healthy thing to do, but also helps us to feel happier. Pets do not spend their time or energy worrying about things in the past or ruminating over things that may happen in the future. Their joy is for the moment, and they express it completely. In fact, they often use whole-body responses to demonstrate their happiness.

Consider the cat that meets his owner at the door with vocalizations and profuse ankle rubbing. The cat feels the need to mark his person and to replace the smells that may have accumulated on the person's ankles during the day with the cat's own, thereby making a statement: "You are mine." Or consider the dog that meets her owner at the door carrying an offering of a favorite toy, wagging her entire body, and then spinning in circles before dissolving into a hugging and petting session. Seldom, if ever, would another person greet us in such an unbridled way. These are the pure forms of love that Konrad Lorenz described.

In our daily lives, we too often stay imprisoned by pain and regrets of the past or worries about the future. We are taught at fairly early ages that it is impolite to express ourselves freely and fully. Yet when faced with a jubilant pet, we are given permission to use higher-pitched voices ("baby talk") and to respond to our pets in ways that most of us would be embarrassed to use in greeting another person. For some people, the only play in their lives may involve playing with their pets.

Pets have long been recognized as "social lubricants." Early studies showed that when people walk down the street accompanied by a dog, they are more likely to be viewed favorably and spoken to by passersby. This finding also held among people in wheelchairs. The presence of a dog was associated with much more positive responses from other people. A pet gives people a nonthreatening subject to talk about. It is perhaps easier to share information about one's pet than about oneself, particularly when first meeting people or talking with people who are not known well. Pet owners like to talk about their pets. Perhaps sharing their pet's funny antics makes owners feel and seem more interesting. Pets can be a medium through which people enjoy talking together.

In dog-walking circles, it is commonly recognized that people stop to chat about their dogs, yet may know relatively nothing about one another as persons except

---

DID YOU KNOW?

- Approximately 62 percent of all U.S. households (71 million) include a pet. These animals include dogs (39 percent of households), cats (33 percent), freshwater fish (13 percent), birds (6 percent), small animals (5 percent), and reptiles (4 percent)
- In 2011, an estimated $50 billion will be spent on pets in the United States.
- More than 1 million people benefit each year from more than 10,000 registered Delta Society Pet Partners animal-assisted activity teams in many settings.

---

through the dogs (e.g., "Snoopy likes to sleep on my chest," "Fluffy and I share our ice cream together every night," or "We don't travel anywhere that Bingo can't go along"). These exchanges help the dog walkers feel connected, and they reinforce the bond that they feel with their dogs. It is common for dog walkers to watch for one another, to be concerned if they do not see one another for a period, and when reconnected to inquire, "Where have you been? We missed you!" These expressions often facilitate descriptions of vacations, major family traumas, and events related to their dogs. It is also clear that dog walkers have unstated rules of behavior around such issues as picking up dog droppings, preventing dogs from jumping on people, or preventing their own pets from accosting other dogs. They may commonly enforce these rules with one another in a friendly way, wanting to maintain the relationship that they have with their dog-walking counterparts, while still adhering to a certain set of standards so that all can have an equal opportunity to enjoy walking their dogs in the chosen location. This unique form of a social network is entirely created around their dogs. Without their dogs, the structure would be quite different, and it is unclear how often these people would even stop to chat, much less how much they might share about themselves with one another.

In today's world of electronic social networking, countless Internet discussion boards related to pets serve as places where people can go to meet others with similar pet interests or concerns—everything from a blind-dog discussion group to cat message boards. A Google search for "pet discussion groups" yielded more than 2 million hits. This mechanism enables our pets to facilitate our social interaction indirectly without even being physically present.

However, when pets are physically present in our lives, our interaction or bond with them has been found to help us emotionally in a number of ways. For example, pet owners are less likely to have depression and anxiety, and less likely to feel lonely than non-pet owners.[8] They have better morale than non-pet owners and can identify the role that their pets play in helping them maintain a healthy emotional outlook.

This result may be due not only to the positive chemical changes described earlier, but also to our pets' unconditional and nonjudgmental acceptance of us, or perhaps our perception of their regard. In one study, people performed better on a complex mathematical test when an unfamiliar dog was present than when either a spouse, a partner, or a self-selected friend was present.[9] This finding may explain why many pet owners talk to their pets about problems in their lives or about their concerns. Not only do the owners know that they will get no argument, but they also may perceive their listener as loving them no matter what they say. Rare is the relationship between people in which anything can be said without fear of repercussions.

The concept of unconditional love may be especially important for older adults, who may be regarded by society as less important given that they are no longer breadwinners. The isolation that can occur in this population as a result of this factor combined with what may be steadily declining functional ability may make pets and the human-animal bond especially important for elderly individuals. Some older adults may make decisions based on owning pets. For example, they may be highly motivated to comply with whatever rehabilitation activity is prescribed so that they can get out of the hospital or rehabilitation facility and return home to their pets.

On the downside, pets are also often a consideration for members of this population in having elective surgeries. Some older adults may have no one to take care of their pets while they are away, so they may put off going into a hospital. (These situations have not been shown by research, but have been reported anecdotally by clinicians taking care of older adults). This situation is unfortunate: if the older adults had someone to help them maintain their pets, they would not have to worry about avoiding health care for fear that their animals will be taken away from them or that no one will take care of the animals in their absence.

Sometimes older adults stay in their homes where they may not be able to get care they need because they do not want to move into a facility where pets are not allowed, thus forcing them to give up their pets. This situation is a difficult one requiring the support of family and friends to find a facility where pets are allowed and to help the older adult with care of the pet so that the person can receive the care he or she needs. Most assistive housing facilities supported by tax dollars allow pets, although a "pet deposit" or fee is often required.

Unfortunately, when older adults become functionally impaired to the point that they are unable to care for their pets independently, it is often decided by their health care providers and family members that "the pet must go." This is an inhumane response to a simple need for some assistance. If an older adult needed a cane or help with getting dressed, this care would readily be provided. However, this same consideration of helping with pet care is often not considered by family members. Too often older adults must surrender their beloved pets to an animal shelter because no one will help them care for their animal companions. As a consequence, they lose a vital component of their social support and source of unconditional love.

One scenario in which this does not occur is at TigerPlace, the aging-in-place retirement residence located in Columbia, Missouri. Started by the University of Missouri's Sinclair School of Nursing with its corporate partner, Americare, Inc., TigerPlace is a pet-encouraging environment where older adults move into an apartment with their pets and never have to move again. Care for the residents is added as they need it. For their pets, a fully equipped veterinary medical examination room staffed by a faculty member from the College of Veterinary Medicine enables owners to walk down the hall to see the veterinarian. In fact, the veterinarian makes monthly house calls for every pet residing at TigerPlace. A special fund provides foster care for pets whose owners pass away. A Pet Assistant makes visits three times per week to check on pet food and water supplies, transport food and pets as needed, clean cat litter boxes, and walk dogs if an owner needs help with this task. TigerPlace is unique in the United States in terms of how it embraces the concept that the human-animal bond can be vital for older adults' well-being. It recognizes how attached older adults are to their pets and how potentially damaging it is for them when the human-animal bond is broken simply because the human side of the equation needs some help.

The older adult–companion animal bond may be one crucial element in helping older adults to stay independent and happy. The concept of attachment has been proposed by theorists as explaining how people become attached to others with whom they feel safe. The nonjudgmental nature of the human-animal bond may create just such a situation in which older adults feel safe.

This nonjudgmental nature is plainly seen in dogs that "work" for their owners. Service animals are vital to the independence of many people with physical or mental challenges. Service animals, as defined by the Americans with Disabilities Act, include "any guide dog, signal dog, or other animal individually trained to provide assistance to an individual with a disability." These highly trained animals perform a myriad of tasks for their owners, such as picking up objects, opening doors, turning on lights, helping with dressing, helping with housekeeping tasks, carrying packs, pulling wheelchairs, and more. They are vital helpers to their owners. Service animals are protected by U.S. federal law, and it is a felony to purposely injure such an animal. They also enjoy special rights, which make their work possible. In particular, service animals cannot be denied access to any public or private location, including restaurants, grocery stores, movie theaters, or taxis. These privileges enable them to do their work in helping their owner go about daily life.

While guide dogs for the blind or hearing service dogs are commonly seen, in recent years service dogs have also begun to play a major role in helping persons with mental illnesses such as post-traumatic stress disorder (PTSD), anxiety, and depression move about with the confidence that their steady helper is there. Very recently, service dogs have been used with children who have autism spectrum disorders (ASD) to ensure the children's safety and help calm and focus the children.

Service animals truly serve a noble purpose in helping their people live their lives more fully. The dogs ask nothing in return except to be cared for, to love and be loved. The bond between a service animal and the animal's owner is a strong one. The owner's quality of life depends on the animal!

In addition, animals support and promote quality of life when they are "used" to help people in various therapeutic settings. Most people are aware of settings where animals are commonly brought to visit, such as hospitals and nursing homes. Their role is often more complex, however, and warrants further discussion.

ANIMAL-ASSISTED THERAPY

There are two levels of interaction where animals are used in structured situations to help people. Animal-assisted activity (AAA) refers to animal visits made by a pet and the handler after they have qualified for this work through a systematic training and testing program. The "gold standard" for such training and testing is provided by the Delta Society (http://www.deltasociety.org/Page.aspx?pid=183).

The goal of AAA visits is distraction, diversion, and companionship for the recipient. The visits usually consist of spontaneous content, with the handler typically "translating" the pet to the person receiving the visit. This usually involves a series of questions about the pet by the visit recipient. The handler provides information about what the breed and age of the pet are, where the pet was obtained, where and how the animal was trained and certified for visits, how long the handler has owned the pet, whether there are more pets at home, whether the pet has any special likes and dislikes, and how long the pet has been making AAA visits. With this type of interaction, there are no specific treatment goals. The pets involved are usually owned by the handlers and live with them, and the handlers are usually volunteers associated with a particular national (e.g., Delta Society) or regional visitation group. Typical recipients of AAA visits include patients in acute care, residents of nursing homes, children in schools, prison inmates, and shut-ins living in their own homes in the community. This type of interaction seems to be most effective in situations that are anxiety provoking for the patient or where loneliness may be a problem.

A common outcome of AAA visits is that the recipient engages in reminiscence about previous pets that he or she has known or owned. This activity may also be therapeutic as fond remembrances of pets are shared with others, resulting in a lively exchange. Such visits also often result in staff members of the particular facility communicating more positively with their co-workers, the patients being served, and the patients' family members.

By comparison, animal-assisted therapy (AAT) entails the specific treatment- and goal-directed involvement of the pet and the handler in the health care of a patient. In the strictest sense, it requires that the handler have professional expertise required to lead the therapy. However, it may also involve a volunteer handler and pet who are directed by a health care professional to participate in certain activities during the therapy. In either case, AAT encompasses a systematic plan for how the pet will be involved in the patient's care based on the individual needs of the patient and how the progress of the patient will be measured. Thus the therapy animal is part of treatment plan.

The goal of AAT is to improve some level of functioning in the patient. This consideration may be physical, as in the case of stroke rehabilitation patients who are relearning to use their affected arms and legs by doing activities that involve the pet (e.g., combing the therapy pet, throwing a ball for the therapy dog, or speaking to the pet), or it may be emotional, as in the case of child abuse victims who are being helped to tell their stories to or through the therapy pet. When pocket pets or birds are used (e.g., in counseling), they may live in the therapy setting. In contrast, when dogs, cats, rabbits, or chickens are used, they live at the home of their owner (i.e., the therapist or the volunteer handler).

AAA AND AAT ACROSS THE LIFE SPAN AND VARIOUS SETTINGS

AAA visits have been studied in many settings and found to provide benefits to the recipients. Such visits seem to help with pain relief in a variety of environments. For example, children who were recovering in the hospital after surgery have been found to have less pain after a dog visit.[10] Adults have also experienced pain relief in response to AAA visits, resulting in fewer pain medications taken. Patients with heart failure were found to have decreased anxiety and epinephrine (the "fight or flight" hormone) levels during and after an animal visit.[11]

Given the chemical changes known to occur when people interact with animals, it is apparent that there may be many situations in which people could benefit from feeling less stressed, more relaxed, nurtured, trusting, and elated through animal contact. Although AAA and AAT have not been formally tested in all of these situations, where such testing has been conducted, the research findings are promising.

In a different form of AAT, children with cerebral palsy aged 4 to 12 years had improved muscle symmetry and decreased spasticity after only a single session of 8 minutes of therapeutic horseback riding.[12] While many therapeutic riding programs are in place across the United States, there has been very little research conducted on therapeutic horseback riding; it is clearly one area where more study is needed.

In long-term care (nursing home) settings, many studies have shown that older adults respond well to AAA visits. In particular, they interact more with one another, visitors, family, and staff members, and staff-to-resident interaction is more positive when a therapy dog is present. AAA is perhaps most effective, however, in helping older adults who have newly relocated to a nursing home to feel less lonely. Particularly during the first six weeks after relocating to a nursing home, older adults may feel a strong sense of depression, anxiety, loss, and betrayal. While group and private visitation have both produced beneficial results in such cases, the preference of an older adult for one or the other needs to be taken into account. As described earlier in this chapter, the extent to which a visitor animal may be a social lubricant in a long-term care setting may be instrumental in helping older adults feel less lonely.

In what may be argued to be a less interactive form of AAA, patients with Alzheimer's disease living in a long-term care facility ate significantly more food when watching fish swim. When investigators placed self-contained aquariums in front of the patients during meal times, they found that the older adults were more likely to sit at the table long enough to consume their food when they could watch the fish.[13] This is clearly a novel application of AAA. The same researchers also found that the residents watched and talked about the fish outside of mealtimes, indicating that the residents were able to break through their confusion while watching the fish.

In an even less traditional situation, prison inmates who participated in a program of puppy raising for a service dog agency and raised a puppy for one year (preparing the dogs to go into training as service animals) in their prison cells had improved self-esteem and feelings that they were responsible for taking control of their own lives to make them better at the end of the experience. This program, in essence, reverses AAA and AAT, in that the inmates were the ones benefiting by living with the puppies, taking care of them and giving them basic obedience training.

The role of AAA and AAT in helping people feel less stressed, less lonely, and more loved and worthy has been widely reported by clinicians working in a variety of settings. Nevertheless, for the field of HAI to truly advance, we need sound research showing specifically which people are benefited, how much exposure to the animal is needed to obtain the maximum benefit, what the actual benefits are (e.g., pain relief, anxiety control, distraction, loneliness relief), and how long the benefits last. A growing body of scientific evidence shows that AAA and AAT are promising therapeutic modalities for those who are receptive to companion animals. Conducting the needed studies will be a complex and costly endeavor, however, given the large number of variables that can influence how people respond to companion animals and the need to account for these variables when conducting the study. For example, a child who has been bitten by a dog may not benefit from AAA or AAT. Likewise, an older adult who believes that animals have no place being inside may not be able to relax and benefit from interacting with an animal in a hospital or nursing home. Thus individual factors must be taken into account when researchers study AAA and AAT, just as they must be taken into account when animals are introduced in health care settings to serve as instruments of therapy. When researchers include these variables in their work, we can rely on the soundness of their findings to show new knowledge.

People and animals have lived together and depended on each other in one capacity or another for thousands of years. Clearly, the human-animal bond is not a recent phenomenon, but the wide array of situations in which it may truly make a difference for people continues to be revealed. These scenarios seem to be limited only by the imagination.

KEY TERMS

Human-animal bond	"A mutually beneficial and dynamic relationship between people and animals that is influenced by behaviors that are essential to the health and well-being of both." (AVMA)
Animal-assisted activity (AAA)	Animal visits made by a pet and the handler after they have qualified for this work through a systematic training and testing program.
Animal-assisted therapy (AAT)	A specific treatment- and goal-directed involvement of the pet and the handler in the health care of a patient.
Assistance/service animal	"Any guide dog, signal dog, or other animal individually trained to provide assistance to an individual with a disability." (http://www.ada.gov/archive/animal.htm)
Delta Society (www.deltasociety.org)	An organization that helps people live healthier and happier lives by incorporating therapy, service, and companion animals into their lives. It provides training and registration of Pet Partner teams who together do AAA and AAT.

REFERENCES

1. Hines, L. "Historical Perspectives on the Human-Animal Bond." *American Behavioral Scientist* 47 (2003): 7–15.

2. American Veterinary Medical Association, available at: http://www.avma.org/issues/human_animal_bond/default.asp

3. Odendaal, J. S. *A Physiological Basis for Animal-Facilitated Psychotherapy.* Unpublished doctoral dissertation, University of Pretoria, Faculty of Veterinary Science, Pretoria, South Africa, 1999.

4. Ham, S. A., and J. Epping. "Dog Walking and Physical Activity in the United States." *Preventing Chronic Disease* 3 (2006): A47.

5. Motooka, M., H. Koike, T. Yokoyama, and N. Kennedy. "Effect of Dog-Walking on Autonomic Nervous Activity in Senior Citizens." *Medical Journal of Australia* 184 (2006): 60–63.

6. Johnson, R. A., and R. L. Meadows. "Dog-Walking: Motivation for Adherence to a Walking Program." *Clinical Nursing Research* 19 (2010): 387–402.

7 Friedmann, E., and S. Thomas. "Pet Ownership, Social Support, and One-Year Survival After Acute Myocardial Infarction in the Cardiac Arrhythmia Suppression Trial (CAST)." *American Journal of Cardiology* 76 (1995): 1213–17.

8. Garrity, T., L. Stallones, M. Marx, and T. Johnson. "Pet Ownership And Attachment as Supportive Factors in the Health of the Elderly." *Anthrozoos* 3 (1989): 35–44.

9. Allen, K., J. Blascovich, J. Tomaka, and R., Kelsey. "Presence of Human Friends and Pet Dogs as Moderators of Autonomic Responses to Stress in Women." *Journal of Personality and Social Psychology* 61 (1991): 582–89.

10. Sobo, E. J., B. Eng, and N. Kassity-Krich. "Canine Visitation (Pet) Therapy: Pilot Data on Decreases in Child Pain Perception." *Journal of Holistic Nursing* 24 (2006): 51–57.

11. Cole, K., and A. Gawlinski. "Animal Assisted Therapy in the Intensive Care Unit." *Research Utilization* 30 (1995): 529–36.

12. Benda, W., N. H. McGibbon, and K. L. Grant." Improvements in Muscle Symmetry in Children with Cerebral Palsy after Equine-Assisted Therapy (Hippotherapy)." *Journal of Alternative and Complementary Medicine* 9 (2003): 817–25.

13. Edwards, N. E., and A. M. Beck. "Animal Assisted Therapy and Nutrition in Alzheimer's Disease." *Western Journal of Nursing Research* 24 (2002): 697–712.

FURTHER READING

Becker, M., and D. Morton. *The Healing Power of Pets*. New York: Hyperion; 2002.

Fine, A. *Handbook on Animal Assisted Therapy and Interventions*. New York: Elsevier; 2010.

Johnson, R. A., and C. McKenney. "Walk a Hound, Lose a Pound: A Community Dog-Walking Program for Families." In *The Health Benefits of Dog-Walking*, ed. by R. A. Johnson, A. M. Beck, and S. McCune. West Lafayette, IN: Purdue University Press; 2011 (In press).

Zeltzman, P., & Johnson, R. *Walk a Hound, Lose a Pound*. West Lafayette, IN: Purdue University Press, 2011.

4

First Aid for Pets

Elisa M. Mazzaferro, MS, DVM, PhD, DACVECC

INTRODUCTION

Whenever a family has a pet, whether the pet is a cat, dog, bird, fish, reptile, or pocket pet, "pet-proofing" the pet's environment is just as important as—or even more important than—providing first aid, so that you can prevent accidents from happening in the first place. In the unfortunate event of an accident, however, this chapter is meant to provide you with guidelines and suggestions about what to do. Thus it describes how to avoid accidents, and how to deal with accidents and emergencies when they do happen. To bolster your knowledge and skills in this area, it is recommended that you take a pet first-aid class from your local veterinary association or Red Cross.

PET PROOFING

Before bringing a pet home, it is important to "pet-proof" the environment to help prevent problems before they occur. A pet, even a newly adopted adult dog or cat, is similar to a small child, in that the animal will be interested and curious to explore her new home environment. Puppies, kittens, and even adult animals can potentially be destructive and chew on carpets, walls, furniture, and electrical cords. Some animals will have the capability to jump onto, or into, countertops and cabinets. New pets may not know boundaries or understand what are acceptable versus unacceptable behaviors.

If you want to make a certain area of your home off-limits to your pet, close the door to that area or purchase an expandable gate to prevent entry. Take care to pick up all items that are off-limits, such as shoes, socks, and laundry that may not have made its way to the laundry basket. Take items such as potpourri, remote control devices, fragile objects d'art, books, candy dishes, and food items off of countertops that are within reach of the new pet so they are not broken or swallowed. Make note of the plants in your house and garden, and make sure they are not toxic if ingested by your pet.

Put safety locks on your cabinets to prevent the pet from getting inside and having access to food, prescription medications, or household chemicals. Also, put safety locks on window screens to prevent animals from falling out of windows.

Electric cords can be very dangerous if the pet chews on them. Loose cords can be secured to the baseboards by small plastic brackets, or they can be enclosed within a length of plastic PCV pipe to prevent chewing and electrocution.

Pet-proofing your outdoors areas also takes time, and sometimes ingenuity. Owners are often surprised by how quickly their pets outsmart them and get into things that they have not thought of. Lawn edging is commonly used in newer garden and landscape projects to prevent grass from encroaching into flowerbeds. It is made of hard plastic or metal, and may include a rubber barrier. While this invention makes it easier to trim your flowerbeds, it also presents a severe hazard to pets and children and causes numerous lacerations that often require surgery. If your yard has any form of lawn edging, even with a protective covering, remove it to protect your pet.

Fence in the area of your yard that is accessible to your dogs, and take care to search carefully for potential escape routes, either over, under, or through fencing. It may be necessary to put chicken wire or other fence material down to the level of the ground and bury it to prevent crafty diggers from escaping. Some dogs may require a fenced-in area with a lid to prevent them from climbing out of your yard. In rural areas, adding a chain-link top to dog runs can also provide protection from wild predators such as large cats, foxes, and coyotes. Removing wasp nests from your yard can also help prevent you and your pet from getting stung by a swarm of insects.

When it comes to first aid, the best course of action is thinking of worst-case scenarios, taking the time to help prevent accidents from occurring, and then being prepared to deal with an accident, if it occurs. As the saying goes, "An ounce of prevention is worth a pound of cure."

THE ANIMAL FIRST-AID KIT

Before an accident happens, it is worthwhile to prepare a first-aid kit for your pets (Table 4.1). To begin, you will need to find a container for your supplies, such as a tackle or shoe box, a plastic container, or even a gallon-sized reclosable zipper-lock bag. Items to have on hand include clean hand towels, duct tape, saline irrigation solution (like you would use for contact lenses), gauze and cotton bandaging material, white surgical adhesive tape, a muzzle appropriate for your pet's mouth, an antibiotic ointment such as Neosporin, hydrogen peroxide, and a digital thermometer.

Table 4.1
Items to Include in Your Pet's First-Aid Kit

Clean towels

Duct tape

Saline irrigation solution

Gauze and cotton bandage material

White adhesive tape

Muzzle

Antibiotic ointment

Hydrogen peroxide

It is also helpful to identify the location of the closest veterinary emergency room (ER) before an accident or emergency occurs. Keep your family veterinarian's number handy, and ask the staff there which facility they recommend in the event of an emergency. Keep that contact name, address, and phone number in your pet first-aid kit. Even better, you can call the emergency facility or use an online mapping system to print out directions beforehand, so you do not waste valuable time getting your pet to the ER during an actual crisis. If you do need emergency services, call ahead to let the staff know that you are coming in. They may be able to give you advice on what to do before coming in and how to transport an ill or injured pet. Ideally, your kit will sit on a shelf, unused and not needed. Because accidents sometimes happen, however, we all need to be prepared.

WILDERNESS FIRST-AID KIT

If you are planning to take your pet on outdoor adventures such as camping or hiking, additional material such as rolled-up newspaper, a cloth sheet, and backpack may come in handy in the event of a fracture that requires splinting, or if you need to carry your pet out from the location of the accident. Rolled-up newspaper can be placed on a leg above and below an obvious fracture, then secured in place with roll gauze and duct tape. Ideally, a towel or sheet can be used as a sling under your dog's body, behind or in front of the broken limb, to help support your pet as you slowly walk to the nearest road or back to your car. The sheet can be tied between straight tree limbs to help carry your pet out. You can also cut the bottom out of a backpack and secure your pet in the backpack with lengths of rope, if you are by yourself and need to carry your pet to safety.

It is always a good idea to let a friend or family member know your plans, including the location where you plan to hike or camp, the estimated time of your arrival and departure at this destination, and your time of arrival at home. In rural areas, sometimes cell phones do not work, so they should not be your only lifeline.

By following these simple guidelines, you ensure that if you are late because of an accident, someone can be alerted to come and find you.

CARDIOPULMONARY RESUSCITATION

Witnessing a pet's death from an accident or illness without having medical personnel on hand to assist in resuscitation efforts is perhaps one of the most stressful things that can happen in a pet owner's life. Pet owners often think that there must be something that they can do to help the animal, some procedure they can use to change the outcome. Cardiopulmonary resuscitation (CPR) can often save lives for humans, particularly in the event of a witnessed heart attack or near-drowning. Unfortunately, television shows such as *Rescue 911, ER, Chicago Hope*, and *Grey's Anatomy* have sensationalized the success of CPR, suggesting that it can save 65 percent of patients (at least on these shows). In real life, however, the success rate for humans is actually much lower—and for animals, it is even lower.

It is important to realize that there are some situations in which performing CPR on your pet may be worthwhile and potentially successful, and other situations in which it is more likely to be unsuccessful, no matter how hard you try. For example, if you witness your pet having a bowel movement and the animal falls over and faints, or stops breathing, the pet is likely experiencing a vasovagal event. CPR, in this case, can be helpful. If your pet nearly drowns, experiences electrocution, or is exposed to smoke in a house fire, CPR may also be successful. If your pet chokes on a bone or other foreign object and you perform the Heimlich maneuver (by compressing the sternum or breastbone toward the pet's spine), the animal may recover. However, if an animal has a terminal condition that is not immediately reversible, such as cancer, kidney or liver failure, or severe trauma, CPR cannot change the outcome.

How to Perform CPR

If you witness acute collapse and your pet is not breathing, place your hand on the chest, just behind the ribs, and feel for a heartbeat. If there is no heartbeat and your pet is not breathing, look inside the mouth to make sure that nothing is obstructing the airway. *Be careful:* many animals will clamp their mouths shut in this situation and you can easily be bitten. Next, place your hand around your pet's muzzle, put your mouth over the nose, and breathe two deep breaths into the nose. Watch to see if the chest rises. Next, place your hands on the chest, just behind the animal's elbow, and push and compress the chest for 50 percent of its diameter while calling for help. Perform 100 to 120 compressions per minute. For smaller animals, such as cats and toy breed dogs, cup your hand around the bottom of the chest, behind the elbows, and compress both sides of the chest at a rate of 100 to 120 times per minute. Intermittently, you can breathe for your pet several times per minute, then resume compressions. If, after 5 to 10 minutes, there is no sign of a heartbeat or breathing, the chance of success decreases dramatically, and attempts at resuscitation should be stopped.

POISON CONTROL HELPLINES

There are a number of poison control hotlines (Table 4.2) that pet owners can call for advice when their animals ingest things that they should not. Notably, a large number of prescription medications that are safe for humans may be toxic to pets. Other pain relievers, such as ibuprofen and naproxen—the active ingredients in Advil and Aleve, respectively—can cause stomach irritation, ulcers, and kidney failure. For this reason, you should never give any over-the-counter or prescription medications to an animal that have not been specifically prescribed by a veterinarian. Even drugs that are prescribed for the pet can be toxic if ingested in

Table 4.2
Websites and Phone Numbers of Pet First-Aid and Pet Poison Helplines

Website Name	URL	Information Available	Phone Number
American Animal Hospital Association (AAHA) Healthy Pet.com	http://www.healthypet.com	AAHA-accredited veterinary hospitals, traveling with your pet, how to find a veterinarian, puppy-proofing your home, pet wellness care, fun facts for kids	
American Veterinary Medical Association (AVMA) Animal Health	http://www.avma.org/firstaid	First-aid tips for pet owners, pet selection, animal brochures, phone numbers for pet poison helplines	
American Society for the Prevention of Cruelty to Animals (ASPCA) Animal Poison Control Center	http://www.aspca.org/pet-care/poison-control	Helpline to get information on pet toxicities, and toxic and nontoxic plants	(888) 426-4435
Pet Poison Helpline	http://www.petpoisonhelpline.com	24-hour service regarding pet toxicities, pet-loss support, food recalls, pet-care tips	(800) 213-6680
Pet Health 101	http://www.pethealth101.com	Adopting a pet, general wellness care, nutrition, poisons, common behavior and medical conditions, "ask a vet" blog	

large quantities. Other household chemicals, toxins, plants, and even foodstuffs, including some fruits, vegetables, and nuts, can also be toxic to pets.

As a rule of thumb, if your pet ingests something that is not her regular food or treat, it is best to contact your family veterinarian, who may recommend that you call a poison hotline. Human poison control assistance is often available free of charge, but these sources may not have the information necessary to assist in the treatment of animals. When you make the call, it is helpful to know the name of the product that the pet ingested or was exposed to, the time since ingestion or exposure, the amount the pet ingested, and the symptoms that the pet is showing. With this information, trained specialists can determine whether it will be necessary to seek veterinary attention.

COMMON INJURIES AND EMERGENCIES

Motor Vehicle Trauma

Among the most common accidents involving pets is an animal getting hit by a car, or what veterinarians call "HBC." All too frequently, animals escape from an enclosed yard, are let loose on purpose, or somehow escape from a leash and collar. The injuries sustained when an animal is struck by a car can range from minor cuts and bruises to death. Many of these injuries can be avoided by keeping your pet indoors, in a properly fenced-in space, or outside only on a leash.

If your pet is struck by a moving vehicle, the animal may or may not be conscious, and may or may not be able to walk. With any trauma, first place a muzzle over your pet's mouth to protect against being bitten. If your pet is unconscious or not able to walk, put the animal on a firm surface like a piece of plywood and place tape over the shoulders and the hips to prevent your dog or cat from attempting to get up, which can cause further injury in the case of a broken back. If you are working by yourself, after you place the muzzle on the dog or cat's face, gently slide the animal onto a board or firm, flat surface, rather than attempting to lift the animal onto the board; lifting can potentially cause further injury to a damaged spinal cord or other fracture.

When an animal has been hit by a car, bruising of the lungs or collapse of the lungs is frequently present. When this happens, the animal's breathing will likely be shallow and labored, and the gums and tongue may appear gray or purple in color. Your veterinarian will also examine the animal for damage to internal organs, including internal bleeding. Broken bones are common in HBC incidents as well.

Even if a pet seems completely fine after being struck by a moving vehicle, it is best to take the animal to the nearest veterinary hospital. Signs of a serious injury such as bruising of the lungs or internal bleeding may not become apparent for several hours after a traumatic event. If an animal is ambulatory and able to walk, place the pet on a leash or in a carrier to prevent excessive activity when transporting the pet to the veterinarian.

Fall from Height

"High-rise syndrome" occurs when an animal falls from height. In urban areas, many times an animal falls from a balcony or out of a window. In more rural areas, animals sometimes fall off of a cliff or a deck or, in the case of cats, from a tree limb. No matter where they fall from, the height of the fall can be associated with significant injury. Curiously, when animals fall from more than three stories, they have a slightly higher chance of survival, as cats and dogs have enough time to right themselves and fall onto their breastbone and legs.

Common injuries from high-rise syndrome include abrasions, broken jaw, broken sternum or breastbone, and fractures of the pelvis. Internal bleeding, collapsed lungs, and rupture of the urinary bladder can also occur. As with other injuries, if an animal is not able to walk after falling from height, the pet should be placed on a firm surface and taped down to help prevent further injury to the spinal cord while transporting the pet to the veterinarian.

Lacerations

Lacerations are most common in the spring and summer months, when animals are outdoors and active; however, this type of injury can occur at any time of year, even when there is snow and ice on the ground. Pet-proofing your backyard can help prevent some lacerations by removing sharp objects such as nails, broken downspouts, and lawn edging from around the garden and flowerbeds. As mentioned previously, even having plastic or rubber material guards over lawn edging may not prevent all lacerations from this source.

If your pet has a laceration or open wound, take a clean cloth or towel and press it over the wound. If significant bleeding is present, keep direct pressure over the wound and take your pet to the nearest veterinary hospital. Never put a tourniquet around a leg to help stop bleeding, as long-term loss of blood supply to the leg could result. If a laceration occurs while you are out hiking on a trail, place a loose-fitting bandage on the animal's leg until you can get your pet to a veterinarian. Once there, your veterinarian can assess the severity of the wound and determine whether it will require stitches. Your pet may also be placed on medication to control pain and prevent infection.

Bite Wounds

Bite wounds may or may not be obvious at the time that they occur. You may or may not witness your pet getting into a fight with another animal. Bacteria from animals' mouths can be very dangerous, however, and cause an infection in a bite wound if left untreated. If you see your pet get into a fight with another animal, check your pet's haircoat carefully for any signs of puncture wounds, abrasions, and lacerations. Even the smallest puncture wound can become infected and turn into an abscess without proper medical treatment.

Clean the wound with saline irrigation solution and antibacterial liquid soap. If the wound is large, take your pet to the veterinarian; otherwise, schedule an appointment with your veterinarian to see whether your pet needs to be started on antibiotics to help prevent infection. Even if a bite wound seems minor or goes unnoticed, watch your pet carefully for signs of swelling or discharge from the skin. Frequently, a small bite or puncture wound initially is small, yet contains bacteria that were injected under the skin. Once the wound scabs over, the bacteria may then multiply and cause an abscess to form. Abscessed wounds and larger bite wounds may require sedation and placement of a drain or stitches, depending on the size, severity, and location of the wound. Antibiotics are essential in helping prevent an infected wound from worsening, and pain medication may be needed as well.

Vomiting and Diarrhea

Vomiting and diarrhea can be caused by a variety of issues, including eating food intended for human consumption, garbage ingestion, toxins, obstruction in the stomach or intestines, bacterial or viral infections, and internal parasites, among other things. In some cases, you may know that your dog or cat has eaten something that the pet should not have. In other cases, you may never know the exact cause of the vomiting or diarrhea, but will need to take action to prevent your pet from becoming dehydrated. Whenever a pet has more than one episode of vomiting or diarrhea, it is best to call your veterinarian and describe what is happening, particularly if the vomitus or diarrhea contains blood. Think about when your pet was last normal. Is your pet vaccinated? Does the vomiting or diarrhea occur after eating? How long after? Does the vomitus or diarrhea have any blood or mucus in it? How many episodes of vomiting or diarrhea have occurred? Has your pet ever had these signs before? If so, when and under which circumstances?

Whenever a dog or cat vomits, it is a good idea to take away food and water for several hours, to give the animal's stomach a chance to rest. If the vomiting has stopped, you can then offer some ice cubes or small amounts of water. After several hours, if the pet does not vomit the water, food can then be offered. If vomiting continues or if your pet does not want to eat, taking the animal to a veterinarian for evaluation is a good idea. Blood work, x-rays, and possibly an abdominal ultrasound may be recommended, in addition to intravenous fluids to combat dehydration.

Dogs and cats can become significantly dehydrated when they have diarrhea. If they are not vomiting, continue to offer water and make sure that they drink. If they are becoming lethargic or if there is blood in the feces, take a fresh sample of the feces along with your pet to the veterinarian. The veterinarian will likely test the feces for intestinal parasites and also look for abnormal bacteria. If your pet is not vomiting and there is no blood in the feces, you can offer a bland diet of brown

---

DID YOU KNOW?

- Pet first-aid classes are often taught by local breed groups and the local Red Cross.
- If your pet has been sprayed by a skunk, carefully rinse the animal's eyes with saline irrigation solution, such as that used for contact lenses. Combine one tablespoon of dishwashing liquid, several drops of vanilla extract, and one quart of hydrogen peroxide, and use this mixture as a shampoo as needed (wear gloves!). If your pet is black in color, dilute this mixture, as the hydrogen peroxide can bleach the haircoat.

---

or white rice mixed with the animal's regular food, or make a mixture of boiled hamburger and rice or boiled chicken and rice, and feed that mixture for several days. The rice should help make the feces more solid. If the diarrhea lasts for more than a day, call your veterinarian.

Over-the-counter antidiarrheal drugs such as Imodium or Pepto-Bismol should not be given to your pet, as these drugs can potentially cause a condition called ileus, in which the intestines do not move very much. Ileus allows any abnormal bacteria an opportunity to overgrow, which can potentially cause even more problems.

Gastric Dilatation Volvulus (Bloat)

Gastric dilatation volvulus (GDV) syndrome, more commonly known as "bloat," causes the stomach to rotate and become distended with gas and sometimes fluid. This condition occurs most commonly in large-breed dogs and deep-chested dogs, such as Great Danes, German shepherds, Labrador retrievers, golden retrievers, Bernese mountain dogs, and Basset hounds, although any age and breed of dog can become affected. GDV is ultimately fatal if left untreated.

Signs of GDV include distention of the abdomen, unproductive retching and unproductive vomiting, and lethargy. In some cases, it may appear that the dog is vomiting white foam. Other dogs may appear to be straining to defecate. The longer the stomach is twisted, the longer it is cut off from its blood supply. If GDV continues for too long, portions of the stomach tissue can die. Time is of the essence with this condition. If your dog shows any of these abnormal signs, take him to the nearest veterinary emergency room. Call ahead to make sure that the clinic is prepared to stabilize your pet and perform the life-saving surgery to untwist the stomach.

Currently, there is no method of feeding, diet, or exercise restriction that definitely prevent bloat from occurring in predisposed breeds of dog. If you have a large-breed dog, it is worthwhile to ask your veterinarian about performing a surgery called prophylactic gastropexy; this procedure sutures the stomach to the inside of the abdominal wall, thereby preventing it from twisting.

Heat Stroke

Heat stroke and heat exertion can develop into a life-threatening emergency very quickly. Some breeds, such as pugs and bulldogs, have inherent problems with their upper airway that predispose them to becoming overheated quickly in hot or humid weather. These animals are not Olympic athletes, and they were not bred to be so. Other dogs and cats—particularly those that are overweight or have acquired problems with their upper airway—may also develop heat-induced illness when exercised, even for a short while, in warm humid weather. As a general rule of thumb, dogs should be exercised during the coolest portion of the day—that is, in early morning and late afternoon or evening near dusk. Like their human friends, dogs should be allowed to become acclimated to the weather, and not be encouraged to become "weekend warriors" or go "full out" after having been sedentary all winter. Exercise your dog for a maximum of 20 minutes, then allow a period of rest in a cool, shady area with plenty of fresh water.

The degree of heat stroke can vary from animal to animal, depending on the ambient temperature, the degree of exercise intolerance, airway issues, and obesity. In general, the longer your pet is allowed to remain overheated, the more detrimental and dangerous that condition is for the animal's body. Some animals will simply become lethargic when experiencing heat stroke, where others will collapse and develop severe neurologic and gastrointestinal problems that can potentially lead to death.

It is helpful to carry a digital thermometer in your first-aid kit so that you can take your pet's temperature, if necessary. For dogs, a normal temperature is in the range of 100.5 to 102.5 °F. If your pet's temperature exceeds 103 °F, rest the animal and stop activity. If at any point your dog's breathing becomes labored or raspy, the animal becomes weak or lethargic, or he vomits, stop activity immediately and cool the animal off. To do this, soak towels in room-temperature (not cold) water and place them over your pet. Cool the dog until his body temperature reaches 103 °F, and then remove the towels, as you do not want your pet to become too cold. Cold water or ice can actually be detrimental, in that the skin is the primary means of dissipating heat. If the blood vessels in the skin become constricted because of contact with ice or cold water, the inner body temperature can continue to rise and damage internal body organs.

Electrocution

Electrical cords are often fascinating for dogs, cats, and other pets that are allowed to remain loose indoors. This is especially true around the winter holidays, when brightly lit Christmas trees and ornaments may tempt even the least curious of cats, dogs, rabbits, and ferrets. When an animal chews on an electric cord, the ensuing electrocution causes not only burns, but also a massive release of adrenaline. Many animals can die from this effect. If they survive the initial event, however, they may develop fluid flooding of the lungs, a condition known as noncardiogenic pulmonary edema.

If you find your pet attached to an electrical cord, pull the plug of the cord to eliminate the source of electricity. If you think that your pet has chewed on an electrical cord, check carefully for burns around the mouth and limbs. The skin around the corners of the mouth and the tongue may appear charred or gray in color. Also, watch for difficulty breathing. Any increase in the rate of respiration or the development of gray or purplish discoloration of the tongue and/or gums may be found when fluid fills the lungs and makes it difficult to breathe. In such cases, immediately call the nearest veterinary emergency hospital, and take your pet in for evaluation. The veterinarian may suggest taking x-rays of the lungs and hospitalizing the animal for observation and possibly oxygen therapy.

Smoke Inhalation

Smoke inhalation and burn injuries are among the most horrible consequences of a house or kennel fire. When an animal is exposed to smoke, the levels of oxygen in the animal's body decrease because the smoke contains toxic substances such as hydrogen cyanide and carbon monoxide. Hot soot particles and the heat from the fire itself can also cause direct thermal damage to the skin, upper airways, and eyes.

Pets sometimes attempt to hide from the source of heat, flame or smoke, so they may be difficult to find in a smoke-filled dwelling. Take the pet away from the smoke and heat source to fresh air immediately—fire fighters and paramedics have access to oxygen that can be delivered by face mask to your pet—and then take your pet to the nearest veterinary hospital for evaluation.

Burn Injury

Thermal and chemical burns can also occur when a pet walks across a hot stove, has prolonged contact with a heating pad, comes too close to a candle or fireplace, or is exposed to a caustic substance. If you think that your pet has come in contact with a hot surface, soothe the burn with cool water. Look carefully for singed fur, blisters, or gray discoloration to the skin. If you see any of these abnormal signs, have the animal evaluated by a veterinarian.

If you think that your pet has walked or rolled through a caustic substance, put on gloves and wash the offending substance from the footpads or fur with lukewarm water. Do not attempt to neutralize the substance with items such as vinegar, baking soda, or lemon juice, as they can also potentially be damaging to the skin.

Seizures

Seizures can be caused by a large variety of problems, including exposure to toxins, low blood glucose (hypoglycemia), liver or kidney disease, infection, or tumors.

In some cases, exposure to a toxin is known. In other cases, animals may have seizures without a known cause. To the observer, a seizure is often quite frightening to watch. When a pet has a seizure, she loses consciousness and often falls to her side. Many animals will chomp their jaws together, have violent muscle spasms, salivate, paddle their legs, and lose control of their bladder and bowels. Some pets will act abnormally before a seizure happens.

There are two important first-aid goals when a pet has a seizure. The first goal is to take precautions so that the caregiver does not get hurt. The second goal is to prevent the pet from becoming injured. To fulfill the first goal, keep your hands away from your pet's mouth during a seizure. In particular, do not attempt to place a rag or stick in the animal's mouth. Some animals will bite their tongue during a seizure, but will not swallow their tongue or have it occlude their airway. For the second goal, whenever possible, place your pet on a soft, padded surface, away from sharp objects, hard furniture, glass, or stairways. If the seizure lasts more than two minutes, or if your pet has multiple seizures in a row, take the animal to the veterinarian.

Always have the cause of a seizure investigated. Your veterinarian will ask you a variety of questions designed to elicit information about the animal's history and likely will recommend blood work and sometimes a screening test for toxins to determine the cause of seizures. In some cases, a pet may be diagnosed with "idiopathic epilepsy," which is the medical term for seizures caused by reasons unknown. Many pets will be placed on medications to help to control the seizures temporarily, and sometimes for the long term.

Insect and Spider Stings and Bites

Many different types of bees, wasps, hornets, and spiders can sting or bite your pet (and you, too, of course). Pets often attempt to play with or bite the flying or crawling critter. In many cases, the sting or bite may be unwitnessed by the animal's owner. If you do witness the incident, carefully remove the stinger from your pet's skin with a tweezers, if it is present and you can find it. The area around the sting may become reddened or swollen, but you can help decrease swelling by placing a cool compress over the area.

More serious reactions to an insect or spider bite may result in generalized signs that are not localized to just the area of the sting. Serious signs of a systemic allergic reaction include swelling of the face, hives, itchiness, vomiting, diarrhea, difficulty breathing, and collapse. If your pet shows signs more serious than localized swelling, take her to the veterinarian immediately. If you live in a rural location far from a veterinary hospital, you can give 1 milligram per pound of Benadryl by mouth once to help treat the reaction. Make sure that the product that you administer contains only the compound diphenhydramine and no other over-the-counter medication that might potentially be toxic for dogs and cats. The veterinarian will administer medications to help stop the allergic reaction and let you know if any further hospitalization or care is necessary.

Snakebites

Snakebites are common in geographic areas that are home to poisonous snakes. It is important to know whether you live in an area of the country that has poisonous snakes.

The most common bites are associated with pit vipers, the family that includes rattlesnakes. Cotton mouths and copperheads also belong to this class of snake, but their bites are less common and less deadly. Pit viper bites cause local tissue necrosis and swelling. Sometimes fang marks or puncture wounds may be visible on the skin near the site of swelling. Signs of pit viper envenomation include localized swelling, bleeding from fang marks, pain at the site of swelling, lethargy, vomiting, diarrhea, and collapse.

Coral snakes are common in the Southwestern United States. Signs of envenomation from coral snakes include local irritation at the site of the bite, followed by weakness, altered mental status, muscle tremors or twitching, and paralysis. The most severe cases can cause difficulty breathing or respiratory arrest.

If you witness your pet being bitten by a snake, take the animal to the nearest veterinary hospital. There is little, if anything, that you can do at home to prevent the venom from spreading. Therapy that includes sucking venom from the wound, placing a tourniquet around a limb, applying ice packs, or using premanufactured snakebite kits not only can be detrimental for the animal but also may cause you to lose valuable time in getting your pet to a veterinarian who can provide life-saving care. If the bite occurs while you are hiking or camping and you are far away from your car, it is best to carry your pet back to safety, if possible. If your pet is too large to carry, walk with your pet on a leash, to prevent the animal from developing over-exertion.

The veterinarian will treat your pet for pain and shock with intravenous fluids, give pain medications, and often recommend antivenin to combat the effects of the snake venom. There is a rattlesnake vaccination available in some areas of the United States; however, to date, there has been no published research that has investigated and proved the vaccine's efficacy or safety in animals, so is not recommended at this time.

COMMON TOXINS

Some toxins are fairly well known. Other substances may be fine for humans, but dangerous for animals. Never give your pet any over-the-counter or prescription medications intended for humans without direct instructions and supervision by your veterinarian. Household plants, chemicals, potpourri, and even fruits and nuts such as raisins, grapes, and macadamia nuts can potentially be toxic to pets. Some sugarless gum products contain a substance called xylitol that can cause life-threatening hypoglycemia, seizures, and liver failure.

As a general rule of thumb, whenever your pet exhibits abnormal signs, it is best to consult with your veterinarian. In those cases in which the toxin is known, an antidote may be available. In other cases, the veterinarian can help treat your pet based on the symptoms. Toxins may cause a wide variety of clinical symptoms. In general, tremors, seizures, excessive salivation, weakness, lethargy, bleeding, vomiting, and diarrhea all may potentially be observed when a pet has been exposed to a poisonous substance. If any of these signs occur and continue, contact your veterinarian immediately.

CONCLUSION

Injuries and accidents are bound to happen from time to time. You can help your pet avoid injury by safeguarding the domestic environment and by keeping a close eye on the animal. To be proactive, pet-proof your house and yard before you acquire a pet. Make note of important telephone numbers such as those for your family veterinarian, local veterinary emergency hospital, and animal poison control hotlines. Keep a pet first-aid kit on hand to use in the event of an emergency. Take a training course in pet safety, first aid, and CPR. With luck, an accident will never happen. If it does, with some pointers, a little advice, and training, you can be prepared to provide aid to your pet.

FURTHER READING

American National Red Cross. "Pet First Aid." www.redcross.org/pubs.
Fogle, B. *First Aid for Dogs: What to Do When Emergencies Happen*. New York: Penguin Books; 1997.
Montiero, M. *Safe Dog Handbook: A Complete Guide to Protecting Your Pooch, Indoors and Out*. Wayside, MA: Quarry Books; 2009.
Schwartz, S. *First Aid for Dogs: An Owner's Guide to a Happy and Healthy Pet*. Hoboken, NJ: Wiley and Sons, Howell Book House; 1999.

5

Dogs: Health, Diseases, and Prevention

Craig Datz, DVM, MS, DABVP, DACVN

INTRODUCTION

Dogs come in all shapes and sizes, yet their health care needs are surprisingly similar. Whether you have a tiny Yorkshire terrier, an enormous mastiff, a playful beagle, or a lazy Basset hound, all dogs require just a few basics: proper feeding, shelter, companionship, and veterinary care for preventing illnesses and treating medical conditions as they arise. Your responsibility for taking care of a new dog starts the minute you bring her home.

This chapter guides you step-by-step in health care for your companion. However, the information presented here is *not intended to take the place of a veterinarian.* Diagnosing and treating canine health problems requires the expertise of qualified, licensed veterinarians who often spend as many years in school as physicians. You should never hesitate to call a veterinary clinic for advice or to simply make an appointment for a check-up whenever you notice a symptom or sign of illness. Chapter 2 offers some tips for finding and working with a great veterinarian who can help keep your dog in the best of health.

BASIC CARE FOR DOGS

Your new pet will provide you with many years of love and companionship. In return, you will need to ensure proper care so that your dog will live a long, healthy life. Pet ownership is a major responsibility. Before bringing a puppy or adult dog into your home, take time to prepare for the new arrival (see Chapter 1 for more information on choosing a new pet).

Almost all dogs need the care and attention that can only be given if they spend most of their time in the house as part of the family. Dogs are social animals and do not like to be isolated, ignored, left alone, or confined for long periods of time. This leads to stress, anxieties, behavioral problems, and even poor health. Having an indoor dog means making sure the environment is comfortable and safe for the animal. At a minimum, dogs need a sleeping area, a place to eat, and room for play and exercise. Access to the outdoors is necessary for housebreaking and avoiding "accidents."

Feeding

Dogs need fresh water in a clean bowl at all times. In larger homes, an extra water bowl or two is helpful. Keep toilet lids closed or bathroom doors closed, as some dogs are attracted to water in toilets, sinks, and bathtubs, which creates a mess and may spread microorganisms that can cause disease. As a small number of dogs are allergic to plastic dishes, choose metal or other types of water containers that are unbreakable and easy to clean.

The food bowl should likewise be kept clean at all times. If your dog is fed one or more meals of dry food each day, be sure to clean the dish daily. If any canned, soft, or sticky dog foods or human foods are given, clean the bowl immediately after eating. Food particles left behind can encourage bacteria or mold growth, which can cause illness in both dogs and people.

Dogs deserve a little privacy and should be left alone while eating. In fact, some dogs will growl or even snap if approached when food is present. If you have more than one dog, be sure that each has an opportunity to eat without being pushed away or bullied by others.

Dental Care

Puppies are born without teeth but soon develop a set of 28 primary (baby) teeth. Between 4 and 6 months of age, they become loose and fall out, to be replaced by 42 secondary (adult) teeth.

You can take care of your pet's teeth by getting in the habit of brushing daily or every other day. Do not use human toothpaste—instead, look for products especially for dogs sold at pet stores and veterinary clinics. Certain chew toys and other products as well as special diets are also available for dental health. Without brushing, most dogs will develop dental tartar buildup, gingivitis (red, swollen gums), bad breath, and infections that can lead to periodontal disease (loss of soft tissue and bone support, loose or missing teeth). Dogs also can suffer from broken or chipped teeth, abscesses, foreign bodies, and a variety of other oral problems. Appropriate diagnostics and treatments are available only from your veterinarian. Do not rely on a groomer or other unqualified person to "clean" or "scale" your dog's teeth, as this practice can be dangerous and will not treat disease.

Play and Exercise

Depending on the breed and size of your pet, you should provide appropriate toys and spend time each day playing games. Dogs need mental stimulation and activities to occupy their time, just like children. Families where everyone is away for long stretches of time should consider whether adding a dog is a good decision. Boredom and isolation can lead to behavioral disorders including separation anxiety, destruction (chewing, digging), and vocalizing (barking, whining, howling).

Exercise is vital for the physical and mental health of both people and pets. A dog is built to run, and she should have lots of opportunities for an active jog or brisk walk. Ideally, a well-trained dog will adapt to a leash and neck collar, harness, or head collar so that it is easy and enjoyable to take the animal out for exercise. Some communities have dog parks set aside for on-leash or off-leash play. Be sure to obey any leash laws and regulations when taking your dog outdoors. Always keep control of your dog, whether on or off a leash, to avoid escapes and accidents.

A fenced yard is convenient when you have a dog. Many dogs will want to go outside first thing in the morning to empty their bladders and check out any new scents or interesting things. However, if the same yard is the only outdoor exposure the dog gets, he will quickly become bored and either want to come back in the house right away or develop behavioral problems. Electric fences are an option for homes without secure enclosures, but are not guaranteed to keep a dog within the perimeter.

In either case, be sure to take the dog for a walk in the neighborhood or anyplace other than the same familiar yard. Daily or twice-daily walks is best, although you should check with your veterinarian about any exercise precautions. Some dogs cannot tolerate strenuous activity such as running for long distances or being outside in hot, humid weather. Puppies, elderly pets, and smaller dogs may tire easily and will not be able to keep up with a long walk or jog.

Housing

While dogs do best by being indoors with the family most of the time, in certain circumstances they must be kept outdoors. This situation is not ideal, and in fact some shelters and breeders will refuse to allow adoption or purchase of a dog if she will be housed outdoors.

You can take certain steps to help an outdoor pet remain healthy. First, make sure the animal has adequate shelter from extreme temperatures (heat and cold), sun, rain, snow, and wind. She will need either an old-fashioned wooden dog house or one of the modern designs available at pet stores. The shelter should be large enough that the dog can turn around and stretch out, but not so large that it cannot be warmed by body heat. The floor should not be plain dirt or grass, as those materials can become wet or frozen. An appropriate platform and bedding must be provided to keep the dog clean, dry, and high enough off the ground during rainy or snowy weather. The water bowl should be large and not easily tipped over. In cold weather, water often becomes frozen, so it needs to be checked several times each day. In the winter, the dog will need more energy to keep warm, so provide plenty of high-quality dog food—up to two to three times more food than the animal eats in warmer weather.

Tying out a dog with a rope or chain is cruel and can lead to choking and getting trapped if the dog wraps himself around a stake or tree. In some communities, leaving a dog tied outside is prohibited, and authorities may charge the owner with animal cruelty if this practice is followed. If you do not have a fenced yard, then resist the temptation to chain the dog outdoors without direct supervision. Instead, take your pet for regular walks on a proper leash. Families that are too busy should find a neighbor or hire a dog-walking service. As noted earlier, if your lives are too hectic for family members to find enough time to take the pet for a walk, then think twice about whether dog ownership is right for you.

Bathing and Grooming

It is a good idea to get your new puppy or adult dog accustomed to an occasional bath and grooming session. Small to medium dogs are easily managed in a bathtub, while larger dogs may need to be washed outdoors. Always use a product intended for dogs, as human shampoos and detergents may lead to dryness, flaking, or irritation. First, thoroughly wet the dog's skin and haircoat with warm water. Then gently work in a small amount of dog shampoo and massage until it lathers. Rinse the animal completely, then towel-dry her hair and skin. If the dog is still not clean or sweet smelling, the shampoo and rinse can be repeated. Avoid the use of hot-air dryers, as they can lead to accidental burns. Brush or comb the dog's hair after drying.

Matting and tangling are common problems in dogs with longer haircoats. Be very careful when using scissors to trim a dog's hair, as it is very easy to cut his skin while trying to remove mats. Instead, use an electric clipper or take the dog to a groomer or veterinarian. Also, be cautious with hair bows, ribbons, rubber bands, or other ornamentation as they can be placed too tight and put pressure on the skin.

Nail trimming can be easy or difficult depending on how cooperative your pet is and whether you have the right tools. You should handle your dog's paws and toes daily to get her used to the feeling. Many dogs automatically pull their feet away when touched, which makes nail care a challenge! Choose an appropriately sized pet nail trimmer and make sure the blades are sharp. Start by trimming a tiny bit of nail from the end, and then try trimming a few more thin slices while checking for the appearance of the "quick"—a gray-to-black soft circular area in the center of the claw that will bleed if cut. Do not forget to trim the dewclaws; many dogs have these digits on their front paws, and sometimes on the back paws as well.

Always trim nails conservatively, because you will soon find that trying to clip too much will lead to a yelp and a bleeding toenail. If that happens, do not panic! Either use a clotting powder (available at pet stores) or make a paste with some flour or cornstarch and a few drops of water. Apply the paste to the end of the claw and the bleeding should stop within a minute or two. Some owners use nail files or emery boards instead of clippers. A quick nail care session every week or two is better than a big struggle on a less frequent basis.

Ear cleaning with a commercial dog product can be done weekly or every other week, depending on the condition of your pet's ears and any history of excessive wax production or ear infections. Fill the ear canals with the cleaner, squeeze and massage the base of the ears for a few seconds, and then use cotton balls to wipe out the excess liquid and wax. If you notice any redness, discomfort, swelling, or odor, avoid cleaning the animal's ears until you can get a veterinarian to check for infection or other problems.

Dogs have two curious structures at the edge of the anus called anal sacs. These sacs can fill up with a bad-smelling fluid or paste and are similar to the scent glands on skunks. If startled or injured, dogs can express their anal sacs, which leads to a smelly mess. You can use a baby diaper wipe to clean around the anal area or cotton balls soaked in rubbing alcohol (do not use on irritated or broken skin). In other cases, the anal sacs may become too full or clogged (impacted) and dogs will "scoot" (drag their rear ends) along the floor to try to relieve the pressure. Groomers and veterinarians routinely express (squeeze out) the anal sacs in dogs and can show you how to perform this procedure at home. Infected and abscessed anal sacs are swollen, red, and painful, and a veterinary visit is needed to treat this serious condition.

CARING FOR YOUR DOG'S HEALTH

While pet owners must first provide the basics for all dogs, including food, water, shelter, exercise, and companionship, much more needs to be done to keep puppies and adult dogs healthy. Some of their needs change with age, while other concerns remain present throughout their lifetime. Although the discussion in this section is divided by age groups, note that there is much overlap between the groups.

Newborn Puppies

If you have a female dog that has just delivered a litter, you will need to help her take care of the puppies until they are ready to be weaned. The two main concerns are warmth and nutrition.

Puppies cannot thermoregulate, which means they will become chilled if separated from their mother or are placed in a cold environment. As long as the house or kennel is at a normal room temperature, newborns will do fine by snuggling with one another and with their mother. If the external environment will be cooler, then a shelter should be provided, such as a box with warm bedding. Electric heaters, pads, and heat lamps can be dangerous and burns are possible, so be very cautious about placing any heat source near a litter of puppies.

Proper nutrition is supplied through nursing the mother's milk. Usually owners do not need to interfere with this natural process. Smaller, weaker puppies may be crowded out by stronger littermates, however, and may need help finding the nipples. The mother needs to eat two to three times more food during the nursing period and have free access to plenty of water to help with milk production. If the puppies are not nursing well or if they are orphans, then owners need to supply milk replacer by bottle- or tube-feeding. It is not difficult to hand-feed puppies, but be sure to have your veterinarian or an experienced breeder show you what to do and what not to do. Commercial milk-replacement products are available at most pet stores.

Young Puppies (Ages 6–16 Weeks)

The most common age at which to acquire a new puppy is 6 to 16 weeks. At this time, puppies have been weaned from their mother's milk and are eating solid food. Ideally, puppies should stay with their mother and littermates until they are 8 weeks of age. Adopting new puppies much before or after 8 weeks may lead to poor socialization.

The first step in caring for your new puppy's health is to take the animal directly to your veterinarian as soon as she arrives. Ideally, you will already have an appointment scheduled for a new-puppy check-up. If you wait too long before visiting the veterinarian, the dog may become ill from common diseases or parasites. Before your visit, gather up all papers, health records, and any medications and take them with you. Most veterinarians ask that you bring a fresh stool (fecal) sample with you, for which a zipper-lock plastic bag or disposable plastic container works well.

While there are some variations in a puppy preventive health program, your veterinary team will do some or all of the following during your first visit.

1. They will first ask questions about your puppy's history, such as when and where the dog was acquired, how he has been feeling, which type of food you are giving the puppy, what the environment is like, whether there are any other pets or people in the household, and so on. They will then want to know if you have noticed any signs or symptoms such as runny eyes, scratching, diarrhea, coughing, or lethargy. After collecting a comprehensive history, they can then investigate any potential problems.
2. Next, the puppy should receive a complete, nose-to-tail physical exam. Your veterinarian will take a close look at the dog's eyes, ears and ear canals, nose, and teeth. He or she will listen to the puppy's heart and lung sounds with a stethoscope and

palpate his abdomen, limbs, and lymph nodes. The skin and coat will be examined carefully, and vital signs such as weight, body temperature, and heart rate will be recorded. After a complete physical, the veterinarian will let you know if your new puppy gets a clean bill of health or whether potential problems were found.

3. Depending on whether the puppy has had any previous vaccinations or medical care, your veterinarian will recommend any necessary procedures. In addition to checking a stool sample, he or she may suggest other diagnostic tests to make sure your puppy is healthy and not infected with parasites or other diseases. Vaccination types and schedules can vary, but most veterinarians will administer a combination vaccine product that protects against several common puppy diseases, including canine distemper, hepatitis, and parvovirus. Other vaccines can be given at the first visit to protect against infectious tracheobronchitis ("kennel cough"), leptospirosis, or Lyme disease in some areas. The injection may sting a little, but most puppies tolerate their check-ups and vaccines very well.

4. Puppies are often born with intestinal worms or acquire them soon after birth. Your veterinarian will most likely administer or dispense a safe deworming medication. In many areas, heartworm disease is common and puppies can be started on preventive medication early in life.

5. After the check-up, vaccinations, deworming, and any other necessary health care, the veterinarian will ask if you have any questions about caring for your new companion. Many clinics offer puppy kits that have product samples and written information about health, common diseases, behavior, and training.

A second puppy visit is typically scheduled approximately three weeks after the first check-up unless there are any concerns that need to be addressed sooner. During the next visit, your veterinarian will repeat the history and physical examination and determine whether more vaccinations, deworming, or other procedures are needed. A third and even a fourth visit may be needed depending on your puppy's age and health. Older puppies will receive a rabies vaccination and license in most areas. Your veterinarian will discuss the best age for spaying or neutering and other important issues during the first year of life.

Back at home, you will need to make sure your puppy is staying healthy, eating well (but not too much!), acting playful, and receiving plenty of rest. Puppy classes may be offered in your area, and they are highly recommended as long as they are led by experience, qualified individuals. Classes are often held weekly for four to six weeks, and your puppy will have a chance to interact with other puppies and their owners. This type of activity is very helpful for socialization. Instructors will go over basic training such as sit and stay, and give helpful advice for housetraining. You may even learn how to trim nails, clean ears, brush teeth, and care for your puppy's skin and haircoat. Be sure to ask around before enrolling in a puppy or training class, and avoid any that use punishment or harsh techniques to enforce desired behaviors.

Puppies can be exposed to bacteria, viruses, and parasites if they spend time outdoors, and some owners are reluctant to take their dog for walks or to visit parks because of this risk. In most cases, this kind of activity is perfectly safe, but be sure to talk with your veterinarian. If you isolate your puppy and do not let her visit with other people, dogs, cats, and so on, the animal may become fearful and poorly socialized.

Older Puppies (Ages 16 Weeks to 1 Year)

Puppies mature quickly, in a short period of time going through their "childhood," "teenage," and young adult phases. You should continue feeding a puppy diet throughout the animal's growth period, which varies from 10 to 12 months in small breeds and lasts as long as 18 to 24 months in large to giant breeds. The older puppy will need increasing amounts of food to keep up with growth, but be careful to ensure that the animal does not gain excessive weight. It is much easier to prevent weight gain than to try to get an older dog to lose the extra pounds.

Your veterinarian will recommend spaying or neutering when the puppy is at or around six months of age. This surgical operation is intended to prevent accidental breeding and unwanted puppies. It has numerous health and behavioral benefits as well, so be sure to schedule this procedure with your veterinarian as soon as it is recommended.

After the puppy series of vaccinations and deworming, additional preventive care visits are not required before one year of age unless recommended by your veterinarian. However, do not hesitate to call for advice or schedule an appointment if you notice any signs of illness or unusual behavior. Obedience and other training classes should be available for older puppies. There are even fun classes and activities such as agility training in which you and your pet can participate together. Continue any heartworm medication prescribed by your veterinarian and apply any flea, tick, or other parasite products as recommended.

Young Adult Dogs (Ages 1–3 Years)

Dogs are usually at their healthiest and most active stage of life during the one- to three-year age period. After the animal is fully grown, you should gradually switch it from a puppy diet to one formulated for adults ("maintenance"). For most adult dogs, preventing obesity is the most important nutritional goal. Young adults love to exercise and play, so provide plenty of opportunities for such activities and outdoor time.

Veterinary check-ups should be scheduled at least once a year, and even twice a year in some cases. For young adults, your veterinarian will set up a vaccination schedule and send you reminders when vaccines are due. After the dog has reached one year of age, the vaccine interval will range from every year to every three years depending on the type of vaccine and other factors. Routine testing for heartworm disease, internal parasites, and other diseases present in your area should be performed as recommended. Your dog may even need her teeth professionally cleaned on a regular basis to prevent dental disease.

Middle-Aged Dogs (Ages 3–7 Years)

There is no consistent definition of "middle age" for dogs, as it depends on the breed and expected life span. Smaller dogs tend to live longer than larger ones, so middle age for these breeds may actually extend up to 10 years. Health check-ups can be done once or twice a year as recommended by your veterinarian. Most dogs of this age have a variable degree of dental disease, ranging from tartar buildup and gingivitis all the way to severe periodontitis. Treatment and prevention of dental disease should be discussed at least yearly with your veterinarian.

Continue providing lots of exercise, but be on the lookout for early signs of arthritis, which include lameness or joint stiffness, slowing down on walks or on stairs, or taking a longer time after a nap to get moving. As with young adult dogs, offer a quality diet, but do not overfeed even if the animal begs. Vaccinations and routine care such as parasite testing should be done regularly at your veterinary clinic.

Older Dogs (Ages 7–15 Years or Older)

When our companions reach their golden years, they need extra attention and lots of tender care. Exercise often declines as dogs become arthritic or tire easily. However, if they are still willing to go for walks and play games such as fetch, there is no harm in continuing mild to moderate activity. Older dogs suffer from changes in their senses such as decreased vision, hearing, and sometimes sense of smell. They will sleep more and may be less tolerant of being handled.

Arthritis is one the most common health problems. Painful, stiff joints are unfortunately very common in senior pets, especially larger breeds. Some owners are in denial because they do not notice their dogs limping or in obvious pain. However, any signs of stiffness, slowing down, reluctance to climb stairs or jump onto the furniture, or not wanting to go for long walks are evidence of the discomfort and pain of arthritis. The good news is that your veterinarian has many treatments available to relieve pain and inflammation, including medication, supplements, special diets, physical therapy, and even unconventional therapies such as acupuncture.

Behavioral changes also occur in older dogs, and they may "forget" their housebreaking and have accidents. At times, they may act confused or even lost in their own homes. Occasionally, the effects of old age can lead to aggression such as growling and snapping, even at family members, or anxiety and stress. Your veterinarian can offer help for many of these behavioral disorders.

At least twice a year, the older dog should have a complete physical exam and other procedures such as laboratory tests (on blood and urine) and x-rays to identify possible problems. Because dogs cannot talk, veterinarians must rely on hands-on exams and diagnostic testing to discover internal problems. Although some older-dog diseases such as cancer, kidney failure, and heart failure cannot always be prevented or cured, many supportive treatments are available that can reduce pain and suffering and help with quality of life.

There may be a time near the end of your dog's life span when you will want to discuss euthanasia with your veterinarian. Euthanasia is a painless, humane way to end suffering and ease the process of passing away when a dog no longer has a good quality of life. If you have had a good relationship with your veterinary health care team, they will be very helpful and compassionate and do what is best for your pet.

COMMON MEDICAL PROBLEMS AND DISEASES

From time to time, you may notice signs of illness in your companion. Often your first thought is to wonder whether the problem is important enough to call or visit the veterinarian. Most veterinary clinics are happy to answer questions over the phone and will help you decide if a check-up is necessary. In some communities, there are even 24-hour hospitals and emergency facilities open at nights and on weekends that can help.

The information presented in this section is simply a general guide to medical conditions that occur in dogs; it is *not* a substitute for proper veterinary care. Also, be wary of information that you find on the Internet, as many websites and email groups dispense inaccurate or even harmful information.

Loss of Appetite

There are many reasons why a dog may stop eating. In puppies, this can be a sign of significant disease; in an adult dog, it may signal that the animal simply is not interested. If your puppy does not act hungry at the normal meal time, call your veterinarian right away. It may be only a minor problem, but puppies do not have the same reserves as adults so they need to be managed right away. In an adult dog, not eating for more than two days is a good reason to call the veterinarian. If you also notice other signs of illness such as lethargy (not active or playful), intestinal upset (vomiting or diarrhea), or signs of pain along with no appetite, call or visit your veterinarian.

Vomiting

Dogs sometimes vomit food or fluids but otherwise act healthy. One or two episodes of vomiting in an otherwise normal dog may not be a concern. Make a note of the time and appearance of the vomit, and if the problem persists for more than a day or two call your veterinarian. Some dogs respond to stomach "rest," which

---

DID YOU KNOW?

The following household items can be poisonous to dogs:

- Human medications, including prescription, over-the-counter, and recreational drugs
- Insecticides and rodenticides
- Foods such as chocolate, grapes, raisins, avocados, and xylitol (an artificial sweetener)
- Plants such as azaleas, yew, oleander, sago palms, and bulbs of ornamental flowers
- Metals, including those in batteries, imported pottery or toys, and coins if swallowed
- Mold-contaminated garbage and compost piles
- Fabric softeners, dishwashing detergents, and potpourri (especially the liquid form)

---

means removing the food and water bowl for approximately 12 hours. This step prevents the dog from continuing to eat and drink on top of an upset stomach. After 12 hours, offer small amounts of water or a few ice cubes to lick. If another few hours pass without any vomiting, offer small amounts of food to see if your pet is interested. Veterinarians often suggest a low-fat, bland food such as cooked white rice mixed with a few pieces of cooked chicken or ground beef (with fat removed) in such cases. If the dog can hold down food, then the next day you can offer the regular diet, but try smaller amounts more frequently. Do not give any medicines unless directed to do so by your veterinarian.

Vomiting can also be a sign of disease or even an emergency. If you see any blood in the vomit (e.g., spots of bright red or dark material that looks like coffee grounds), or if the dog continues to vomit even after you remove the water bowl, a visit to the veterinarian is in order. At home, you can check for dehydration by gently feeling the animal's inner lips and gums to see if they are moist. If they are dry and sticky, then the dog is moderately dehydrated. If your dog acts like she is trying to vomit but nothing comes up, or if she is restless (pacing and will not lie down), that could be an emergency, so check with a veterinarian, no matter whether it is day or night.

Diarrhea

In healthy dogs, stools are formed and have a consistent color and appearance. Soft stools are a sign of mild diarrhea and may look like pudding. Severe diarrhea may be liquid or even bloody. Puppies may have slightly soft stools, which can be normal, but diarrhea is a sign of many common diseases in both puppies and adults. If your dog is otherwise acting normally and eating well, then diarrhea may be temporary. You can call your veterinary clinic for advice, and the staff there might suggest bringing a stool sample in for analysis. As with vomiting, some dogs will improve if you simply give the intestinal tract a rest. You do not have to remove the water if the dog is not vomiting, but do not feed the animal for 12 to 24 hours; after that, offer small amounts of bland food. Your veterinarian may suggest home treatment or medication for mild diarrhea, but do not use human antidiarrheal drugs unless directed to do so by your veterinarian.

What are some common causes of vomiting and diarrhea? The first thing to consider is whether the dog may have eaten something recently the pet should not have. Dogs are clever enough to get into human food or the trash, or pick up toys or objects and swallow them. Intestinal worms are very common in dogs, especially puppies, and diarrhea is a typical sign of this problem (you rarely see worms passed in the stool, so bring a sample to your veterinarian for microscopic testing). Infections such as parvovirus are often seen in puppies and young dogs, in which they lead to lethargy, no appetite, vomiting, and diarrhea (which may be bloody). Bacterial or protozoal infections are possible. Even stress, such as a change in diet or environment or a trip to the boarding kennel, can result in intestinal upset. In older dogs, diarrhea raises a greater concern for metabolic diseases or cancer, so be sure to visit your veterinarian for vomiting or diarrhea that lasts more than a couple of days.

Skin Disease

Skin and haircoat problems are second only to intestinal disease as a common health care condition in dogs. The first sign of such problems you may notice is scratching more than usual, or chewing or licking at areas of skin. On closer exam, you may discover loss of hair, a rash or reddened areas, flaky or greasy skin, or lumps and bumps. While there are many causes of itchiness, the most common ones are parasites such as fleas, allergies, and skin infections.

Fleas can usually be seen crawling on the skin, often around the rump and tail base or around the thighs (although they may live anywhere on the body). They leave behind a telltale sign called "flea dirt," which is excreted material that resembles black pepper flakes. Some dogs are allergic to flea bites and scratch or chew excessively even if no live fleas can be found. Your veterinary clinic can suggest an effective program to get rid of fleas, which involves treating the dog, any other animals in the house, and the environment.

Allergies often result in itchiness. Dogs can be allergic to almost anything in the outdoor environment, including grass, trees, and pollen, or to indoor materials such as plants, molds, and dust mites. If your dog scratches only during certain times of the year, environmental allergy (also called atopy or atopic dermatitis) is likely.

Dogs that scratch year-round may be allergic to something indoors or to a food or food ingredient. Your veterinarian is well equipped to treat allergies, with medication, shampoos or topical agents, or special diets. In severe cases, the veterinarian may do allergy testing and prescribe immunotherapy (small amounts of the allergic substance given by injection to reduce sensitivity).

Skin infections, hair loss, and other conditions may not result in scratching, so any changes in your dog's skin or coat should prompt a call to the veterinarian. Swelling, lumps and bumps, discoloration, odors, or excessively moist or dry areas are all reasons to visit your veterinarian.

Ear Disease

Scratching at the ears, head shaking, a head tilt, an unusual odor, or a discharge from the ear canals most likely indicates an ear infection. Dogs may suffer from a variety of diseases affecting the ears (sometimes in addition to skin disease), and you should visit your veterinarian for an exam and diagnostic tests if you suspect that your dog has such a condition. Some problems are easy to treat, such as ear mites, whereas others are more difficult to cure, such as deep bacterial infection. Ear infections may be itchy, painful, or both, so be gentle when checking or cleaning your dog's ears. Your veterinarian may prescribe topical medication such as drops or ointments along with other drugs. Routine ear cleaning can be helpful in preventing ear infections and severe long-term consequences, so follow your veterinarian's recommendations for regular cleaning of your dog's ears.

Heart Disease

Fortunately, sudden heart attacks or strokes in dogs are rare, but these animals can develop heart problems that are slower to cause clinical signs. Congestive heart failure can occur in older dogs, usually smaller breeds, and lead to coughing and exercise intolerance. Puppies can be born with congenital heart disease, which may require treatment or even surgery. Heartworms are a problem in much of the United States, but are easily prevented (see the section on heartworm disease later in this chapter for more information).

Neurologic Problems

Dogs can be diagnosed with seizure disorders such as epilepsy. If your dog suddenly starts shaking or convulsing and falls over, the incident may be a seizure. Do not try to intervene, as you may be bitten or scratched involuntarily. Instead, call your veterinarian for instructions. Most seizures stop within a few minutes. If the convulsions continue for more than five minutes, it is best to carefully transport the dog to a clinic or emergency facility for immediate treatment. Other potential problems with the nervous system include spinal disease, such as a slipped disk that can lead to pain, weakness, or even paralysis, and vestibular disease, which that causes a head tilt or inability to walk or stay balanced.

Reproductive System Disorders

Almost all experts recommend spaying and neutering pet dogs. These routine surgical procedures safely remove reproductive organs (ovaries and uterus, testicles), which results in a healthier, more well-behaved pet. Your veterinarian can advise you on the best time to schedule this surgery, which is typically performed before the dog reaches six months of age. Dogs that are not spayed or neutered are at higher risk of infection, cancer, and other diseases.

Some dogs are purposely allowed to mate to produce litters of puppies. This practice is best left to people who are experienced in dog breeding and have adoptive homes available for the puppies when they arrive. Before considering breeding, make sure your dog receives a clean bill of health from a veterinarian, including being checked for inherited diseases (such as hip dysplasia), parasites, and infections such as brucellosis.

Pregnancy in the dog lasts approximately nine weeks, and in the final week or so the female will look for a nesting area. The birthing process is divided into three stages, and you should be familiar with both normal behavior and signs of complications. For example, if a dog is in labor (having contractions) for more than two hours without delivering any puppies, she should be taken directly to a veterinarian for an emergency assessment and possible cesarean section (C-section). While nursing, some female dogs develop mastitis (infection of the mammary glands) or eclampsia (low blood calcium). Your veterinarian is the best resource for helping you navigate the complicated breeding, birthing, and lactating periods.

Cancer

Just like people, dogs can get many types of cancer that may or may not be recognizable. Lumps, bumps, swellings, and color changes of the skin or haircoat, for example, might indicate cancer. Tumors can also develop internally, leading to various signs of illness. Some types of cancer are benign (localized), while others are malignant (can metastasize or spread to other parts of the body). Veterinarians now offer comprehensive treatment for most types of cancer, including surgery, radiation, and chemotherapy. If your clinic does not routinely manage cancer cases, ask for a referral to a specialty hospital.

Parasites

Many dogs, especially those that spend time outdoors, are exposed to internal and external parasites. Regular check-ups with your veterinarian are necessary to ensure they your dog does not become colonized with these organisms. Almost all puppies are born with worms and require regular treatment with deworming medication. Older puppies and adult dogs should be checked for worms routinely and ideally treated monthly with medication that also prevents heartworm disease.

The best way to check for internal parasites is to bring a fresh fecal (stool) sample to your veterinarian. If the animal is infected with roundworms (an easily treated condition), you may see worms in your puppy's stool that look like thin noodles. The other common worms observed by owners are tapeworms, which look like grains of rice; they are also easily treated by your veterinarian. Keep in mind that some types of worms are zoonotic (contagious) to people and can cause disease, especially in children. The best way to avoid zoonotic worms is to wash your hands before eating and avoid coming in contact with fecal material.

External parasites of dogs include fleas, ticks, mites, and lice. Fleas (discussed earlier in this chapter) are tiny wingless insects. Ticks come in a variety of sizes and are usually attached to the skin. Mites are invisible but can cause skin disease. Lice are very rare. Complete flea control is possible by using products recommended by your veterinarian and making sure you are vacuuming and cleaning up the animal's environment. Ticks are more difficult to control and may need both topical (drops, sprays, collars) treatment and environmental control. Skin and ear disease caused by mites may lead to itching, hair loss, crusting, and secondary infections. Your veterinarian will need to use a microscope to look at skin and hair samples to identify the mites. Effective treatments for mites and lice are available.

VACCINE-PREVENTABLE DISEASES

As noted earlier in this chapter, it is very important to take your dog to the veterinarian on a regular basis for check-ups and vaccinations. Fortunately, safe and effective vaccines are available to prevent a number of diseases in our canine companions. Some of these are called "core" vaccines; they should be administered to all dogs. In contrast, "noncore" vaccines are optional depending on whether the diseases are common in your area and whether your veterinarian recommends their use.

Core Vaccines for Dogs

Distemper is a serious, often fatal disease that is caused by a virus. Puppies are more commonly infected than adult dogs, and the virus can be spread from other dogs or wildlife such as skunks and raccoons. Signs of distemper usually occur within one week of exposure and include runny, crusty eyes and nose, coughing, vomiting, poor appetite, and depression. As the disease gets worse, puppies may develop nervous twitches and seizures. There is no effective treatment but veterinarians can use various types of supportive care. Vaccination is highly effective at preventing distemper infection, so be sure to take your new puppy to a veterinarian for the first vaccine at six to eight weeks of age and follow the recommended booster schedule. Adult dogs should receive booster vaccinations every few years.

Parvo (more formally, parvovirus) is another common disease caused by a virus that is highly contagious to puppies and can be fatal. Puppies are easily exposed to the virus, as it is widespread in the environment. Signs of illness appear within three to five days after infection and include depression, not eating, vomiting, and diarrhea (which can be bloody). As with distemper, there is no cure, but veterinary care is often successful in treating affected dogs. Parvo vaccines are very effective and are usually given at the same time as distemper vaccination, starting at six to eight weeks of age. Boosters are important, and your veterinarian will recommend a schedule for rechecks. As with distemper vaccines, parvo vaccines are boosted in adult dogs every few years.

Hepatitis, or adenovirus, is often covered through a combination vaccine that also includes distemper and parvo. This viral infection can affect very young puppies and cause liver failure and death. Although hepatitis is not as common as the other infectious diseases, it is important to vaccinate all puppies against this disease and to give boosters to adult dogs as recommended by your veterinarian.

Rabies is not as common today in dogs as in the past but does still occur. It is much more prevalent among wildlife—particularly bats, skunks, and raccoons. Infection occurs through bite wounds, so never allow your dog to play with or fight with wild animals. State and local laws regulate rabies vaccination and licensing, so be sure to talk to your veterinarian or animal control officer and make sure you comply with rabies vaccine requirements. A dog exposed to wildlife may require quarantine and a rabies booster vaccination, and a dog that bites a person will very likely need to be quarantined for 10 days.

Noncore Vaccines for Dogs

Bordetella is a type of bacteria that causes coughing and other signs of respiratory disease in dogs. This infection is highly contagious and often spreads in situations where dogs are crowded, as in an animal shelter. In most puppies and dogs, the disease is not serious, but sometimes it leads to pneumonia and it can be fatal. Your veterinarian may use antibiotics or other forms of treatment if your pet develops this disease, and you should keep your dog away from other dogs until he recovers. Both injectable and intranasal (nose drops) vaccines are available but are not always effective in preventing infection. Some combination products also protect against parainfluenza, a viral infection that is very similar. Talk to your veterinarian about the pros and cons of *Bordetella* and parainfluenza vaccination.

Leptospira are a group of related bacteria that are usually spread to dogs from the environment, especially if wildlife are present. The disease caused by infection with these pathogens, known as leptospirosis, can cause depression, fever, and poor appetite, and sometimes severe complications such as liver or kidney failure.

Antibiotics and other treatments are available, but in areas where leptospirosis is common your veterinarian may recommend regular vaccination. The leptospirosis vaccines are not always completely effective but can be helpful. Humans are at risk of infection as well; in people, leptospirosis can cause flu-like symptoms or more serious disease.

Lyme disease is common in the northeastern and upper Midwestern areas of the United States. This bacterial infection (*Borrelia*) is spread by deer ticks to dogs, humans, and other animals. Affected dogs generally have signs of fever, poor appetite, and lameness. Antibiotics are effective for treatment, and your veterinarian may recommend regular vaccination if the disease is widespread in your area.

Vaccines are also currently available for *coronavirus*, which is a disease of young puppies that causes mild diarrhea, and *canine influenza*, which can cause coughing and sometimes leads to pneumonia. Talk to your veterinarian about the risks of these diseases and benefits of vaccination. While they may not be necessary for all dogs, in some situations these and other newer vaccines can be important.

OTHER INFECTIOUS DISEASES

A large number of bacterial, protozoal, and fungal diseases may affect dogs, and vaccines are not currently available for most of them. Table 5.1 provides a sample list but does not include every possible infectious disease. Always talk to your veterinarian whenever you have questions or concerns about these or any other infections.

Heartworm Disease

In many parts of the world, dogs are exposed to heartworms through mosquito bites. This infection is more common in the southern United States, but has also been found throughout North America and most other countries. Mosquitoes can spread microscopic larvae (baby worms) from infected dogs or wildlife every time they bite. Cats, humans, and other animals may get heartworm disease as well, although this condition is very rare in humans. After a mosquito bite, it takes at least three months and sometimes longer for the larvae to develop into adult worms, which find their way into blood vessels leading from the heart to the lungs. Signs of heartworm disease include coughing, weight loss, getting tired easily when exercising, and sometimes congestive heart failure.

A simple blood test for the presence of heartworms should be done annually, starting as early as six months of age. In some areas, testing may need to be done more often, especially if proper prevention is not being followed. Dogs that test negative can be started on medications from your veterinarian that are very effective in preventing heartworm disease. Available products currently include chewable tablets as well as liquids that are applied to the skin. They are most often

Table 5.1
Other Infectious Diseases of Dogs

Disease	Cause (Agent)	Means of Transmission
Babesiosis	*Babesia canis* or *gibsoni*	Ticks, other dogs
Blastomycosis	*Blastomyces dermatitidis*	Environment
Brucellosis	*Brucella canis*	Other dogs (especially breeding dogs)
Campylobacteriosis	*Campylobacter jejuni*	Other animals, environment, raw meat
Coccidiomycosis	*Coccidioides immitis*	Environment
Coccidiosis	*Isospora canis*	Other dogs, environment
Cryptosporidiosis	*Cryptosporidium canis*	Other dogs, environment
Dermatophytosis (ringworm)	*Microsporum canis*, others	Other animals, environment
Ehrlichiosis	*Ehrlichia canis*, others	Ticks
Giardiasis	*Giardia*	Other animals, environment
Hepatozoonosis	*Hepatozoon canis or americanum*	Ticks
Histoplasmosis	*Histoplasma capsulatum*	Environment
Leishmaniasis	*Leishmania donovani*	Sandflies, other dogs
Rocky Mountain spotted fever	*Rickettsia rickettsii*	Ticks
Salmonellosis	*Salmonella*	Other animals, environment, raw meat

used monthly, either year-round in some areas or just during the mosquito season in other areas.

If your dog tests positive for heartworms, your veterinarian can offer treatment that is usually very successful. Be sure to follow the instructions carefully, especially those concerning restriction of exercise. Do not attempt to treat heartworms with over-the-counter medications or remedies found on the Internet—none are effective and some may even be harmful. Fortunately, lung damage from heartworms can be reversed over time, and your dog should live a normal, healthy life after treatment.

CONCLUSION

Dogs are indeed "man's best friend" and give unconditional love to people of all ages around the world. Your responsibility when caring for your pet includes food, shelter, companionship, and health care. By following the suggestions in this chapter and the rest of this book, you will be well on your way to being the kind of owner your dog deserves! Establish a relationship with a veterinarian early on, and always ask his or her advice when you have questions about your dog's health.

FURTHER READING

Brevitz, B. *The Complete Healthy Dog Handbook*. New York: Workman Publishing; 2009.

Eldredge, D. M., L. D. Carlson, D. G. Carlson, J. M. Giffin, and B. Adelman. *Dog Owner's Home Veterinary Handbook*. 4th ed. Hoboken, NJ: Wiley/Howell Book House; 2007.

Kahn, C. M., and S. Line, eds. *The Merck/Merial Manual for Pet Health*. Rahway, NJ: Merck Publishing Group; 2007.

Kay, N. *Speaking for Spot*. North Pomfret, VT: Trafalgar Square Books; 2008.

6

Cats: Health, Diseases, and Prevention

Craig Datz, DVM, MS, DABVP, DACVN

INTRODUCTION

Cats are the most popular household pets in the United States for many reasons: they are easy and inexpensive to care for, they are happy living indoors, and they provide endless entertainment. Originally, cats were domesticated for the purpose of rodent control, but now we simply enjoy their companionship.

This chapter begins by discussing basic care of cats, and then describes some common medical diseases affecting these animal companions. Always consult your veterinary clinic health care team for specific advice, as this chapter is not intended to substitute for the care of a qualified veterinarian.

BASIC CARE FOR CATS

Whether you acquire a fluffy new kitten or a sleek adult cat, you will need to follow some simple steps to get ready for the new arrival. Your cat will provide you with many years of friendship, and in return you will be responsible for her care so that your pet will live a long, healthy life.

Housing

Cats can live indoors, outdoors, or both in and out. To ensure that these animals will have a healthy, long life, however, it is best to keep your cat indoors. This way, your pet will avoid the accidents, injuries, and illnesses commonly observed with outdoor cats, such as being hit by a car, chased by a dog, getting into a cat fight, or becoming lost.

Indoor pets have only a few needs. Cats prefer having quiet, secure resting places where they will not be bothered by children, other animals, or too much activity.

They should have a clean area for a food and water bowl, and at least one litter box. Add a few toys, a place to scratch, and some fun time with you and the family, and your cat will be happy!

Feeding

In choosing dishes for your cat's food and water, you may want to avoid plastic as it may introduce an off-taste or even cause skin irritation. Metal or ceramic or other unbreakable materials are ideal.

Clean and refill the water bowl daily, and keep in mind that some cats prefer drinking water from a lightly dripping faucet. If you do not mind your pet jumping into the sink or bathtub to get a drink, it is perfectly okay to let the water drip a minute or two.

The food bowl should likewise be kept clean at all times. If the cat is fed one or more meals of dry food each day, be sure to clean the dish daily. In addition, if any canned foods are given, clean the bowl immediately after eating. Food particles left behind can encourage bacteria or mold growth, which can cause illness in both cats and people. Please do not offer unlimited food to your cat! More and more cats are becoming overweight or even dangerously obese because their owners leave dry food out continuously. (For more information on feeding cats, see Chapter 11.)

Environmental Enhancement

One disadvantage of keeping cats indoors is that their exercise and play options are limited. Your active, playful kitten that scampers around the house can grow into a lazy adult cat that seems to sleep all day and all night. We now know the importance of providing a stimulating indoor environment for these pets, and you should try to make your home as "cat-friendly" as possible. This reduces both stress and the risk of several medical and behavioral problems. Here are some suggestions:

- Create "hiding places" by offering boxes or allowing the cat access to closets or under a bed.
- Have various perches including windowsills, climbing trees, or even space in a bookshelf, as cats like to jump up.
- Remove any toxic houseplants, as curious cats will often nibble on them. Instead, offer "cat grass," which is available at pet stores. Also hide any string, rubber bands, yarn, hair ties, shoelaces, tinsel, or similar objects, as cats care notorious for investigating, playing with, and even swallowing these items. Their ingestion can block the cat's intestinal tract and lead to a life-threatening condition that often requires immediate surgery.
- As cats love to explore and solve puzzles, place a few cat treats or kibbles of food in out-of-the-way locations (like an Easter egg hunt!).

- A laser pointer moved slowly along the floor or walls often attracts cats, who will stalk and pounce on the red dot. Because there is no reward for "catching" the light, however, felines will quickly tire of this game. Dragging a string or old shoelace through the house will get your met moving!

Most importantly, learn to read and respect your cat's mood. When the cat is sleepy, let him take a nap. If he is ready to play, your pet will come to you for attention or start running and jumping. But if he is grooming ("taking a bath"), the animal will want to be left alone for a while.

Litter Boxes

Unlike dogs, who need to be walked outside to urinate and defecate, cats prefer a clean litter box in a quiet location. If you have more than one cat, you should have one litter box for each cat plus an additional one (for example, three cats means four litter boxes).

The most common types of litter are plain clay and clumping. Usually, clay litter is the least expensive and is adequate for most cats. It may be dusty when poured out. Clumping litter has a finer, sand-like texture and is often preferred by cats. Avoid heavily scented or unusual types of litter.

Use the largest, deepest litter box possible, as cats like to circle around and scratch at the litter before eliminating. Too small an area limits their movement, and they may respond by eliminating just outside the box or in different parts of the house. If you are unable to find a large cat litter box at the store, consider using a plastic storage container, as these items are often available in more shapes and sizes.

Whichever type of litter and box you use, remember to scoop and discard the liquid and solid wastes at least once a day. In addition, once a week or every other week, dump all of the litter, clean the box, and refill it with fresh litter. Covered litter pans may not be a good idea, as odors are trapped and you may forget to clean a dirty box as often as needed. Self-cleaning boxes are also available but tend to be expensive, and the noise may frighten your cat.

Grooming

Cats are very clean animals and may not need much attention; however, long-haired cats sometimes require brushing and combing to prevent tangles and mats. Regular brushing also helps during shedding season (spring and summer) and gives you a chance to check for fleas, ticks, or any skin problems. A nice feature of cats is that they like to give themselves baths. They have roughened tongue surfaces that they use to remove dust, dirt, oils, dead skin cells, and other debris and to smooth down their haircoats; therefore, cats do not need to be regularly bathed.

Toenails should be trimmed to help avoid puncture wounds and scratches—usually once or twice a month is sufficient. Nail trimming can be easy or difficult depending on how cooperative your cat is and whether you have the right tools. You should handle your cat's paws and toes daily to get her used to the feeling. Offer a tiny tasty treat as a reward or positive reinforcement for letting you touch the feet and trim the nails. Choose an appropriately sized pet nail trimmer and make sure the blades are sharp. Most cats have light-colored translucent nails that allow you to see the blood vessel in the center and avoid cutting into it. Start by trimming a tiny bit of nail from the end, then try trimming a few more thin slices while checking for the appearance of the "quick," or the blood vessel. If bleeding occurs, do not panic! Either use a clotting powder (available at pet stores) or make a paste with some flour or cornstarch and a few drops of water. Apply the paste to the end of the claw, and the bleeding should stop within a minute or two.

Cats instinctively scratch at or around various surfaces as a marking behavior. Many owners will not want their furniture, carpets, curtains, or other belongings destroyed by an enthusiastic scratching cat. Declawing is a surgical operation in which the claws and nail beds are amputated so that they will not grow back. This procedure is illegal in some areas and should be performed only by licensed, qualified veterinarians, as mistakes can lead to complications. Lameness, infection, damage to footpads, and regrowth of claws are some of the problems seen after declawing surgery. Although anesthesia and pain medications are used to minimize the trauma, cats may still have sore feet for days to weeks after the procedure. Instead of declawing, it is safer and preferable to train your kitten or cat to use appropriate scratching areas in the house. (For more information on managing this normal behavior, see Chapter 9.)

Toothbrushing is also an essential part of keeping your cat healthy (see Chapter 2 for more on dental care). It can be made into a positive experience by providing lots of praise and petting, or even a treat!

Outdoor Cats

While cats can thrive and have long, healthy lives if kept indoors, there are some situations where pet cats are allowed to go outdoors or even stay outside. You may have a safe, fenced-in yard or live in a quiet neighborhood with no loose dogs. People living in rural areas often end up with "barn cats," that are content to roam and control rodents as long as they have access to safe housing in case of bad weather or a threat. A small number of cats have significant behavior problems such as aggression or inability to use a litter box, and so end up being kept outdoors or in a garage. Owners have also been known to train their pet cats to walk on a harness and leash and can be observed strolling with them outdoors. An outdoor fenced-in patio or protected perching area can allow for fresh air and sunshine while avoiding injuries and accidents.

Are there any advantages to letting cats outside? Possible benefits include encouraging exercise, mental stimulation, and the ability to express instinctive behaviors such as stalking and pouncing. An indoor pet does not always have the opportunity to "act like a cat." In other words, instead of the animal having to hunt and catch food, we automatically fill our pets' bowls with no effort needed. Instead of running, jumping, and burning calories, indoor cats may choose to sleep all night and nap all day. Alternatively they may express their stalking and hunting behavior by attacking ankles as people walk by. A lack of mental stimulation in an indoor environment often leads to boredom and in some cases behavioral problems.

Even with these potential challenges, keeping your cat indoors is still the ideal option. No one wants to see a companion injured or become lost. The best of both worlds is to keep your pet inside but do your best to make the indoor environment mimic the best qualities of the outdoors—fresh, stimulating, exciting, and full of opportunities to play, exercise, explore, and just be a cat!

CARING FOR YOUR CAT'S HEALTH

All cats need the basic care of food, water, and shelter. In addition, proper medical care and prevention of illness are necessary to keep cats healthy. The needs of kittens are somewhat different than those of adult cats, and senior citizen cats have their own requirements. This section is divided by age groups, but there is much overlap among the various groups.

Newborn Kittens

If you own or come across a female cat that has just delivered a litter, you will need to help her take care of the kittens until they are ready to be weaned. The two main concerns are warmth and nutrition.

Kittens cannot thermoregulate, so they will become chilled if separated from their mother or placed in a cold environment. Newborns will keep warm enough by snuggling with one another and with their mother. A box or small enclosed area with warm bedding is fine, but be careful with electric heaters, heating pads, and lamps, as they can be dangerous and cause burns.

Most female cats are good mothers and will lie still while kittens suckle. Stress, such as loud noises, too many people or dogs around, or any perceived threats, will interfere with nursing. If the mother is scared or just uneasy, she may move her kittens one by one to a different location by picking them up by the scruffs of their necks with her front teeth. Smaller, weaker kittens can be pushed aside by stronger littermates and may need help finding the mother's nipples for nursing.

The mother needs to eat two to three times more food during the nursing period and have free access to plenty of water to help with milk production. If the kittens are not nursing well or if they are orphans, you will have to supply milk to them by bottle- or tube-feeding. It is not difficult to hand-feed kittens, but be sure to have your veterinarian or someone experienced with kittens show you what to do and what not to do. Commercial milk-replacement products are available at most pet stores.

Young Kittens (Ages 6–16 Weeks)

Kittens are weaned onto solid food at 5 to 6 weeks of age, and a good time to find new homes is when they reach 8 to 10 weeks of age. Adopting kittens at too young an age may lead to poor socialization or even illnesses. Older kittens can still make perfect pets, but may need a little more time to get accustomed to their new home.

The first step in caring for your new kitten's health is to take the animal directly to your veterinarian as soon as she arrives. Ideally, you will already have an appointment scheduled for a check-up. If you wait too long before visiting the veterinarian, the kitten may become ill from common diseases or parasites. Before your visit, gather up all papers, health records, and any medications and take them along. Most veterinarians ask that you bring a fresh stool (fecal) sample with you. A zipper-lock plastic bag or disposable plastic container works well. As most kittens instinctively use litter boxes, it is easy to collect a stool sample.

While there are some variations in a kitten preventive health program, your veterinary team will do some or all of the following during your first visit.

1. They will first ask questions about your kitten's history, such as when and where you obtained the cat, how he has been feeling, which type of food you are using, what the cat's environment like, and whether there are any other cats, dogs, or other pets or people in the household. Staff members will also want to know if you have noticed any signs or symptoms such as runny eyes, runny nose, sneezing, head shaking or scratching at the ears, vomiting, or diarrhea. After collecting a comprehensive history, they can then investigate any potential problems.
2. Next, your kitten should receive a complete, nose-to-tail physical exam. Your veterinarian will take a close look at her eyes, ears and ear canals, nose, and teeth. He or she will listen to the kitten's heart and lung sounds with a stethoscope, and palpate her abdomen, limbs, and lymph nodes. Her skin and coat will be examined carefully, and vital signs such as weight, body temperature, and heart rate will be recorded. After a complete physical examination of your kitten, the veterinarian will let you know if he gets a clean bill of health or whether any potential problems were uncovered.
3. Depending on whether the kitten has had any previous vaccinations or medical care, your veterinarian will recommend any necessary procedures. In addition to checking a stool sample, he or she may suggest other diagnostic tests to make sure your kitten is healthy and not infected with parasites or other diseases. One common test involves collecting a few drops of blood to test for feline leukemia virus (FeLV). Vaccination types and schedules can vary, but most veterinarians will administer a combination vaccine product that protects against several common diseases, including feline panleukopenia, rhinotracheitis (herpesvirus), and calicivirus. Other

vaccines can be given at the first visit to protect against other diseases as well. The injections may sting a little, but most kittens tolerate their check-ups and shots with only an occasional meow!

4. Kittens can acquire intestinal worms soon after birth. Your veterinarian will most likely administer or dispense a safe deworming medication meant to kill parasites. In some areas, heartworm disease is endemic; although it is mainly a dog disease, this condition occasionally can spread to cats through mosquito bites. Several safe medications are available to protect kittens and cats from heartworms and other parasites.

5. After the check-up, vaccinations, deworming, and any other necessary health care, the veterinarian will ask if you have any questions about caring for your new companion. Many clinics offer kitten kits that have product samples and written information about health, common diseases, and behavior.

A second kitten visit is normally scheduled approximately three to four weeks after the first, unless any concerns need to be addressed sooner. During the next visit, your veterinarian will repeat the history and physical examination and determine whether more vaccinations, deworming, or other procedures are needed. A third and even a fourth visit may be needed depending on your kitten's age and health. Older kittens will receive a rabies vaccination and license in most areas. Your veterinarian will discuss the best age for spaying or neutering and other important issues during the first year of life.

Back at home, you will need to make sure your kitten is staying healthy, eating well (but not too much!), acting playful, and receiving plenty of rest. You may be able to find kitten classes ("kitty kindergarten") led by experienced individuals who have had training in feline behavior. Kittens should be actively socialized, which means exposing them to different people, animals, environments, and situations such as loud noise, car rides, being in a carrier or kennel, and being handled (picked up and petted). Invite people and well-behaved children and pets to your house to see and play with your new kitten. You may want to take your pet along to visit others if you have safe transportation such as a cat carrier. If you isolate your kitten and do not let her interact with other people, dogs, cats, and so on, the animal may become fearful and poorly socialized. At the same time, because kittens can become overwhelmed with attention and activity, allow your pet to get away and hide or take a well-deserved nap after a busy day.

Older Kittens (Ages 16 Weeks to 1 Year)

Kittens grow up quickly and can reach "puberty" at 5 to 6 months of age. Full growth usually occurs when they are 10 to 12 months old. Continue feeding a kitten diet throughout your pet's growth period. She will need more and more food to keep up with growth and activity, but be careful that your kitten does not gain excessive weight. It is much easier to prevent weight gain than to try to get an older cat to lose the extra pounds.

Your veterinarian will recommend spaying or neutering at or around six months of age. In addition to preventing accidental breeding and unwanted kittens, this procedure provides numerous health and behavioral benefits, so be sure to schedule it with your veterinarian as soon as it is recommended.

After the kitten series of vaccinations and deworming, additional preventive care visits are not required before one year of age unless recommended by your veterinarian. However, you should not hesitate to call for advice or schedule an appointment if you notice any signs of illness or unusual behavior. Continue any heartworm medication prescribed by your veterinarian and apply any flea, tick, or other parasite products as recommended.

Young Adult Cats (Ages 1–3 Years)

Cats are healthy and playful during their young adult years. One of the most important things you can do to ensure a long, active life is to choose a high-quality diet formulated for adult cats. Do not overfeed! Cats do not need extra food unless they are growing, pregnant, or nursing. Otherwise, cats rarely require high-calorie diets, unlike dogs that may be running or working or otherwise active all day. While it is tempting to leave dry cat food out and let your pet nibble away, many cats will overeat and gain unnecessary weight, which leads to health complications and a shorter life span. Instead, use a measuring cup for dry food or give a certain amount from a can, and be consistent.

Veterinary check-ups should be scheduled at least once a year and even twice a year in some cases. Ask your veterinarian which schedule he or she recommends. For young adults, your veterinarian will set up a vaccination schedule and send you reminders when vaccines are necessary. After your cat reaches one year of age, the vaccine interval will range from every year to every three years depending on the type of vaccine and other factors. Routine diagnostic testing may be recommended to check for parasites, viral diseases, and internal conditions such as kidney or bladder disease. Most veterinarians also recommend regular dental care for adult cats, which may involve annual check-ups and cleanings.

To avoid the "lazy cat" syndrome, in which your companion seems to want to sleep all day and all night, make your indoor environment as rich and stimulating as possible. As noted earlier, cats thrive on interesting activities such as running, jumping, climbing, hiding, solving puzzles, chasing real or imaginary objects, and even playing "fetch" like dogs. Your cat needs both physical and mental "workouts" to keep him active and healthy.

Middle-Aged Cats (Ages 3–9 Years)

Some cats slow down noticeably in the middle part of their life, demonstrating less playfulness and activity. Indoor cats are especially prone to being bored, overweight, and no longer interested in kitten games. It is important to continue visiting your veterinary clinic once or twice a year even if your pet seems perfectly healthy. Many medical, behavioral, nutritional, and dental problems are more easily and inexpensively managed or even prevented when caught early. Any necessary vaccinations and diagnostic tests can be done during wellness veterinary visits. Laboratory tests, including routine tests on blood and urine samples, can give valuable information about the overall health of your companion.

Keep an eye out for your cat slowing down, being less willing to run and jump, or having excessive sleep time, as these may be signs of the onset of arthritis. Just like humans and dogs, older cats frequently become arthritic and suffer from joint and bone pain. Unfortunately, owners often fail to recognize this problem and simply attribute it to "old age." Be sure to report any changes in your cat's health and behavior to your veterinarian.

Older Cats (10–15 Years or Older)

Most cats are slow to show signs of aging and may appear to be normal and healthy past the age of 10 years. Other cats may have episodes of illness or chronic medical problems in their geriatric years. More than ever, you should plan on scheduling twice-yearly check-ups with your veterinarian. He or she will help you care for your cat and offer advice, diagnostic tests, and treatments that can prevent and manage illness.

Older cats may want to be left alone and can become intolerant of children. Part of the reason is that eyesight, hearing, and sense of smell decline with age. A cat may be easily startled if she does not see or hear your approach. Napping takes priority, and an older cat should be allowed to have a quiet, comfortable place to rest. With advancing age, her dining habits may change, such that the cat may need more canned cat food and less dry or different varieties to tempt her to eat. Cats often suffer from a number of dental diseases that can cause discomfort and pain, which in turn may lead to less appetite and weight loss. Arthritis is often present, which results in stiff, painful joints. Older cats may no longer be able to climb staircases, jump onto furniture, or even make it to a litter box if it is far away or too high. Never punish a cat for missing the litter box; instead, try to determine why the problem is happening and make adjustments, such as adding extra boxes with lower sides in more areas of the house.

Older cats, like dogs, may suffer from diseases such as cancer, kidney failure, and heart failure. These conditions cannot always be prevented or cured, but many supportive treatments are available that can reduce pain and suffering and help with quality of life.

There may be a time near the end of your cat's life span where you will want to discuss euthanasia with your veterinarian. Euthanasia is a painless, humane way

---

DID YOU KNOW?

- Cats communicate by rubbing and "marking" objects, people, or even other animals. This behavior releases special scents called pheromones from glands located in their cheeks and other areas of the body.
- The predatory behavior of cats toward birds and small mammals will not be curtailed by offering them more food. The motivation to hunt is not a direct result of hunger.
- Contrary to popular belief, cats are not nocturnal, but crepuscular, being most active at dawn and dusk.
- Households with multiple cats should have one litter box more than the total number of cats.

---

to end suffering and ease the process of passing away when a cat no longer has a good quality of life. If you have had a good relationship with your veterinary health care team, they will be very helpful and compassionate and do what is best for your pet.

COMMON MEDICAL PROBLEMS AND DISEASES

From time to time, you may notice signs of illness in your feline companion. Often your first thought is to wonder whether the issue is important enough to call or visit the veterinarian. Most veterinary clinics are happy to answer questions over the phone and will help you decide if a check-up is necessary. In some communities, there are even 24-hour hospitals and emergency facilities open nights and weekends that can help.

The information presented in this section is simply a general guide to medical conditions that occur in cats; it is *not* a substitute for proper veterinary care. Also, be wary of information that you find on the Internet, as many websites and email groups dispense inaccurate or even harmful information.

Loss of Appetite

Cats can be finicky eaters and it can be difficult to know if they are sick or just holding out for something that tastes better. Kittens should readily eat commercial diets, whether dry or canned, at least two or three times per day. Any cat younger than one year of age that stops eating should be evaluated right away by a veterinarian. Older cats may appear not to eat all day, but if food is left out they will normally get enough. If you are sure that your cat has not eaten in more than 24 hours, a call to your veterinarian for advice is in order.

Vomiting

Cats sometimes vomit food, fluids, hairballs, or even small objects, such as bits of string, but otherwise act healthy. An occasional bit of vomiting in an otherwise normal cat may not be a matter of concern. Make a note of the time and appearance, and if the problem persists more than a day or two, call your veterinarian. Hairballs have a tubular shape and consist of balled-up hair (normally with no odor). Your veterinarian may suggest laxatives or a special diet for ongoing hairball problems. If you notice three or four instances of vomiting in a single day, or if the cat is lethargic or hiding, take him directly to a veterinarian. You may want to remove the cat's food and water bowls for six to eight hours to avoid repeated eating/vomiting episodes. Do not give any medicines unless directed by your veterinarian.

Vomiting can also be a sign of disease or even an emergency. If diarrhea occurs at the same time or if you see any blood or dark material in the vomitus or diarrhea, call your veterinarian. At home, you can check for dehydration by gently feeling the animal's inner lips and gums to see if they are moist. If they are dry and sticky, then the cat is moderately dehydrated.

Diarrhea

In healthy cats, stools are formed and have a consistent color and appearance. Soft stools are a sign of mild diarrhea and may be semi-formed or look like pudding. Severe diarrhea may be liquid or even bloody. If your cat is otherwise acting normally and eating, then diarrhea may be temporary. Your veterinarian might suggest bringing in a stool sample in for analysis.

What are some common causes of vomiting and diarrhea? The first thing to consider is whether your pet may have eaten something recently he should not have. Cats are not as likely as dogs to pick up and chew unfamiliar objects. Nevertheless, cats are by nature very curious and may nibble on houseplants, bits of spoiled food or garbage, pieces of string, ribbon, yarn, tinsel, fabric, or toys. Both indoor and outdoor cats may acquire bacterial infections, intestinal worms, and other parasites that can lead to vomiting and diarrhea. Stress, such as a change in diet or environment, can also result in intestinal upset. In older cats, there is a greater concern for metabolic diseases (e.g., kidney or liver insufficiency, diabetes, thyroid gland disorders) or cancer, so be sure to visit your veterinarian if your pet experiences vomiting or diarrhea that lasts more than a few days.

Skin Disease

Cats are clean animals that spend a lot of time grooming themselves. Disorders of the skin and haircoat may lead to itching and scratching, so you may notice excessive licking and grooming. While itchiness has many potential causes, the most common ones are parasites (such as fleas) and allergies.

Fleas can be seen crawling on the skin, often around the rump and tail base or around the thighs (although they may live anywhere on the body). They leave behind a telltale sign called "flea dirt," which is excreted material that resembles black pepper flakes. Some cats are allergic to flea bites and may scratch or chew excessively even if no live fleas can be found. In fact, it is more common not to actually see fleas on itchy cats because they are determined and efficient groomers. Your veterinary clinic can suggest an effective program to get rid of fleas, which involves treating the cat, other animals in the house, and the environment. Never use flea products intended for dogs on your cat, as many of them are toxic; cats can go into seizures or even die if certain flea or tick products are accidentally applied.

Allergies are less common in cats than dogs but can still cause misery. Cats can be allergic to almost anything in the outdoor environment, including grass, trees, and pollen, or to indoor material such as plants, molds, and dust mites. If your cat scratches only during certain times of the year, environmental allergy (also called atopy or atopic dermatitis) is likely. Cats that scratch year-round may be allergic to something indoors or to a food or food ingredient. Your veterinarian is well equipped to treat allergies. He or she may use prescription medication, shampoos or topical agents, or special diets for this purpose. In severe cases your veterinarian may perform allergy testing and prescribe immunotherapy (small amounts of the allergic substance given by injection to reduce sensitivity).

Skin infections, hair loss, and other conditions may not result in scratching. Any changes in your cat's skin or coat; any swellings, lumps and bumps, discoloration, or odors; or excessively moist or dry areas are good reasons to visit your veterinarian.

Ear Disease

Unlike dogs, cats rarely develop a buildup of ear wax or ear infections, so routine ear cleaning is not necessary. However, shaking or tilting of the cat's head or scratching at her ears most likely indicates a problem. Many kittens have ear mites, which are microscopic parasites that live deep in the ear canals and cause intense itching. Adult cats can have ear mites as well if they are exposed to other cats or spend a lot of time outdoors. While you may find ear mite medication at pet stores, it is always best to visit the veterinarian for a proper diagnosis and effective treatment. Cats can also have other ear problems such as polyps (overgrowth of tissue), bacterial infections, hematomas (pockets of bloody fluid), foreign bodies, and even cancerous tumors, so be sure to take your pet to the veterinarian for an expert check-up instead of trying to treat the condition at home.

Bone, Joint, Spinal, and Muscle Disorders

A sudden lameness in a cat can result from injury, whereas a more gradual onset suggests a chronic, ongoing problem. If you notice your cat holding a foot or leg up or not bearing full weight, try checking for obvious causes. If the cat will hold still, gently palpate her feet and toes, and look for any toenail problems. Move your hands up the leg and squeeze gently to see if there is a sore area. Infections and abscesses are common causes of limping in cats. Be careful when palpating sore areas, as the cat may scratch or bite. Your veterinarian can do a more comprehensive physical examination and may recommend x-rays or other tests to definitely determine the cause of the lameness. Lastly, never give human medicines such as aspirin, acetaminophen (Tylenol), or ibuprofen to cats; many over-the-counter drugs are toxic or even fatal to them.

Respiratory Diseases

Kittens are very susceptible to upper respiratory infections. Two of the common causes are herpesvirus (rhinotracheitis) and calicivirus (see the section on vaccine-preventable diseases later in this chapter). While there are currently no cures available for viral infections, your veterinarian will be able to do an exam to determine the probable cause and severity and suggest treatment options.

Older cats occasionally have allergic bronchitis, or asthma, that usually results from environmental exposure to allergenic substances. Signs of this disease include coughing and rapid or open-mouth breathing. Cats with asthma may have trouble breathing and should be taken directly to a veterinary clinic on an emergency basis. Lung infections and pneumonia are not common, but cats with difficulty breathing may have a buildup of fluid around the lungs. Always consult your veterinarian as soon as possible if your cat's breathing pattern changes or if she stops eating and becomes lethargic.

Eye Problems

If your cat's eyes have a watery or thick discharge, or if they appear red, swollen, or squinting, this could be a sign of a significant disorder. Some eye problems can lead to blindness if left untreated, so call or visit your veterinarian as soon as possible. Common causes of red, painful eyes include injuries, scratches, allergies, foreign bodies, infections, or even more serious conditions such as glaucoma. You can gently clean around your cat's eyes with a moistened cotton ball if you notice discharge, but be sure to take your pet to the veterinarian for a check-up and diagnostics. Diseases of the eye should be taken seriously, as they can worsen rapidly.

Dental Disease

Kittens are born without teeth but soon develop a set of 26 primary (baby) teeth. When the kitten is between 4 and 6 months of age, they become loose and fall out, to be replaced by 30 secondary (adult) teeth.

You can take care of your cat's teeth by getting in the habit of brushing daily or every other day. Do not use human toothpaste. Instead, look for products especially for cats sold at pet stores and veterinary clinics. They are made with cat-friendly flavors such as poultry. Without brushing, most cats will develop dental tartar buildup, gingivitis (red, swollen gums), bad breath, and infections that can lead to periodontal disease (loss of soft tissue and bone support, loose or missing teeth). Cats also can suffer from broken or chipped teeth, abscesses, and a variety of other oral problems.

Resorptive lesions are a common dental problem in cats, but one that is often overlooked. Similar to cavities in humans, they involve a gradual erosion or complete loss of enamel and dental tissue. These lesions are very painful when touched, and currently the only effective treatment is complete extraction of the affected teeth. Appropriate diagnostics and treatments are available only from your veterinarian.

Heart Disease

A variety of conditions can lead to heart failure and even sudden death in cats. Diseases of the heart muscle (hypertrophic, restrictive, or dilated cardiomyopathy) can be seen in adult cats, while kittens may be born with congenital heart defects. Signs of heart disease in cats may include coughing, difficulty breathing, vomiting, loss of appetite, and weight loss. Blood clots may form and can stop circulation to parts of the body, especially the rear legs, as a result of severe heart conditions. Additionally, an improper or unbalanced diet may be deficient in taurine, an important amino acid found in protein; such a deficiency can lead to heart failure.

Neurologic Problems

The brain and nervous system can be affected by trauma, infection, disease, or other less common conditions. Some cats may have seizure disorders such as epilepsy, in which you may notice a sudden onset of staring, stumbling, or convulsions. Seizure is an emergency, and you should take your cat to the veterinarian immediately if it occurs. A loss of limb function or paralysis can result from spinal cord trauma or disease. Older cats occasionally develop a head tilt or walk in circles as a result of vestibular (inner ear) disease. Unusual behaviors, especially in older cats, may indicate infection, inflammation, or even cancer of the central nervous system (brain).

Urinary Disorders

Because indoor cats use litter boxes for elimination, it can be easy to tell if something is wrong with your cat's urinary system. The first sign of trouble may be finding urine outside the litter box. Another sign may be frequent trips to the litter box, or squatting with only a few drops of urine coming out. If you use clumping-type litter, you may notice several small areas instead of large clumps. Vocalizing (meowing or crying) while in the litter box is a sure sign of pain or distress. Blood in the urine may be visible as reddish flecks or a pink to tan color. Some cats even squat and leave small puddles of urine in bathtubs, sinks, bedding, or piles of laundry.

No matter the cause of the problem, call or visit your veterinarian. Bladder diseases range from mild to severe, especially in the case of male cats, who can become "blocked" (unable to urinate because of an obstruction in the bladder or urethra). In fact, if you have a male cat, you should be on the lookout for signs of urinary obstruction, which include all of the previously mentioned issues (straining in the litter box, vocalizing) along with vomiting, lethargy, and a painful abdomen if picked up. Some owners mistake straining behavior for constipation, which is not as likely to occur in cats.

Your veterinarian will first try to determine whether the urinary disorder is primarily behavioral or medical. (For more information about behavioral reasons for eliminating outside the litter box, see Chapter 9.) After a physical examination, your veterinarian will obtain a urine sample to check for various disorders and may order blood tests, x-rays, ultrasound, or other diagnostics. Interestingly, one of the most common causes of bladder disease in cats is stress. When cats are upset, angry, or scared, or when they encounter changes in their household or environment, their nervous systems can overreact, leading to idiopathic feline lower urinary tract disease. This medical term describes cats with frequent urination, sometimes with blood, and signs of pain or discomfort in which no obvious medical cause (such as infection or bladder stones) can be found. While cats of all ages can be affected, this disorder most commonly occurs in young to middle-aged adult cats. Your veterinarian may treat such disease with medications or special diets, but you should also analyze your cat's environment and lifestyle to see if any recent changes may have caused stress.

A common urinary disease in older cats is kidney failure. The kidneys are responsible for conserving water in the body and eliminating waste products. Over time, a cat's kidneys can gradually lose their ability to function, resulting in increased urine output and increased water consumption. You may find yourself filling the water bowl more often and scooping out bigger clumps of urine from the litter box. Cats usually develop some loss of kidney function between the ages of 10 and 15 years, but you may not notice any signs until months or years after the disease starts. Your veterinarian can diagnose kidney disease with simple blood and urine testing. At this time, there is no cure for failing kidneys except for kidney transplantation (performed at a few specialty centers); however, the veterinary staff will have several suggestions to help your cat feel better and slow disease progression. These approaches may include special diets, medications, supplements, and even at-home fluid therapy. Even when their kidneys not working optimally, cats can often still live a long time.

Reproductive System Disorders

Almost all experts recommend spaying and neutering all pet cats, and your veterinarian can advise you on the best time to schedule the surgery, most often before the cat reaches 6 months of age. Female cats can be ready to mate and produce kittens as early as 5 to 6 months of age; males usually mature between 6 and 10 months of age.

If you are dealing with a pregnant cat, there are a few steps you can take to ensure that both mother and kittens will be healthy. Pregnancy lasts approximately nine weeks, and in the final week or so the cat will look for a nesting area. You should be familiar with both normal behavior and signs of complications. After cats go into labor (active contractions), no more than two hours should go by before the mother delivers each kitten. If you see contractions but no kittens, take your cat directly to a veterinarian for an emergency assessment and possible cesarean section (C-section). Cats prefer to be left alone during the birthing process and may resent too much human interaction. In fact, the mother may stop her labor or pick up her kittens one at a time and move them to a different location if she feels bothered or threatened in her birthing and nursing box or confined area. Your veterinarian is the best resource for helping you navigate the complicated breeding, birthing, and nursing periods.

Parasites

To prevent and treat internal or external parasites, your cat will need regular check-ups with your veterinarian. Kittens should be dewormed for common intestinal parasites starting before six weeks of age. Older kittens and adult cats should be checked for worms routinely and ideally treated monthly with medication that also prevents heartworm disease. The best way to check for internal parasites is to bring a fresh fecal (stool) sample to your veterinarian. A common worm observed by owners is the tapeworm, which can pass in the stool or even where your cat sits or naps. The egg packets look like grains of rice. These worms are also easily treated by your veterinarian. Keep in mind that some types of worms are zoonotic (contagious) to people and can cause disease, especially in children. The best way to avoid zoonotic worms is to wash your hands before eating and avoid coming in contact with fecal material.

External parasites of cats include fleas, ticks, mites, and lice. Fleas are tiny wingless insects that can be seen moving around on the skin, often around the tail base and rear legs. Ticks come in a variety of sizes and are usually attached to the skin. Mites are invisible but can cause skin or ear disease. Lice are very rare. Complete flea control is possible by using products recommended by your veterinarian and by routinely vacuuming and cleaning up the environment where the cat lives. Ticks, mites, and lice are more difficult to control and may require topical treatment and environmental control. Keep in mind that many antiparasite products that are safe for use in dogs are highly toxic to cats and can cause illness or even death.

VACCINE-PREVENTABLE DISEASES

Veterinarians now have effective vaccines for cats that can help prevent a number of infectious diseases. The available vaccines are divided into "core vaccines," which should be given to all cats, and "noncore vaccines," which are optional depending on your cat's risk of infection and effectiveness of the vaccine. Your local veterinarian will design a vaccine program that maximizes protection while avoiding unnecessary vaccinations.

Core Vaccines for Cats

Panleukopenia, also called feline distemper, is a serious and often fatal disease that mainly affects kittens. It is caused by a parvovirus and can be spread from other cats, certain wildlife, and even dogs. Kittens that are affected with panleukopenia will stop eating and have severe vomiting and diarrhea. Veterinarians can treat this disease with supportive care, but there are no effective antiviral medications. To prevent panleukopenia, all kittens should be vaccinated starting at six to eight weeks of age, and then receive boosters as recommended by your veterinarian. Adult cats may need booster vaccines every few years.

Rhinotracheitis (herpes) and *calici* are two viral diseases that are common in kittens but can also affect adult cats. These infections are easily spread among cats, especially if they are housed close together. Their usual signs include reddened, runny eyes, runny nose, sneezing, and sometimes fever and loss of appetite. While vaccinations are available to help prevent these two viral infections, they are not completely effective. Instead, vaccinated cats will exhibit milder clinical signs and a shorter time of illness. All kittens should be vaccinated at six to eight weeks of age, and then receive boosters as recommended. An especially harmful type of calici virus has been recently discovered that can cause severe illness and death, especially in cats housed in shelters. Your veterinarian can advise you on the best ways to prevent exposure of your cat to respiratory viral infections.

Rabies is more common in cats than in dogs, and all kittens and adult cats should be vaccinated against this infection as required by state and local laws. Because wildlife such as bats, skunks, and raccoons can spread rabies to cats through bites, cats should be kept away from wild animals. A cat exposed to a wild animal will likely need a rabies booster vaccination and then be placed under quarantine. If contact with a wild animal does occur, take your cat to your veterinarian for evaluation. Additionally, all cat bites to humans should be reported to animal control authorities, and a 10-day quarantine for your cat will likely be necessary.

Noncore Vaccines for Cats

Feline leukemia virus (FeLV) is spread from cat to cat. This infection is found most commonly in kittens born to infected mothers and in cats that have contact with strays or other outdoor cats. Some cats exposed to FeLV will not become ill, as their immune systems can fight off the virus. Other cats, especially kittens, will develop diseases associated with decreased immunity (such as frequent infections) and even certain types of cancer. A simple blood test is available to detect FeLV, but the prognosis for sick cats is poor. Many FeLV-infected cats will die within two to three years after diagnosis. Others may remain healthy but can transmit the virus to other cats. All kittens and newly acquired cats should be tested for FeLV and kept isolated from other cats if they test positive. Vaccination is available and highly recommended for all kittens and any adult cat that is considered at risk of exposure to the virus.

Feline immunodeficiency virus (FIV) also spreads from cat to cat, usually through bite wounds (fighting). Kittens may be obtain the infection from their mothers in utero, but this is much less common than with FeLV. As with FeLV, a blood test can detect exposure to FIV. Newly acquired cats, especially strays, should be tested for this virus as soon as possible. Some cats that test positive will remain healthy and live a normal life span, whereas others are at risk of decreased immunity and may develop serious diseases. In either case, those animals with the virus should be isolated from other cats so that they will not spread the infection. Vaccination is available and your veterinarian may recommend it for outdoor cats at risk of getting into fights. Unfortunately, current vaccines are not completely effective and can produce false-positive results on the blood tests.

Feline infectious peritonitis (FIP) is a rare but fatal disease of cats caused by a mutated (changed) type of coronavirus. Kittens are more susceptible to FIP than adult cats. Signs of the disease can include not eating, weight loss, fever, depression, and fluid accumulation in the abdomen (swollen belly) or in the chest cavity (which can cause difficulty breathing). The virus is spread from cat to cat, most often in shelters or catteries where many cats are housed together. There are currently no effective treatments for FIP, and vaccination is available but unreliable.

Bordetella and *Chlamydophila* are types of bacteria that can cause respiratory infections in cats. It can be difficult to tell these conditions apart from rhinotracheitis and calici viral infections, and they may occur at the same time. Such bacterial infections are usually milder and can be treated with antibiotics from your veterinarian. Vaccinations are available but are not completely effective and not as commonly recommended as the viral vaccines.

OTHER INFECTIOUS DISEASES

Cats can be exposed to some other infections, but vaccines are not available for every disease. Your veterinarian is the best source of information on which diseases are known to occur in your area.

CONCLUSION

Cats were originally domesticated to help with rodent and pest control, especially on farms and in areas where food products were stored. Over time, they have worked their way into our homes, our bedrooms, and even our laps. While cats are somewhat more independent than dogs and can survive without humans, we should provide them with the best care so that they will live long, healthy lives. Cats do not require much to be happy—a safe environment and shelter, cat food, clean water, a litter box, some toys and opportunities to play, and plenty of comfortable spots for napping. In return, cats share loving affection, companionship, and entertainment that helps keep us healthy and happy.

FURTHER READING

American Society for the Prevention and Cruelty to Animals. "Seventeen Poisonous Plants." http://www.aspca.org/pet-care/poison-control/17-common-poisonous -plants.html

Eldredge, D. M., D. G. Carlson, L. D. Carlson, and J. M. Giffin. *Cat Owner's Home Veterinary Handbook*, 3rd ed. Hoboken, NJ: Wiley/Howell Book House; 2007. Indoor Cat Initiative. Available at: http://www.vet.ohio-state.edu/indoorcat.htm

Indoor Cat Initiative. http://www.vet.ohio-state.edu/indoorcat.htm

Kahn, C. M., and S. Line, eds. *The Merck/Merial Manual for Pet Health*. Rahway, NJ: Merck Publishing Group; 2007.

Wexler-Mitchell, E. *Guide to a Healthy Cat*. Hoboken, NJ: Wiley/Howell Book House; 2003.

7

Ferrets, Rabbits, Rodents, and Other Small Mammals: Health, Diseases, and Prevention

Daniella R. Yaakov, DVM, and Jeffrey L. Rhody, DVM

INTRODUCTION

Many species of small mammals are kept as pets, with their numbers increasing yearly. Two of the many benefits to keeping small mammals are that they usually need less room than some of the larger pets (such as cats and dogs) and, therefore, can be kept in smaller homes, and they do not need to be walked regularly, although they do need exercise. Small mammals can create amazing bonds with their caregivers and provide a great deal of satisfaction and pleasure as pets, just like dogs and cats.

Of the small mammals that can be chosen as pets, each is a different species with different biology and different needs. To care for these animals properly, it is important to know about their origin, their needs, and their behavior, and to be familiar with some of their common diseases and signs of disease. Many of these species are prey species and will hide signs of disease until they are no longer able to do so; therefore, it is important to recognize subtle signs of illness and to know as much as possible about these pets. This chapter is designed to provide some basic information about the more commonly kept species and their common diseases.

A person who chooses to keep these animals as pets should research the species and learn as much about them as possible from reliable sources. In addition, finding a veterinarian who is comfortable with these species and has experience with them should be done early. Do not wait until a problem appears. Your veterinarian can be a good source of information not only about diseases and early signs, but also about the husbandry and proper keeping of these pets. He or she can also help direct you to reliable sources of information.

FERRETS

The scientific name of the ferret is *Mustela putorius furo*, from the Latin: *furonem* = "thief"; *putor* = "a stench." Ferrets are members of the family *Mustilidae*, which includes badgers, skunks, and otters, among other animals.

Natural History

Ferrets are small carnivores, thought to have been domesticated more than 2,000 years ago. It is unclear exactly who their wild ancestors were, and several different species have been proposed as their progenitors—mainly the European ferret, the European polecat, and the steppe polecat. The original use of ferrets at the time of their domestication was for hunting—they were sent into burrows to chase out rabbits, a practice that continues today. Other uses of ferrets have been in medical research, such as in studying influenza, which also infects and causes disease in ferrets.

Ferret Biology Basics

The average reported life span of a ferret is five to eight years in the United States. Males are typically larger than females, weighing up to 2 kilograms; females weigh up to 1 kilogram (spayed and neutered ferrets tend to be smaller than intact ones).

As carnivores, these animals have teeth that are suitable for killing and chewing live prey. Their fang teeth (also known as canine teeth) are well developed, and the baby teeth fall out and are replaced by permanent teeth by three months of age. Ferrets have a relatively short, simple gastrointestinal tract, and their respiratory system is suited to burrowing, with a large lung capacity compared to their body size. They also have a very good sense of smell and hearing; however, their eyesight is relatively poor.

Ferrets have sebaceous glands in their skin; these glands secrete a waxy/oily matter that is secreted on the skin and gives these animals a typical musky smell. This odor can be reduced, but not eliminated, by spaying and neutering.

Husbandry

Ferrets are fun, active, and curious pets. They will explore every nook and cranny, so their environment needs to be ferret-proofed against dangers such as electric cords, exposed rubber or foam items, and toxic substances. Some people choose to keep ferrets in a cage; in such a case, the cage should be as large as possible. Ferrets will climb, and cages should allow for this behavior. A safe cage is free of jagged edges, escape-proof, and made from safe, nontoxic materials. Good cages are easy to clean. If the cage is located outdoors, it should be protected from the elements and predators. Some people prefer to dedicate a ferret-proofed room for their pets.

Ferrets like to burrow and hide. A soft-lined pouch or a soft shirt provides a comfortable place to sleep, and they are often happy to rest in a hammock. Enrichment activities will keep a ferret's brain active. Ferrets were domesticated to hunt rodents and other small mammals, so you can satisfy the urge to hunt by providing foraging opportunities. In addition to putting some food in their food bowls, place food in various spots around their environment so they have to scavenge to find it. Tunnels and boxes can be fun for a ferret to explore. Of course, ferret-safe toys can be helpful when these animals are left alone or when playing with their owner. Litter box training is possible, although they will generally pick the corner of the room they prefer to use and will happily use a litter box if placed there. Additionally, ferrets are not good at cooling themselves down, so they need to be protected from extreme heat.

As carnivores, ferrets need a diet high in protein and fat. The source of protein should be high-quality, animal-based protein. Low-quality protein (such as bone meal) and plant proteins are inappropriate, because ferrets cannot effectively digest them. Ferrets are also unable to easily digest carbohydrates, so the carbohydrate content of the food should be minimal. Many options for feeding ferrets are available. Most caregivers prefer to use kibble marketed for ferrets, of which there are many different brands. Some people like to feed their ferrets whole prey or different types of freeze-dried meat diets intended for ferrets. Treats should be meat based as well.

Owners should monitor their ferrets for signs of illness. Given that owners tend to know their pets better than anyone else, any change from normal should be considered important enough to warrant a call to your veterinarian. Specific signs to watch for include decreased appetite, a change in character or amount of feces or urine, lo of hair or scratching, coughing, sneezing, trouble breathing, weakness in the rear legs, excessive sleepiness, and pawing at the face or mouth. If any of these signs or any others of concern are noted, owners are advised to have their ferret seen by their veterinarian.

Common Diseases and Problems

Foreign Body Ingestion

Young ferrets are very curious and love to hunt. While hunting, playing, or exploring, however, they may swallow objects that they find. Ferrets seem to have a preference for ingesting rubber, but certainly do not limit themselves to this material. A foreign body ingested by a ferret will do one of four things: (1) it may go through the gastrointestinal tract and cause no clinical signs and no harm, (2) it may stay in the stomach and cause irritation to the stomach lining, (3) it may sit in the stomach and cause an intermittent blockage of flow to the intestine, or (4) it may lodge somewhere along the gastrointestinal tract (usually the small intestine), causing a partial or complete obstruction.

Ferrets younger than one year of age are very prone to ingesting foreign bodies that can cause a small intestinal obstruction. Owners may notice their pet is just not acting right, but more often the ferret becomes very weak, and when handled acts limp and depressed. In a dog or cat, you would expect to see vomiting, but for some reason this sign is not common in ferrets with obstructions. Such an ill ferret needs veterinary attention as soon as possible, and owners should take these pets to their veterinarian right away.

Older ferrets are more prone to hairballs and chronic intermittent obstructions. Common signs of these problems include weight loss, lack of appetite, diarrhea, a decrease in activity, playing and exploring, and sometimes vomiting. These clinical signs are often noted over a period of weeks to months.

To diagnose a foreign body, your veterinarian will perform a complete physical examination, including palpation of the abdomen, and may also recommend radiographs and an abdominal ultrasound. Because the types of objects ferrets swallow are typically difficult to see on x-ray film, these tests may be inconclusive. Often the diagnosis is made during an exploratory surgery. Prior to surgery, blood work should be performed to check for any problem that might rule out the use of general anesthesia. Medication to stabilize the animal may needed prior to administration of anesthesia and surgery. It is important to correct dehydration and sometimes manage nausea and pain before intervening surgically. If the obstruction is discovered early and if no surgical complications occur, ferrets usually make a quick and full recovery.

Adrenal Gland Disease

Adrenal gland disease (AGD) in ferrets is caused by the excessive production of hormones by the adrenal gland. These excess amounts may be produced by adrenal glands that are either hyperplastic (enlarged and active) or neoplastic (cancerous). AGD is very common in pet ferrets, and despite years of research into what causes the disease, only unproven hypotheses about its etiology exist. There is an association between age of onset of AGD and the age at which the animal is spayed or neutered, but the role of spaying or neutering in causation is complicated by the presence of AGD in the rare non-neutered or non-spayed ferret. Photoperiod (length of daylight versus nighttime) may play a role in altering the ferret's hormone production. Other potential factors include genetics and social group interactions.

The average age at which ferrets develop AGD is four years, but the condition has also been seen in ferrets younger than one year old. Signs of AGD include alopecia (usually starting on the tail and progressing forward), pruritus (itchiness), aggressive or sexual behavior in spayed or neutered individuals, an enlarged vulva, and difficulty urinating. This diagnosis may often be suspected by your veterinarian based on clinical signs and physical examination. If needed, confirmation of the diagnosis can be made with a blood test that measures ferret sex hormone levels; however, even this test will miss the diagnosis in some ferrets. Your veterinarian will also perform tests to rule out other concurrent problems. Ferrets that are older than three to four years of age are very prone to have more than one disease problem at a time.

Treatment of AGD can be either medical or surgical. Surgical therapy offers a chance to cure the disease. Because surgery can be risky and very expensive (depending on which adrenal gland is involved and the presence of concurrent disease), some ferret owners choose medical therapy instead. Medical therapy will not halt the growth of the adrenal glands, but it can help control the symptoms caused by the excess hormones.

The prognosis for adrenal gland disease is generally very good. Quality of life for ferrets with treated AGD is typically good, but may suffer greatly in three situations:

- If severe itchiness is present, ferrets can self-mutilate their skin by scratching. Anti-itch medications do not work in the ferret, so medical or surgical therapy should be pursued.
- In males, the effects of the hormones cause the prostate to become enlarged, potentially leading to difficulty urinating, infection, or complete obstruction. Ferrets with these issues should receive medical and/or surgical therapy. Urinary obstruction needs immediate surgical intervention.
- In chronic, severe AGD, excessive estrogen may suppress the bone marrow and cause severely low red blood cell counts. This condition is a medical emergency that may require surgery for its correction.

Epizootic Catarrhal Enteritis

Epizootic catarrhal enteritis (ECE; also known as "green slime disease") is an inflammation of the intestine thought to be caused by a viral infection. Ferrets can contract the infection through contact with infected ill ferrets or ferrets that are not sick but still carrying the disease. A common time to see this disease is upon introduction of a new ferret to the home. In such a case, the new ferret may not show any clinical problems, but the ferrets already in the home get sick. There have even been cases where owners have visited other ferrets (or played with them in a pet store) and brought the disease home to their own pets on their hands or clothes.

Ferrets with ECE generally have diarrhea, which is often green and slimy, or the feces seems to contain granules like bird seed. Infected ferrets can also have hepatitis. Some ferrets seem to be mildly affected, but often when they reach the veterinarian they appear weak, dehydrated, and very ill. Any generally weak ferret with ECE is likely to drag her hind legs. Chronically affected ferrets often lose weight and will refuse to eat well.

Diarrhea, weakness, dehydration, and weight loss are all nonspecific signs and can be caused by many different conditions. Some tests are indicated to help narrow down the list of potential diagnoses: blood tests to check for signs of inflammation, anemia, and signs of liver involvement, and radiographs or ultrasound of the abdomen to check for organ involvement. Currently, a definitive diagnosis can be made only by examining biopsies of internal organs (intestines, liver, and lymph nodes). Given that treatment is mostly supportive, a definitive diagnosis is not always needed.

Treatment involves rehydration, which may require intravenous or subcutaneous fluids, for a few days. Gastric protectants help with nausea and gastric pain. In some cases, antibiotics are used. As with people who have a viral infection, it is important that the ferret take in fluids and food to help support the body to make a quick recovery. If the ferret is not eating, syringe assist-feeding of a diet appropriate for a pure carnivore may be necessary. If ECE is caught early before weight loss and severe liver disease ensue, the prognosis is fair to good. Some ferrets may develop chronic liver and intestinal inflammation, and chronic or severe cases of ECE are usually associated with a poorer prognosis. Ferrets that recover may continue to spread the infection and may have recurrent illnesses during times of stress.

Insulinoma

An insulinoma is an insulin-producing tumor of the pancreas that occurs commonly in ferrets over three years old. The excess insulin lowers the blood sugar to dangerous levels, making ferrets seem less active or more sleepy than normal. They can also stare blankly, drool, paw at their mouths and/or drag their hind legs. When the blood sugar level gets very low, they can have epileptic grand-mal type seizures. These seizures cause semi-consciousness, increased leg movements, and sometimes urination or defecation.

The diagnosis of an insulinoma can be made based on the medical history from the owner, clinical signs, and a demonstrably low blood sugar. The blood sugar needs to be measured more than once, and the ferret may need to fast for as long as four hours before testing. The initial tests for diagnosis should also assess for infection and liver disease; however, as stated previously, ferrets commonly have more than one disease at a time, and broader-spectrum tests are needed to look for other problems.

An insulinoma is often quite small (usually microscopic), so the tumor can be difficult to identify with radiographs or ultrasound. Measuring blood insulin levels is controversial and, in these authors' experience, unnecessary. The results of such tests are difficult to interpret and can lead to a delay in proper treatment. A definitive diagnosis requires surgery and removal of tissue for a biopsy.

Insulinomas in ferrets will eventually progress and become uncontrollable. Frequently, the tumor is widespread within the pancreas, and sometimes the liver as well. Surgical treatment can provide a longer disease-free interval of time than medication alone, but eventually most ferrets will need medical therapy. Ferrets generally do not live longer than 18 months after a diagnosis is made, although one author (Rhody) has seen some animals live for 2 years or longer. The medicine most commonly used to control blood sugar is prednisolone, which is administered orally once or twice daily. Fortunately, ferrets usually do not suffer side effects from this medicine, unlike dogs and people.

Preventive Medicine

Preventive medicine encompasses all that veterinarians can do to keep a pet ferret healthy. It includes vaccinations, periodic examination, spaying and neutering, and periodic blood tests.

Two vaccines are specifically licensed for and used in ferrets in the United States: rabies and canine distemper. In some states and countries, ferrets are required by law to be vaccinated yearly against rabies. Currently, only one rabies vaccine is approved for use in ferrets in the United States. Because canine distemper virus is a highly fatal illness in ferrets, all young ferrets should receive this vaccination as youngsters (starting at 6 to 8 weeks of age). Yearly boosters are often recommended based on an assessment of the risk of contracting the virus. The vaccine that ferrets receive for distemper is not the same as the vaccine that is given to dogs. If the canine combination vaccine is given to a ferret, severe and potentially fatal reactions could occur. The ferret vaccine is not available all over the world, and care should be taken to ensure the correct vaccine is used. Ferrets should remain at the veterinary office for 20 to 30 minutes after receiving any vaccination, as they tend to have a high incidence of adverse reactions to vaccines.

Spaying female ferrets before or during the first heat (which can be at age six months to almost a year, depending on season of birth) is recommended for many reasons. Females go into heat as young adults and produce large amounts of estrogen, and they do not stop producing estrogen until they are mated. If they are not mated, the ferret may develop a bone marrow problem related to the excess estrogen. This problem can be fatal and needs emergency medical and perhaps surgical treatment for survival. Spaying also prevents uterine and ovarian disease. Neutering male ferrets is performed primarily to reduce aggressive behavior and to reduce the odor from the skin secretions, which can be very strong. Female ferrets that are spayed also have less of an odor.

After purchase, ferrets need a general physical examination by a veterinarian, including a check for ear mites, and most will still need vaccinations. All pet ferrets should receive annual veterinary examinations. After the animal reaches three to four years of age. your veterinarian will likely recommend exams once to twice a year and annual blood tests so that any medical problems can be diagnosed early.

Ferrets do not require a lot of space; they can be affectionate and amusing; and they tend to easily adapt to a home with a busy schedule. If they are housed and fed properly, and care is taken to monitor for signs of disease, they can be very rewarding pets.

DID YOU KNOW?

- Female rabbits are called does, males are called bucks, and the offspring are called kits.
- Guinea pigs can develop food preferences when young and may not adjust well to changes in their diet.
- Rabbits and guinea pigs can have pigments in their urine, which causes the urine to appear pink, red, orange, or other colors.
- A scared chinchilla may urinate at an attacker as a defense, or may release fur that is grasped, leaving a bald area.
- Rat incisors have a yellowish color that is due to iron pigments.

RABBITS

The scientific name of the house rabbit is *Oryctolagus cuniculus*. It comes from the Latin words *Oryctolagus* = "burrowing hare" and *cuniculus* = "underground passage." These animals are also known as domestic rabbits or European rabbits. They belong to the family *Leporidae*, which includes hares, pikas, and other mammals and are a completely different species from the wild cottontail rabbit found in the United States.

Natural History

Rabbits are herbivorous hindgut fermenters, meaning that plant matter is broken down by single-cell organisms in their cecum and converted into usable energy. They originally came from the Iberian Peninsula, and the process of their domestication started approximately 2,000 years ago. By the seventeenth century, they were completely domesticated. Rabbits were initially domesticated as a food source by monks. Later, they were carried in ships by explorers as a source of fresh meat, a practice that introduced them on many continents. Rabbits started to be kept as pets in the Victorian era. Today, besides being common pets, they are still raised as meat, used in medical research, kept as show animals, and raised for their wool.

Rabbit Biology Basics

The average reported life span of a rabbit is 5 to 6 years, with some reports of these animals living as long as 15 years. Many different breeds of rabbits (more than 70 recognized breeds) exist, with a large variety of sizes and colors. A miniature rabbit can weigh as little as 1 kilogram, and giant breeds can exceed 7 kilograms.

As herbivores, rabbits have teeth that are suitable to consumption of a high-fiber herbivorous diet. These includes long incisors (four upper and two lower, with the second pair of uppers arranged behind the first pair), and pre-molars and molars; rabbits do not have canine teeth. All of their teeth continue to grow and be worn down throughout the rabbits' life.

Rabbits have a relatively long and complex gastrointestinal tract. The cecum accounts for approximately 40 percent of the gastrointestinal volume, and is where a large part of the digestion takes place. Numerous types of microorganisms are found in the cecum, which break down cellulose into components that rabbits can then absorb. Some of the nutrients go through the remaining gastrointestinal tract and are passed as cecotrophs (also called night feces), which are eaten directly from the anus and then digested and absorbed in the upper gastrointestinal tract. The cecotrophs are completely different feces than the hard, fibrous pellets that are passed, and have no nutritional value. Due to their reliance on microorganisms to digest plant material that would otherwise be indigestible to them, rabbits are sensitive to antibiotic treatments. In fact, some antibiotics can cause drastic changes in the balance of these microorganisms, thereby endangering the life of the rabbit.

Rabbits are obligate nasal breathers, with a very small thorax relative to their body size, which means they have a small lung capacity. Their senses are well developed, including acute hearing and very good peripheral vision (almost 360 degrees due to their laterally placed eyes), which allows them to be more alert for predators. Rabbits also have a number of scent glands—one on their chin, and others in the inguinal area and around the anus.

Rabbits are born hairless and helpless, usually in a nest built by the doe. The mother goes in to allow the kits to nurse once to twice a day, but otherwise stays away from them. The pregnancy is short, approximately 30 days.

Husbandry

Rabbits are often shy at first, requiring time to overcome their natural fear of predators (who include people). The more they are handled (gently) as youngsters, the more interactive and curious they seem to be. Rabbits are social animals, living in groups in the wild. In captivity, they can get along very well together, generally in pairs. This congeniality is not guaranteed, however, and especially with older individuals, the introduction of a new rabbit can take time and effort.

Indoor rabbits should be given hiding spot and a safe area to go to. If allowed to roam freely in the house, care must be taken to prevent them from coming to harm, as they may chew carpets, electrical wiring, and other objects. Rabbits kept outdoors need to reside in hutches or enclosures that fully protect them from predators as well as from the elements. They are good diggers, so if they live on the ground, fences need to be dug very deep or flooring needs to be put down that prevents them from digging out of the enclosure.

In the wild, rabbits live in burrows, so they generally appreciate hiding areas and dark areas. For activity, natural activities such as digging and gnawing should be provided. Gnawing can be done on natural materials such as nontoxic wood. Their burrows in the wild include a latrine area, which the rabbits use as a toilet, so litter box training is usually intuitive with them; they do, however, use some feces as territorial markers.

A correct diet is one of the most important things owners can provide to their pet rabbits. Proper food can decrease disease and behavioral problems, and help keep rabbits generally healthy. For these herbivores, the most important component in the diet is a good-quality grass hay (such as Timothy hay or brome hay). In fact, this can be the only thing fed to rabbits and still be nutritionally complete for them (in the wild, they eat mainly wild grasses). In addition to the hay, which should be available at all times and should make up at least 70 percent of the rabbit's diet, dark leafy greens can be fed (approximately one cup of greens per kilogram of body weight per day). Pellets can be fed but are not necessary, and in some rabbits can cause problems. If pellets are fed, they should be high quality, preferably based on a grass hay, and the amount should be limited (one-eighth cup per kilogram of body weight per day), as pellets tend to contain a large amount of carbohydrates and can predispose the rabbit to certain gastrointestinal problems. Fruit and other high-sugar foods are not recommended, as they can also lead to gastrointestinal problems; however, very small amounts of fruit can be given as a treat.

Common Diseases and Problems

Ileus

Ileus (also referred to as gastric stasis) is not a specific disease, but rather one of the most common signs of disease seen in rabbits. Any rabbit with a decreased appetite and decreased fecal production can be considered to have ileus. When a rabbit stops eating for any reason or the animal's gastrointestinal motility is reduced for any reason, there will also be a reduction of feces produced. When this happens, the intestines can fill with gas, which can be very painful. Generally, the contents of the gastrointestinal tract also become dehydrated as the fluids are absorbed. The most common causes of ileus in rabbits are dental disease or an inappropriate diet with a lack of fiber or an excess of carbohydrates. However, any problem can cause this condition: disease, pain, stress, a reaction to anesthesia or sedation, or a change in the environment.

Clinical signs of ileus, besides a lack of eating and a reduction in fecal production, can include smaller, drier fecal pellets, a decrease in activity, and sitting in a hunched position. The rabbit may also hide more than usual, and her gastrointestinal tract may produce audible sounds (borborygmus).

The diagnosis of ileus is a relatively simple one, based on the clinical signs. Nevertheless, your veterinarian will review the husbandry to assess the diet and other possible causes of this problem, and may offer further diagnostic tests to determine the underlying cause. These tests will be based on the findings of the exam and history and may include blood tests, radiographs, a sedated oral exam, and diagnostic imaging of the skull.

Treatment of ileus includes feeding and rehydration. Feeding is often accomplished with special foods that can be made into a slurry and fed by syringe. Rehydration can be accomplished with fluids given intravenously, subcutaneously, or orally, depending on the degree of dehydration. Other treatments to consider are pain management, encouraging motion (motion may encourage gastrointestinal motility), and in some cases drugs that help with gastrointestinal motility (there is a lack of information about how or if these medications work in rabbits). In addition to this supportive care for the ileus, identification and treatment of the underlying cause is of extreme importance. Remedying the problem may be as simple as adjusting the diet, or as complicated as surgical procedures to manage dental disease. The prognosis is determined by the underlying disease or problem that caused the ileus in the first place.

Dental Disease

Dental disease is, unfortunately, very common in rabbits. Although it is usually seen in older rabbits, this condition can be seen at any age. Because rabbits' teeth grow constantly, anything that causes them not to wear down properly can cause problems. Malocclusion (a lack of appropriate meeting between the teeth) is quite common and may be caused by genetic factors, inappropriate diet, a combination of the two, or other factors. As the teeth continue to grow, points can form within the mouth, causing sores on the tongue or inner cheeks. The part of the tooth that is located within the jaw can grow further into the bone and affect the roots of other teeth and the health of the jaw. Infections can travel around the tooth and into the bone and surrounding tissues, forming an abscess and leading to osteomyelitis (infection of the bone).

Signs that suggest dental disease include a change in eating habits, such as preferring softer foods and ignoring harder foods; dropping food while chewing; a change in chewing habits; teeth grinding; drooling or a wet chin; ileus; abscesses or masses anywhere on the face or chin; and general signs of discomfort.

To diagnose dental disease, a complete oral exam is needed. This can begin with an awake rabbit (the incisors are easy to evaluate this way), but as the mouth of rabbit is small and very difficult to open wide for a good view, a sedated or anesthetized exam is often needed to evaluate the molars. In addition, because some of the disease process occurs within the bones and the soft tissues surrounding the mouth, skull radiographs or a computed tomography scan (CT) are necessary to completely evaluate the teeth and surrounding tissues. Additional diagnostics may be offered, such as blood tests, to check for concurrent disease and evaluate the rabbit's general health.

Treatment depends on the severity of the problem. Sometimes a procedure in which all of the teeth are shortened under anesthesia is enough to manage the problem. In other cases involving severe infection in the bone or soft tissue, surgery is needed to remove all of the diseased tissue. Rabbits cannot be cured of dental disease, but the disease can often be managed with treatments. In addition to addressing the teeth, concurrent problems such as ileus need to be addressed as a part of the medical management.

Uterine Adenocarcinoma and Other Uterine Disease

Uterine adenocarcinoma, a malignant tumor in the uterus, is the most common type of cancer seen in rabbits. It occurs in older unspayed females (three years or older). Thankfully, this tumor is quite slow to metastasize to other organs. Other diseases of the uterus are also possible, and a biopsy can help differentiate them from uterine adenocarcinoma, but the treatment is the same for them all.

The signs related to uterine adenocarcinoma can be subtle. In a breeding female, a decrease in fertility may be noticed. In nonbreeding females, signs may include occasional bleeding from the vulva (the blood may mix with the urine) or general signs of weakness. In advanced disease, there may be signs due to metastases, such as difficulty breathing if tumors arise in the lungs (a common site of metastasis), or neurological signs if metastases to the brain occur.

Diagnosis of uterine disease generally includes an abdominal radiograph, an abdominal ultrasound, or both. The appearance of an enlarged uterus indicates disease, although it cannot diagnose the exact disease. Prior to surgery, your veterinarian will recommend taking steps to rule out metastasis such as a chest radiograph. Treatment for uterine disease consists of surgery. Removal of the uterus and ovaries is curative unless the tumor has already metastasized.

Upper Respiratory Infections

Upper respiratory infections (URI) are seen quite often in rabbits of all ages, including very young ones. URIs involve an infection of the nasal passages, may also affect the eyes and trachea, and may develop into lower respiratory infections involving the lungs (pneumonia). Multiple causes of URIs have been suggested—mainly bacterial infection—but there may also be other causes, including environmental issues (e.g., dust, lack of good ventilation). Rabbits with URI produce a nasal discharge that is usually thick and white; they can also have ocular discharge, difficulty breathing, and general signs of illness, including ileus.

Diagnosis of a URI is based on the presence of signs of the disease. To determine the cause, an investigation of the environment and diet should be performed, and diagnostic tests should be run. Ideally, the bacteria involved should be identified by obtaining a culture; because culturing the nasal discharge is not usually fruitful, samples are often needed from deep tissue (surgically obtained from the sinuses).

Treatment usually includes an antibiotic—preferably based on a culture, but often tried empirically. In addition, changing the substrate in the cage to something less irritating to the respiratory passages may help, as may improving air flow in and around the cage. URIs often respond well to treatment, but usually are not completely cured and may return throughout the rabbit's lifetime.

Head Tilt

Head tilt is a common problem seen in rabbits of all ages, affecting the sense of balance and causing signs related to a loss of balance. It may have any of several causes: infection of the middle ear (which includes the vestibular system), noninfectious problems of the vestibular system, and processes affecting the brain. Signs of this disease can be either subtle or very severe. The affected rabbit can have a mild tilt of the head to one side, can have a severe tilt in which the head is rotated 90 degrees or more, or may be unable to stand due to rolling and a loss of balance. The rabbit may have an irregular gait or exhibit increased eye movement from side to side (nystagmus). In addition, general signs of disease may be present, including ileus.

Diagnosis of a head tilt can be made based on the signs; however, it is important to attempt to identify the cause. This may require blood tests and imaging of the skull (radiographs or a CT scan) to assess the inner ears for damage.

Treatment consists of supportive care: feeding as necessary, a padded area for protection if the rabbit is rolling, and treatment of the eye on the side facing down, as it is sometimes damaged (i.e., scratched or irritated) by facing downward. Sometimes specific medications such as antibiotics or anti-inflammatory agents are used. It is also possible to use medications that may stop the sense of vertigo. In addition, if a clear diagnosis is made, then specific therapy may be recommended, such as surgery to clean out the inner ear.

Rabbits with this condition can do quite well. Although some will remain with a certain degree of head tilt, they may otherwise function completely normally. Other rabbits, in contrast, deteriorate despite treatment.

Abscesses

Rabbits often develop abscesses around any infection. This can occur at any age and in any area or organ in the body. The type of immune cells that rabbits have and use to fight infection create a very thick kind of pus, which eventually becomes surrounded by a capsule. The combination of these two components is meant to keep the infection from spreading to the rest of the body, but in doing so usually prevents the entrance of antibiotics into the area. Whenever a rabbit has an infection (e.g., external skin wounds, dental disease, infection that spreads to internal organs), an abscess or multiple abscesses may form.

Any lump or bump on a rabbit's skin should be viewed with suspicion as an abscess. If such lumps appear on the head, they are most likely related to dental disease. Abscesses can also form in the lungs, liver, and other organs, and the signs seen will be specific to the system affected (i.e., abscesses in the lungs will cause signs in the respiratory system).

Your veterinarian will likely perform a needle aspiration of material from within the lump to make a diagnosis. With an abscess, this material will appear thick and white and, when examined under a microscope, will show cells typical of infection and bacteria. Internal abscesses can be identified through the use of ultrasound and an aspiration of the contents (if possible, due to the location). The cause of the abscess should also be determined (as related to dental disease, bite wounds, or immune problems, for example), which may require additional testing.

Due to the thick nature of pus, rabbit abscesses can be frustrating to treat. Attempting to open them and flush out the pus often results in recurrence. Surgical removal of the entire abscess and capsule is often the treatment of choice, together with treatment of the underlying cause. Sometimes the infection may have penetrated the surrounding tissues. In such cases, as much infection as possible is first removed, then beads containing antibiotics are placed in the wound so that a constant level of antibiotics remains in the area to clear up any remaining infection. Culturing the content and capsule of the abscess can help your veterinarian select the appropriate antibiotic.

Preventive Medicine

In the United States, there are no recommended vaccines for rabbits. In Europe and Australia, some rabbits are vaccinated against myxomatosis and rabbit viral hemorrhagic disease—both of these viral diseases are associated with high morbidity and mortality. Spaying female rabbits, which is usually recommended when they are approximately six months of age, can increase their life span as it prevents uterine disease and uterine tumors. In males (and some females), neutering (spaying) may reduce some unwanted behaviors such as territorial aggression or territorial marking; if these behaviors are well established, however, the surgery may not change them.

The most important factor in keeping rabbits healthy is appropriate husbandry. With the proper diet and environment, and care and attention paid to early and mild-seeming signs of disease, rabbits can make wonderful, loving, and entertaining companion animals.

GUINEA PIGS

Guinea pigs (scientific name: *Cavia porcellus*) are also known as cavies, where *porcellus* in Latin refers to a small pig. There are many explanations for this name, including the sounds guinea pigs make and their body shape.

Natural History

Domesticated from similar species in the Andes in South America, the currently known guinea pig species does not exist in the wild. Their wild predecessors, however, continue to live in small groups in grassland areas in South America. Guinea pigs, which were brought to Europe as pets in the sixteenth century, were domesticated as a food animal and are still used for this purpose in South America.

Guinea Pig Biology Basics

Guinea pigs live an average of 4 to 6 years. Males are usually larger than females and weigh up to 1.2 kilograms, with females weighing up to 0.9 kilogram. These mammals are herbivores and hindgut fermenters, with a gastrointestinal tract and dietary needs similar to those of rabbits. Guinea pigs have only four incisors: two upper and two lower. Like rabbits, their teeth grow continuously and are worn down throughout their lives (open rooted or hypsodont).

Guinea pigs are unable to synthesize vitamin C for themselves; as a consequence, similar to humans, they need an external source of vitamin C. Their pregnancy is relatively long (approximately two months), and the pups are born quite developed and covered in fur.

Husbandry

Guinea pigs can live in groups if enough space is provided. If the group includes multiple males, however, subordinate cavies may not be allowed access to food or water; thus care must be taken to ensure that all animals receive adequate access to these necessities. Guinea pigs are usually housed in cages, and hiding areas are important to allow them to feel safe. Also, guinea pigs have many different types of vocalizations, and learning to recognize them can help interpret their behaviors.

The diet should consist mainly of good-quality grass hay, with the addition of dark leafy greens and vitamin C–rich vegetables. Pellets can be fed in small amounts but should not make up the bulk of the diet. If fed, pellets should be of high quality and based on grass hay—mixes with dried fruit, pieces of corn, and other materials can lead to the pet choosing the unhealthy foods and consuming an unbalanced diet.

Common Diseases and Problems

Dental Disease

A common problem seen in guinea pigs is dental disease. Malocclusion (when the teeth do not meet properly) is sometimes seen; when it occurs, the teeth do not wear down properly. The overgrowth of the lower molars is another problem to which guinea pigs are susceptible. With this condition, the tongue may become entrapped, as these teeth tend to grow toward each other, meeting over the tongue and forming a "bridge." Overgrown roots also occur occasionally and can lead to pain, infection, and abscesses, similar to what occurs in rabbits. One possible cause of dental disease is a lack of vitamin C in the diet, which leads to the teeth being loose within their sockets. When dental disease is present, the guinea pig may stop eating and develop ileus. He may also be selective about his food (choosing softer food items), drool excessively, lose weight, and drink more water.

To diagnose the dental problem, a thorough oral exam is needed, which requires sedation or anesthesia. The roots of the teeth and surrounding bone and soft tissues need to be evaluated as well, which will require radiographs or a CT scan of skull. Blood tests and whole-body radiographs will help assess for complications such as hepatic lipidosis (a condition in which fat is utilized by the starving body, and some of that fat is deposited in the liver, causing disease in the liver) (a and other concurrent diseases.

Treatment of overgrown teeth, an entrapped tongue, infections of the bone, and other dental disease involves trimming the teeth down under anesthesia, and sometimes surgically removing the infected areas. Supportive care should be given until the guinea pig recovers, including syringe feeding, fluids, and pain management measures. Dental disease usually requires periodic treatments, as it is not a curable disease; nevertheless, it can be managed successfully.

Ovarian Cysts

Ovarian cysts—a very common problem in intact female guinea pigs—can be seen in animals as young as one and half years old. Cysts can develop spontaneously in the ovaries and grow to large sizes. Signs of ovarian cysts include a symmetrical loss of fur over the sides of the body, an enlarged abdomen, and general signs of discomfort. Diagnosis by your veterinarian can be made by palpation of large ovaries, and an ultrasound is the most reliable tool to evaluate the cysts. Treatment consists of surgical removal of the ovaries and uterus (similar to spaying), although some medications are available that may reduce the cysts, and other treatments are sometimes used when surgery is not possible.

Scurvy

Scurvy comprises a deficiency of vitamin C, a nutrient that is vital for the formation of healthy connective tissues (collagen). Without normal collagen, many tissues would suffer damage. Although some pelleted foods for guinea pigs list vitamin C as an ingredient, it is important to recognize that with exposure to light and air, and over time, vitamin C dissipates. Thus pellets and supplements added to water should not be relied on as a sole source of vitamin C.

Signs of scurvy include dental disease (collagen is important to anchor the teeth), skin disease, skin wounds, lameness (scurvy can affect the joints), and a reduction in the effectiveness of the immune system, which can allow many types of secondary infections.

Treatment depends on the organs affected, but supplementation with vitamin C is the main goal. It can be achieved through use of injections, syrups, and adjustment of the diet. Pain management, supportive care, wound management, and other necessary medical interventions may all be part of the treatment plan, depending on the severity of the illness and the condition of the animal. Recovery is related to the severity of the scurvy, as the damage that occurs is not reversible. As a consequence, if quality of life is severely affected, it may not be possible to improve it.

Urinary Calculi

Urinary bladder stones are a problem often seen in guinea pigs and can be very frustrating for owners. A guinea pig with bladder stones may show signs of discomfort (hunched position or vocalizations), especially when passing urine, and may have difficulty passing urine. Additionally, blood or blood clots may appear in the urine. Bladder stones can usually be seen on radiographs, as they generally contain calcium. It is also important to evaluate the urine for the presence of infection (bacterial), as this type of disease can be a complication of a bladder stone and can cause similar signs.

Treatment includes fluids and syringe feedings, as guinea pigs often stop eating and drinking when they are ill. Pain management is also an important component of treatment, as stones and the concurrent inflammation can be quite painful. Unfortunately, the stone will usually not pass on its own and instead must be surgically removed. Re-formation of a stone is quite common and can happen very rapidly, sometimes even within weeks after surgery.

Preventive Medicine

Prevention of disease in the guinea pig is mostly about good diet and husbandry. Knowing your pet well and identifying any early signs of disease can have a major impact on the outcome. There are no vaccines that are used in guinea pigs. Spaying and neutering at any age can have many benefits, including preventing unwanted litters, reducing fighting, and preventing or treating ovarian disease such as cysts.

Guinea pigs can make wonderful pets—they are vocal, active, and engaging animals that can bond to people well, but they are also masters at hiding signs of disease. They can be quite sick before they show signs, so monitoring their body weight, their activity level, and the size, shape, and amount of feces can help to identify problems early on.

CHINCHILLAS

The scientific name for the chinchilla is *Chinchilla laniger*, where *Chinchilla* means "little Chincha." These mammals were named after the Chincha people of the Andes.

Natural History

Chinchillas are kept as pets, as fur animals, and lab animals. In their natural habitat, the Andes mountains, they have been hunted until they are near extinction. Chinchillas were first imported and kept as pets in the 1920s.

Chinchilla Biology Basics

Chinchillas are very similar to guinea pigs in their anatomy and physiology, but in one area they differ: they are capable of synthesizing vitamin C on their own, so they do not need supplementation with this nutrient. Chinchillas traditionally come from higher up in the mountains, so they are less tolerant of heat and humidity. For this reason, the ambient temperature where they are housed should not exceed 80 °F (27 °C).

The reported life span of chinchillas is 10 years, but there have been reports of them living much longer. Males tend to be slightly smaller than females, weighing 400 to 500 grams, while females weigh up to 600 grams. Females have a long pregnancy (almost 3 months), and the young are born precocious with fur and opened eyes.

Husbandry

Chinchillas are very active and able to leap and jump; thus they require large cages to allow them to engage in this activity. Multilevel cages can be used—and chinchillas will certainly take advantage of them. Hiding areas are also important to these animals, so such features should be provided in their housing structure.

The dietary requirements for chinchillas are similar to those of guinea pigs and rabbits. Pellets formulated for chinchillas are usually longer and narrower, allowing them to hold the pellets in their front paws while eating.

One thing that is unique to chinchillas is their requirement for a special fine sand to care for their fur coat. This material can be bought or made by mixing silver sand and Fuller's earth. The sand should be made available for the chinchilla to roll in, accomplished by putting the sand dish in the chinchilla's cage for a short period every day (approximately 20 minutes). The dish should not be left in the cage permanently, as it can get quite dirty.

Common Diseases and Problems

Dental disease is commonly seen in chinchillas and is similar to that seen in rabbits and guinea pigs. Heat stroke in chinchillas that are exposed to high temperatures and high humidity is a life-threatening problem, which needs immediate attention. Affected animals will breathe rapidly, lie down, be listless, and have very red mucous membranes and ears. These animals should be cooled down gently (not in an ice bath) while seeking immediate veterinary care.

Fractures of the back legs may also seen, especially in cages where running wheels are present, which allow the chinchilla's thin leg to slip through and be caught. These injuries are often complicated fractures, which can prove challenging to repair.

Preventive Medicine

There are no recommended vaccines for chinchillas. Spaying and neutering can be used to prevent unwanted breeding and behavioral problems such as territoriality.

As prey animals, chinchillas usually hide signs of illness. For this reason, even mild signs of illness need to be taken seriously and your pet taken to your veterinarian for a thorough examination before the animal's condition worsens.

RATS

The scientific name for the pet rat is *Rattus norvegicus*, but this animal is also known as the brown rat, common rat, and sewer rat. The scientific name means Norway rat, although the origin of these mammals is not actually in Europe.

Natural History

Originally a burrowing animal from Asia, rats made their way around the world and adapted to an urban environment in the early 1700s. Initially domesticated as a research animal, they have since become a common pet.

Rat Basic Biology

Rats are omnivorous, which means they will eat just about anything. Their teeth are suited to gnawing (done principally with their incisors) and chewing (using their pre-molars and molars). The incisors are open rooted and grow throughout the life span; however, the molars do not.

The reported life span of rats is 2.5 to 3.5 years. Males are larger than females, weighing 450 to 500 grams, and females weigh 250 to 300 grams. Pregnancy is short—3 weeks, with the pups born hairless and helpless.

Husbandry

The cage in which your rat lives should provide adequate room for moving around, as rats are active and like to climb. Hiding areas should be provided. Rats are good at gnawing, so the cage should be checked occasionally for signs of wear. Safe, nontoxic, untreated wood or straw baskets can be used as gnawing toys, which should be available at all times. Bedding should be nontoxic and as dust free as possible. Recycled-paper products seem to be the least irritating of the available types of bedding.

The diet of your pet rat should consist mainly of a formulated diet meant for rodents, which can be found in most pet stores. These products provide the most balanced nutrition. Although seed mixes are marketed, they allow the rat to choose the high-fat, unhealthy components and ignore the rest, creating an unbalanced diet; thus they are not recommended.

Common Diseases and Problems

The most common problem seen in female rats is mammary tumors, which can, interestingly enough, occur anywhere on the body, including on the shoulders and sides. These growths can become very large. Luckily, such tumors are usually benign and do not metastasize. Their surgical removal can be curative; however, there is a high rate of recurrence. Spaying or ovariactomy (removal of the ovaries) reduces the risk of recurrence, and prevents the initial occurrence of these tumors if done before they appear.

Respiratory disease is also quite common in rats. It may have multiple causes, including bacteria, viruses, and combinations of these pathogens, with the disease affecting either the upper or lower respiratory system, or both simultaneously. Signs of respiratory disease in rats include difficulty breathing, sneezing, nasal and ocular discharge (the discharge from the eyes can appear red in color, due to the presence of a pigment in the tears, so do not worry that your rat is bleeding), weight loss, and a hunched posture. Diagnosis by your veterinarian may include radiographs of the chest to evaluate the lungs, tests for specific organisms, and an evaluation of the environment. Treatment for respiratory disease may include administering antibiotics, making a change in the rat's environment (including increasing the humidity), decreasing dust in the cage, and keeping the cage clean and well ventilated.

Preventive Medicine

There are no recommended vaccines for rats. Spaying and neutering can be used to prevent unwanted breeding and behavioral problems such as territoriality, and greatly reduce the occurrence of mammary tumors.

FURTHER READING

Fox, J. G., ed. *Biology and Diseases of the Ferret*, 2nd ed. Baltimore, MD: Williams & Wilkins; 1998.

Harkness, J. E., and J. E. Wagner, eds. *The Biology and Medicine of Rabbits and Rodents*, 4th ed. Baltimore, MD: Williams & Wilkins; 1995:13–71.

Lewington, J. "Ferrets." In: *Clinical Anatomy and Physiology of Exotic Species*, edited by B. O'Malley. Edinburgh: Elsevier Saunders; 2005:237–61.

O'Malley, B. "Small Mammals." In: *Clinical Anatomy and Physiology of Exotic Species*, edited by B. O'Malley. Edinburgh: Elsevier Saunders; 2005:163–236.

Quesenberry, K. E., and J. W. Carpenter, eds. *Ferrets Rabbits, and Rodents: Clinical Medicine and Surgery*, 2nd ed. Philadelphia, PA: WB Saunders; 2003.

8

Birds: Health, Diseases, and Prevention

Niklos Weber, DVM, DABVP (Avian, Canine, Feline)

INTRODUCTION

Pet birds are becoming more popular in these days of improved breeding practices and availability of better medical care. Much more is known today about the dietary requirements of different species and disease processes than was understood 20 years ago, so it is much easier to prevent and treat disease, and birds live much longer than they formerly did. Problems still exist in determining when a bird is sick, however, because it is quite difficult for most owners to ascertain subtle signs of the beginning of an avian illness.

This chapter mostly deals with pet parrots, but includes some information on passerines (e.g., finches, canaries, mynahs), columbines (doves and pigeons), poultry (e.g., chickens, turkeys), and waterfowl (ducks and geese). Many of the health problems that are discussed relate to other problems (e.g., liver failure can lead to feather picking), and some processes such as inflammation and immune suppression are common aspects of many diseases. These systemic effects occur because everything is connected in a living animal, and problems in one organ or system can greatly affect other systems that might otherwise seem disconnected.

THE BASICS OF BIRD HEALTH AND ILLNESS

The determination of illness in birds is more difficult than in dogs and cats for three reasons. First, birds have not been "domesticated" for as long as dogs and cats. As a consequence, birds are generally not as "comfortable" around humans, so they do not show weakness as readily as most dogs and cats. Second, for the most part birds are prey species, and in the wild obviously weak individuals will be culled from the flock by predators. Thus their instinct for hiding illness for as long as possible confers advantages in their natural setting. Third, most avian species have evolved to live in flocks with distinct dominance hierarchies, and any member that shows weakness is immediately relegated to a lower status. As a lower dominance state corresponds to fewer breeding opportunities and an inferior food selection, birds strive to avoid this state at all costs.

When birds are sick for long periods of time, they are subject to a great deal of stress, both in fighting the disease and in striving to hide it. Chronic stress of this type causes levels of certain hormones to increase, which suppresses the immune system, usually exacerbating the bird's health problems and predisposing it to infections. The increased amounts of stress hormones induce changes in metabolism and the way the bird absorbs and deposits fat, sugar, and protein. They also cause over-usage of certain vitamins and minerals, which results in deficiencies.

Fortunately, avian medicine has advanced in leaps and bounds over the last decade. Avian veterinarians have developed many new diagnostic and therapeutic techniques in recent years and have researched new drug doses and nutritional requirements. For example, the use of endoscopes, intraosseous fluids (intravenous fluids given into the bone), complete blood workups on very small samples, safe anesthesia, and other techniques are now commonplace in avian medicine. There is even a specialty board (the American Board of Veterinary Practitioners) that certifies Specialists in Avian Practice. Currently, birds receive veterinary care on par with that of dogs and cats. Occasionally, even ducks and chickens receive computer-assisted tomography (CT) scans and magnetic resonance imaging (MRI). The goal of this chapter is to help bird owners better prevent diseases in their pets and to educate them about when to seek timely and suitable assistance.

THE VETERINARY VISIT

During a visit to the avian veterinarian, certain tests will be part of what is called a "minimum database"—that is, the group of tests needed to give a good basic idea of the bird's health. If their results do not suggest a diagnosis outright, the tests will provide a direction in which to investigate further. The minimum database usually consists of a complete blood count, serum chemistry panel, fecal exam (float for parasite eggs, direct smear, and bacterial Gram stain), choanal swab (cytology and bacterial Gram stain of the slit in the top of the mouth that communicates with the sinuses), and full-body x-rays. Many birds will need sedation so that all of these samples may be collected. Additional tests often include crop swabs, specific bacterial and/or viral tests, and endoscopy. Some avian veterinarians will include some of these tests in their "new bird" package or yearly package. It is important to have records of the minimum database every year for healthy pet birds because some normal birds will have blood values outside the published normal range, which can be misleading. Also, birds are so good at hiding illness that the only way some diseases can be diagnosed early enough to effect a cure is to run tests on birds that appear to be normal.

A complete blood count examines the number and nature of all cells in the blood: red blood cells, white blood cells, and thrombocytes. Red blood cells carry oxygen to the tissues, white blood cells fight infection and are involved in inflammation, and thrombocytes help the blood to clot. A serum chemistry panel measures the levels of 12 to 15 enzymes and electrolytes in the blood and shows whether certain organs (e.g., liver, kidneys, pancreas) are damaged or not working well. X-rays can depict the shape of the organs and bones in the body and show whether foreign bodies or areas of infection are present in the air sacs. Fecal examinations determine the bacterial balance of the gastrointestinal tract and will reveal any parasites that may be present. Choanal swabs reveal inflammation or infection and characterize the bacteria causing upper respiratory infections.

COMMON MEDICAL PROBLEMS OF BIRDS

By far, the most common problems seen in avian medicine are problems related to poor nutrition. A vast number of disorders are related to nutritional deficiencies, the majority of which are seen in birds fed seed-only diets. Other health concerns that often arise in pet birds include toxicities (especially lead or zinc), reproductive-related problems (such as egg binding), trauma, infectious diseases, and behavior problems.

Diets and Nutritional Problems

Nutritional diseases are common in parrots mostly when they are fed seed diets, but also occasionally when they are fed inappropriate foods. Some species-specific diet-related diseases have also been identified, such as iron-storage disease in mynah birds. In this disease, mynahs' livers cannot process the amount of iron in a typical commercially available pelleted diet, and the excess collects in the liver, causing liver failure. Nutritional disease in chickens, turkeys, and waterfowl is uncommon because most people feed them appropriate pellets, and passerines and doves are granivores (seed eaters) so seed mixes are appropriate for members of these bird families.

Parrots fed seeds become deficient in a number of major nutrients, including vitamin A, calcium, zinc, iodine, magnesium, and certain amino acids. Zinc and magnesium and some amino acids are vital for proper immune system function, and a deficiency in these nutrients results in immune suppression and infections. Calcium is necessary for egg laying, nerve conduction, and muscle contraction, so a calcium deficiency usually results in egg problems (including egg binding), muscle weakness, and seizures. Iodine is necessary for thyroid function, and deficiency of this nutrient (common in budgerigars) can result in hypothyroidism, obesity, and goiter. Vitamin A is necessary for formation of the lining of the sinuses and respiratory tract in addition to proper immune system function; its deficiency commonly results in sinus infections, which tend to extend into the bone and cause bone damage. When infections progress this far, they can become extremely difficult to cure.[1]

Seed diets are also high in fat, which is why birds prefer them to pelleted diets. Just as a typical child (or adult) will select fast food over a plate of more nutritious vegetables, so a bird will choose to eat the high-fat "junk food" over any kind of pellets. High-fat diets lead to obesity in parrots, which is associated with hepatic lipidosis (fatty liver disease) and liver failure, as well as the same kind of heart disease, arterial plaque, and arteriosclerosis that humans can develop.

Ideally, parrots should be fed the same foods they eat in the wild, but this is usually not feasible because the native diets of most parrots consist of rain forest plants, seeds, and nuts. Much research has been done since the 1960s into a proper balanced diet for these birds, and this research has been applied to formulate a number of different pelleted diets. The best options are all organic and use human food-quality ingredients. Such diets are generally well accepted by most parrots. In addition, seeds formulated with supplements of missing nutrients and formed into balls are available; these products work well for small birds that refuse to eat anything except seeds. Successful use of these diets requires that the birds eat the entire ball of seeds and supplements so they receive the correct levels of all of the nutrients; otherwise, they could remain deficient in some nutrients. Small amounts of table food are acceptable as treats, but should be limited to the size of a grain of rice daily. Foods to avoid include chocolate, caffeine, avocado, and all meat.

Toxicities and Foreign Bodies

In addition to dietary issues, other preventable health concerns for cage birds that bird owners should be aware of include toxicities, foreign body ingestion, and trauma.

When left alone out of their cages, parrots like to chew on whatever they can get. This behavior can lead to lead or zinc toxicity from eating lead paint, the weights from window dressings, the lead in stained glass windows between the colored panels of glass, and zinc from anything that is galvanized. Old cages will sometimes be galvanized as well, and the birds can pick the drips of zinc off of the cage bars. Birds such as chickens that live in the yard will pick up anything shiny and commonly develop zinc toxicity from ingesting nails and staples. These items can also perforate the bird's gastrointestinal tract.

Signs of lead and zinc toxicity include lethargy, fluffed-up appearance, weight loss, heavy breathing, and bloody stools. Diagnosing heavy metal toxicity is fairly straightforward: your avian veterinarian will draw blood and send the samples to outside laboratories that measure the lead and zinc levels. Your veterinarian will also run some blood tests in-house to determine if the bird is anemic or has any other problems, and will take x-rays to see if any metal is present in the stomach or crop.

Treatment for heavy metal toxicity consists of medications called chelators that bind to the metal atoms and let the body flush them out. Chelators are available in injectable and oral forms. Severely affected birds may need blood transfusions or surgery, but many times successful treatment can be accomplished with medications only.

Other foreign bodies that cage birds tend to ingest include plastic, drywall, wood, parts of bird toys, and child toys or small pieces thereof. Some of these items are visible on x-rays, but others are not. Some may require surgical removal. Birds can also eat parts of toxic plants, but usually they simply chew the leaves up rather than ingest them, so actual poisoning from plant ingestion is rare.

Inhalation of toxins is both very common and very dangerous to pet birds. The respiratory tract of birds is built for a one-way flow of air through the lungs. Birds have structures called air sacs throughout their body cavities that extend up their necks and into the bones of their wings and legs. When a bird inhales, the air bypasses her lungs initially and fills the air sacs in the back half of her body. When she exhales, that air goes into the lungs, where oxygen is transferred into the blood in a one-way "countercurrent" flow, which is much more efficient than the oxygenation system in mammals. When the bird inhales again, the air goes from the lungs to the air sacs in the front half of the body, and then exits the body on the next exhalation. Without this highly efficient system, birds would not be able to fly. Unfortunately, the extensive air sac arrangement and the efficiency of the oxygen exchange make birds much more sensitive to inhaled toxins, especially if particulates are involved. Recall that coal miners once used birds to determine when the toxic gas levels in the mines were nearing dangerous levels for the miners—levels that would kill a bird.

The most common toxin is probably cigarette smoke, which is extremely dangerous for birds and can cause a number of problems. Many birds experience recurrent respiratory infections due to the weakening of the respiratory lining and immune system from exposure to such smoke. They will commonly pick their feathers, probably because their air sacs are irritated, which makes their skin itchy from underneath. The small particulates in cigarette smoke (which also damage humans' lungs) are deposited in the air sacs and lead to foci of inflammation and infection, which weaken the bird's immune system and lead to other problems. The toxic gases in cigarette smoke are also absorbed much more efficiently in birds than in humans, leading to carbon monoxide inhalation and other toxicities. Smoke from wood stoves or forest fires is similarly dangerous to birds.

Another inhalant toxin important for pet birds to avoid is polytetrafluoroethylene (PTFE; commonly known by the brand name Teflon). If a Teflon pan is left on the stove, particles of PTFE may become aerosolized from the pan and can be inhaled by birds. These particles can cause severe inflammation in birds' respiratory tracts and commonly lead to death. There is no treatment for Teflon poisoning.

Trauma

Most types of trauma to birds are fairly simple to prevent by monitoring the bird when he is out of his cage and keeping him caged when the owner is not home. Some birds will fly into boiling water on the stove or hot water in a shower or bathtub and can get severely burned. Birds that are not supervised may be injured by children or other pets. Ceiling fans are very dangerous to birds, and cockatiels in particular tend to fly toward them. Cockatiels also like to sit on top of doors, so that their toes may be cut off if someone unknowingly closes the door. Some owners like to sleep with their birds, but this practice is not recommended, as many of these birds eventually get inadvertently crushed by their owners in the night. Birds living outside are commonly injured by predatory wildlife, so it is very important to keep birds that live outside in a predator-proof enclosure.

Respiratory Conditions

Certain respiratory diseases are very common in pet birds. Generally, many of these conditions may be overlooked for long periods of time if they are not immediately life threatening. Some owners may even think that certain clinical signs (such as sneezing or poor feathering) are normal for their birds, especially if the bird was exhibiting the clinical signs when they purchased it. Additionally, the clinical signs of many respiratory diseases are subtle to absent, and not readily apparent to most bird owners.

Poor nutrition, as mentioned earlier, commonly leads to upper respiratory infections. Most parrots on seed-only diets have some degree of upper respiratory infection because of the delicate nature of the avian respiratory tract, breakdown of the respiratory lining from vitamin and mineral deficiencies, and suppression of the immune system. Upper respiratory infections are manifested as nasal discharge or crusting around the nostrils, sneezing, coughing, wiping the beak on the wings (and a corresponding wet or crusty spot on the top of the wing), swollen eyes or cheeks, and eye discharge.

Upper respiratory infections are fairly simple for your avian veterinarian to diagnose. During the exam, your veterinarian will look at the roof of the bird's mouth, where the choana is. The choana, as described earlier, is a cleft in the upper palate that communicates with the sinuses and nasal cavity and has small papillae along the edges. If these papillae are not sharp (rounded off) or gone, the bird likely has an upper respiratory infection. The veterinarian can swab the choana and look at the material under the microscope to get an idea of the type of bacteria involved in the infection; he or she may also culture the sample to determine which kind of antibiotic will work best.

Sinus infections develop when an upper respiratory infection becomes chronic. These problems sometimes present as swollen cheeks and eyes. The sinuses have drainage holes that become plugged when infection is present; this condition then progresses to sinus distention, which causes pain and irritability. Sinus infections can be difficult to diagnose and treat because the sinuses are extensive structures located throughout a bird's skull. Generally, x-rays are needed to locate the filled sinuses, and flushing under anesthesia combined with long-term antibiotics is necessary to treat them. Additionally, infections in the sinus cavities usually penetrate into the bone, where some antibiotics will not reach.

Obesity

Another disease related to poor diet is obesity. Birds are very intelligent, but have evolved to eat as much high-energy food as they can; foods high in fat have the most energy, so birds will choose the higher-fat option if given a choice. In seed-based diets, the mixtures always include some seeds that are higher in fat (such as sunflower seeds, safflower seeds, and peanuts) than others, and birds will always eat those items first. The best place to see excess fat on birds is on the breast muscles; the fat will bulge on either side of the breastbone, whereas a normal bird's muscles will be flat to somewhat lower than the breastbone.

High-fat diets cause a few additional problems for birds. They easily become obese to the point where they cannot fly anymore. When this happens, birds can damage their keels (breastbones) if they attempt to fly and fall. Parrots tend to develop plaque in their arteries much like people do, and plaque can lead to atherosclerosis, heart attacks, strokes, and aneurysms. Severely affected arteries will become calcified, and at that point they can be seen on x-rays. Birds with such problems need their diets changed and sometimes require medication for long periods of time.

Obesity in birds often leads to liver disease as well. Hepatic lipidosis (fatty liver) is common in avian species and can become life threatening. Through a variety of mechanisms, the liver in an obese bird stores fat instead of processing it normally, to the point where the fat buildup causes damage to the liver cells. Cell death in the liver leads to liver failure such that the liver cannot perform any of its usual functions, including removing toxins from the bloodstream and making proteins that help blood to clot. Ammonia and other toxins can accumulate as well, making the bird very sick and even causing her death. Less affected birds can develop a myriad of secondary problems such as blood clotting problems and skin problems, as well as edema from portal hypertension (high pressure in the blood vessels leading through the liver toward the heart because the swollen liver compresses the veins and fluid subsequently leaks into the tissues).

Diagnosis of fatty liver is fairly simple. The bird may be jaundiced (have a yellow tint to the eyes and skin) or have difficulty breathing. An avian veterinarian will find elevated liver enzymes and cholesterol on the blood work results and will see an enlarged liver on x-rays and endoscopy. Treatment consists of medications to support the liver and a diet change to reduce fat. Some birds will need blood transfusions or hand-feeding while their liver recovers.

Feather Picking

Many birds exhibit "feather picking," the destruction or removal of their own feathers. Many Internet sites reiterate the common misconception that most birds who pick their feathers do so because of primary behavior disorders (i.e., boredom, anger, or other anthropomorphic concepts). This is not the case, as most feather picking has an underlying physical cause—usually some disorder that causes the bird to be itchy or irritated, either on the surface of the skin or underneath. Skin infections, superficial irritation from sprays or other topical substances, feather follicle and shaft infections, liver disease, and parasites such as *Giardia* (a common protozoal parasite) can all cause itching of the surface of the skin. Allergic skin disease may exist in birds as well, but this diagnosis remains controversial and is not yet well characterized. Air sac and lung infections or inflammation, liver disease, other organ infection, other parasites, and some kinds of cancer can also cause itching underneath the skin.

Feather picking must be differentiated from generalized skin or feather problems, which is simple to do: feather-picking birds have normal skin and feathers on their heads because they cannot reach their own heads. Once it is determined that the bird is picking his own feathers, a myriad of diagnostic tests can be performed. The minimum database must be performed to rule out parasites, liver failure, kidney failure, and other systemic diseases. Virus tests are very important to rule out psittacine beak and feather disease (PBFD) and herpes virus (Pacheco's disease), two highly contagious diseases for which there is no cure. If any abnormalities are found on the minimum database, endoscopy or other more invasive tests may be indicated.

Contrary to popular belief, mites are *not* a common cause of feather picking in parrots, although secondary skin infections are common in these birds. A skin scrape may help determine whether a bacterial or fungal infection is present, and a Gram stain will help characterize the kind of bacteria present so that an initial antibiotic can be selected. Many of these bacterial infections should be cultured so that an appropriate antibiotic can be chosen for long-term treatment.

Another simple test is a feather follicle cytology and culture. In this test, a young feather that has some blood and fluid still in the shaft is plucked and the material from inside the feather shaft is extruded onto a slide. This material is examined under a microscope to see if any bacteria, yeast, or inflammatory cells are present. An additional sample is collected in a sterile fashion and submitted for a bacterial culture. A very small amount of bacteria can cause problems in a feather shaft, and culturing is important in finding bacteria that may not be visible on a microscope slide.

DID YOU KNOW?

- The oldest parrot on record lived to 104 years old.
- There are more than 350 species of parrots, ranging from 3¼ inches (pygmy parrot) to 40 inches (hyacinth macaw) in length.
- Chickens outnumber humans on earth by 4 to 1.
- The fastest recorded homing pigeon in the United States finished a 102-mile race in 1 hour 1 minute, with a flight speed averaging more than 100 miles per hour!
- Crows and ravens frequently use tools and can solve logic puzzles.

Occasionally, the underlying cause of the feather picking is not found on the minimum testing. In these cases, skin biopsies are indicated. A skin biopsy is performed under general anesthesia most of the time, with small pieces of skin being surgically removed from the affected (feather-picked) area as well as from an unaffected area. Feathers are included in these samples so that the pathologist can evaluate the feather follicle and shaft in case the problem arises from those areas. The unpicked areas will give the pathologist a baseline for that particular bird and can show abnormalities in birds with systemic diseases. The pathologist can perform special stains on the samples to look for yeast and certain types of bacteria, and can also perform viral testing for PBFD and herpes.

If all of the tests in the feather-picking bird are normal, and there is no history of exposure to inhalant toxins, the bird can be considered to be a behavioral feather picker. These birds may have some anxiety that causes them to pick their feathers, or they may have too much time on their hands so they preen their feathers excessively to the point of plucking.

Parrots in the wild spend most of their time during the day foraging for food. As food is scarce and flight requires a constant source of energy, they have evolved to search for food almost constantly and store it in a specialized pouch in their esophagus called a crop. Most birds can store enough food to keep their energy up overnight and through the next morning of foraging. If a bird is kept in a small area and is given food in an easily located bowl without having to work for it, she has nothing to do and may get bored, sometimes leading to excessive preening and feather picking. The remedy for this problem is to provide these birds with foraging opportunities. Food can be hidden in progressively more difficult puzzles for the bird to solve, from wads of paper to cardboard boxes filled with shredded paper to blocks of wood the bird has to destroy to get to the food item. These puzzles can be spread over a "playground" with ropes, ladders, and other obstacles that have to be worked through for the bird to reach the food. Setting up such diversions can be very labor intensive for the bird owner, but if the problem is inadequate foraging, it is the only solution.

Behavior Problems

Behavior problems are very common in parrots. In addition to feather picking, owners often complain about are biting, screaming, inappropriate sexual behaviors, aggression toward people other than the owner, and destructive behaviors. Any of these behaviors can contribute to expansion of the unwanted bird population and even euthanasia, and all of these behaviors are perfectly normal in wild birds. Most of these behaviors can be modified into a more acceptable form with some work on the owner's part, but some are more difficult than others to alter.[2, 3]

To change unwanted behaviors in parrots, the behavior of the wild parrot must be understood. Some species have certain behaviors particular to them, and they also must be understood, but in general parrot behavior can be thought of as a triangle. Wild parrots spend approximately equal amounts of time devoted to three different behaviors: foraging for food, preening themselves and flock mates and bathing, and engaging in social interaction with the flock. If one or two of these activities become too easy for the bird and takes less time than one-third of the day, the bird spends excessive time engaging in one of the other behaviors. This imbalance will result in a bird that preens excessively (or a feather picker) or a bird that craves more social interaction. It seems almost impossible for a cage bird to find a way to forage excessively. Birds that crave more social interaction can develop unwanted sexual behavior such as regurgitation, masturbation, and egg-related problems, or they can develop separation anxiety if the flock or perceived mate (human owner) is frequently absent and start screaming excessively, as wild parrots do to reestablish contact with their flock.[3]

It is beyond the scope of this chapter to go into detailed instructions for modification of every unwanted behavior in parrots, but some general points can be made. Beginning when they are young, parrots should be socialized with as many people and other pet birds (that were tested negative for viruses, of course) as possible. This socialization should be continued for the life of the bird. Well-socialized birds tend not to get separation anxiety, do not develop pair bonding or phobias, and are much more "well adjusted." They also almost never "like only one person," "hate men/women," or exhibit other preferential behaviors.[2]

Biting can be normal and understandable when a bird is coaxed to go to the hand and then the hand is moved away. In the wild, if a bird tries to get on a branch that suddenly moves in the wind, he will grab on with his beak so it does not fall. If a bird bites in an aggressive fashion, it is usually either scared of something or guarding a mate. Occasionally, a bird will bite a human if he sees another bird that it has aggression toward—it may be trying to guard his mate/owner or territory in these cases, and the aggression is misplaced onto the owner. A bird will also bite to defend himself if he feels threatened, which is also understandable. Socialization will usually prevent birds from being fearful of new people or new surroundings.[2]

Destructive behavior is usually related to foraging instincts, but certain birds like to shred items apparently for fun rather than for food. Wild birds that live in large flocks, such as cockatoos, will shred the trees they roost in at night. When captive birds do not have enough toys to destroy in their cages, they sometimes turn to their feathers and shred those instead. These behaviors are relatively easy to change: simply remove the bird from the item getting destroyed, or vice versa. There are many toys made specifically for birds to destroy, and many others are simple to make at home.[3]

Anxiety due to inappropriate mating behavior is very common in pet parrots. Because parrots are so charismatic and sociable, as well as demanding of attention, many owners inadvertently cause their birds to become sexually bonded to them. Birds seem much happier when owners are playing with them, but the owners do not realize what certain behaviors signify. Some behaviors that may seem innocent to humans are mating and bonding behaviors in birds, performed only with their mates. These include kissing, petting or scratching the bird's head and back, and hand-feeding. Because the human does not react as expected to the subsequent more advanced sexual behaviors the bird demonstrates in response (such as regurgitation and masturbation), this failure leads to anxiety for the bird, which does not understand why the pair bond is not leading to its logical conclusion of mating and eggs. Some birds will pick their feathers because of the anxiety; others will scream or bite. This inappropriate pair bonding can also lead to reproductive problems in female birds.[3]

Reproductive Problems

Female birds that are reproductively stimulated lay eggs, even if they have not been fertilized. Some birds, such as chickens, are stimulated by day length only, whereas others require a mate to begin the egg-laying process. Most parrots will produce eggs only when they have some kind of pair bond with another member of their flock, which can be another bird, a human, or even another pet. Some species such as cockatiels and lovebirds are easily stimulated and lay eggs at the slightest provocation; other species are quite difficult to get to lay eggs.

Constant stimulation of female reproduction can cause a number of problems. Chronic egg laying can deplete a bird's calcium quickly, especially if she has poor nutrition. African Greys are especially sensitive to calcium depletion and can develop weakness and seizures from low calcium levels. Egg laying also takes a large amount of energy, and birds can lose weight from excessive egg production. Additionally, the stress involved in egg production can suppress the immune system and predispose the bird to fatty liver and other maladies.[1]

When a bird produces excessive numbers of eggs and experiences the stress and energy usage involved with egg laying for a protracted period of time, there is a greater chance of abnormally shaped eggs and damage to the uterus. Abnormally shaped eggs can become stuck in the uterus; if the uterus is damaged or infected, normal eggs can get stuck as well. This condition of an egg stuck in the oviduct is called "egg binding" and is usually an emergency situation. The bird will strain to lay the egg and, much like a mammal giving birth, will become rapidly exhausted. Exhaustion and the toxins that build up in the bird's system from damage to the uterus and prolonged muscle contraction can send the bird into shock and lead to circulatory system collapse, which can easily result in the bird's death. Birds in this state require intravenous (or intraosseous) fluids, antibiotics, and pain medication. It is important to remove the egg, but stabilizing the bird's condition is more important in the immediate moment. It is also important to run blood tests to see if the calcium level requires correction, and if there is evidence of infection or other organ failure.[1]

An egg that cannot be laid without assistance can be removed via various methods. The best care in the short term is to provide the bird with a warm, humid, stress-free environment. It is also very important to make sure the bird is well hydrated, so fluid therapy may be required. If the bird has a low calcium level, she should receive an injection of calcium as well. Many birds will lay their eggs with only these techniques. Administration of some hormone medications used in mammals may help, but it is unclear how much an avian uterus responds to these hormones. If it still does not respond, after the bird is stable the egg can be removed by other means. One strategy is to anesthetize the bird, lubricate the egg, and attempt to pass it manually. If it still will not pass, the egg can be penetrated with a large needle and the contents aspirated out with a syringe. If done carefully, the egg can be imploded with this technique and then it will pass easily. This procedure can be very dangerous, however: if the egg is not imploded correctly, pieces of the shell can lacerate the uterine lining and kill the bird. For this reason, such removal is considered a last resort in birds that may otherwise die and should be performed by an avian veterinarian with an adequate amount of experience in doing this procedure.

Uterine infections can also happen secondarily to chronic stimulation of reproductive hormones. Chronic infections cause the immune system to use up most of its reserves, and bacterial infections always secrete numerous kinds of toxins (which can cause liver, kidney, blood, and neurologic problems) into the circulatory system. Additionally, chronic infections can cause scarring and thickening of the uterine lining. Chronic inflammation can also become "precancerous" and eventually develop into cancer. Antibiotics may sometimes cure this problem, but at other times extensive scarring may have already occurred, which can cause infertility and lead to egg binding.

Another problem that chronic egg-laying birds can develop is egg yolk peritonitis. Egg yolk peritonitis occurs when an ovulated ovarian follicle (which normally ends up as the yolk in the finished egg) slips past the part of the oviduct that is supposed to catch the yolk as it is ovulated. The yolk ends up free in the body cavity (known as the coelomic cavity) of the bird. Most of the time this condition is benign, but in some cases it can cause inflammation or result in infection. There is usually a fairly severe fluid buildup in the cavity, which can restrict the bird's ability to breathe. Egg yolk peritonitis can quickly become life threatening, especially if it becomes infected. Treatment requirements depend on how critical the bird's condition is and may range from the need for extensive fluid therapy, to surgery, to outpatient therapy.

In all cases of reproductive diseases in birds, the minimum database is vital to rapidly determining which process is occurring. Infection must be identified quickly so that treatment can begin, and concurrent abnormalities must be identified so problems such as low calcium levels can be corrected. Some additional diagnostics may also be necessary, especially in cases of abdominal enlargement. If the coelom is full of fluid, it will appear the same as a tumor or mass on x-rays, so it is important that an ultrasound examination be performed to differentiate fluid from solid tissue. Additionally, a fine-needle aspiration may be done on the fluid or mass. In this technique, a needle is advanced into the mass or fluid pocket and some of the contents are drawn out with a syringe and then examined under the microscope. For solid masses, the aspirate consists of cells from the mass; they can be examined to determine whether the mass is benign or malignant and what kind of tissue the mass arises from. For fluid pockets, the fluid can be analyzed for the presence of inflammatory cells and bacteria. Endoscopy of the coelomic cavity can be performed in cases where there is a mass in the reproductive tract to visualize and biopsy.

Cancer and Other Growths

Cancer is fairly rare in birds but is increasing in frequency with the recent advancements in medicine and nutrition, which have allowed pet birds to live longer and encouraged owners to pursue more extensive diagnostics and therapeutics. The more common forms of cancer include cancer of the reproductive tract, kidney, skin, and intestinal tract. Cancer can also occasionally occur in many other places in the body. Most of the time, avian cancer is a disease of older birds, but there are a few exceptions. In ducks and geese, leukemia is much more common than in parrots, and chickens can get a virus that causes leukemia and another that causes cancer of the nerves. Parrots, especially Amazons, can develop intestinal papillomas, which may be associated with a virus, although these tumors are usually found in older birds.

Kidney cancer is common is certain species, such as lovebirds and budgerigars. This kind of cancer does not usually cause clinical signs until the tumor enlarges to the point where it affects nerves leading to the leg. Certain nerves running across the surface of the kidneys lead to the legs, and once the tumor reaches a large enough size it can stretch or compress a nerve, causing lameness or weakness. Affected birds assume a typical stance on their perch: their legs are spread apart and sometimes one leg will stick out to the side to the point where the bird cannot use it. This leg also tends to be weaker, and the bird cannot grip as well with the affected foot. Presumptive diagnosis can be via x-rays, but most of the time the diagnosis is not considered definitive without endoscopy and biopsy of the tumor. There is currently no surgical treatment for kidney tumors in birds due to the extensive nerve and blood vessel involvement in and on the tumor. Chemotherapy has not been attempted but probably would not help due to the type of tumor commonly found.

Skin masses are fairly common in birds as well. Benign masses such as feather cysts are frequently observed in canaries and other passerines. Feather cysts in parrots may be a sign of the more insidious PBFD. Birds can also develop other types of tumors, such as squamous cell carcinomas, adenomas, or other malignant or benign tumors. Pox virus can lead to the development of wart-like masses on the skin, which can spread to other parts of the body or other birds. If the pox virus gets into the water supply, it can infect the lining of the mouth and respiratory tract of multiple birds and cause severe losses in a flock.

Another benign mass often found in obese birds with nutritional deficiencies is called a xanthoma. Xanthomas are yellow masses that usually appear on the wings, which can become quite large. They are not tumors in the strictest sense, but rather consist of conglomerations of cells that are full of cholesterol. It is thought that poor nutrition and high-fat diets predispose birds to xanthomas. Fine-needle aspiration of these masses is usually diagnostic; the cholesterol-containing cells are easily identified. Although surgical excision of these masses is curative, they will usually disappear on their own over a period of months if the nutritional deficits are corrected with an appropriate diet.

Avian papillomatosis is usually a disease of older birds and is very common in Amazon parrots. It is believed to be caused by a virus that can lay dormant in the bird for years. Papillomas are wart-like masses inside the intestinal tract, typically in the cloaca or colon. Usually the first sign of cloacal papillomas is frank (red) blood in the bird's stool. The bleeding can be extensive, or it can be minor and intermittent; most of the time it progresses to more severe bleeding that occurs more frequently. An affected bird will also become lethargic and may not want to eat. On physical examination, a papilloma may be visible in the cloaca, but a speculum may be necessary to visualize it if it is in the upper cloaca. Occasionally the papilloma may progress to a liver tumor, which suggests a poor prognosis for the bird. Another potential problem is multiple papillomas located farther up the intestinal tract, where it is impossible to visualize them via endoscopy; in such a case, contrast x-rays may be required to find the masses.

Treatment for solitary papillomas consists of surgical excision. Excision may not be curative due to the probable viral cause of the disease, but it will curtail the clinical signs and the bleeding for days, sometimes years. Some studies suggest that a diet high in capsicum (hot pepper) can prevent recurrence of papillomas, but this relationship has not been definitively proven.

Skin and Feather Conditions

Skin diseases are not uncommon in pet birds. Some birds kept with other birds in a cage or aviary that is too small can be victims of trauma—the other birds will pick the feathers from the back of their head, sometimes causing bleeding or even death. Birds that enter the incorrect nest box may also be subjected to similar trauma. Birds can also bite one another's beaks and toes; lovebirds tend to bite the toes of birds that land on their cages, and larger birds such as cockatoos sometimes bite and severely damage their mates' beaks.

Mites are common in small birds such as budgies and canaries but are uncommon in larger birds. The "scaly leg mite" will cause thickening of the skin on a bird's legs and nares, leaving tiny holes through which the mites can breathe. Mite infestations are usually easily treated with injectable medication or topical administration of a miticide, but care must be taken because many of the compounds available on an over-the-counter basis can be dangerous.

Feather abnormalities may be noted as well. Cysts and malformed feathers can be the first sign of PBFD or can result from infections of the feather follicle. One very common problem, especially in cockatiels, is broken blood feathers. Cockatiels sometimes get "night terrors" and thrash around their cages when they become scared by something at night. If they happen to be molting, this behavior can damage blood feathers, which are new feathers that are growing in that still have a blood supply. When they break a blood feather, it tends to bleed copiously; because the blood feather is usually located on the wing, the bird flings blood everywhere as it flaps. Sometimes it is difficult to get the bleeding to stop, especially if the bird is scared, but some cornstarch or styptic powder applied copiously to the bleeding area usually works. The old method of treating blood feathers involved removal of the feather. This technique is painful and can result in follicle damage, however, so this treatment has fallen out of favor and it is now recommended to leave these feathers alone.

Foot Conditions

Foot problems are not uncommon in birds. Obese parrots, especially ones who have sandpaper on their perches, can develop bumblefoot (infectious pododermatitis). Bumblefoot is a chronic infection of the bottom of the foot from a wound or cracking of the skin, complicated by obesity and nutritional deficiency. This condition is common in poultry and waterfowl as well, in which it results from contamination of wounds and inappropriate flooring; it tends to be very difficult to treat.

Birds with leg bands can get dead skin buildup under the bands and the foot can lose blood circulation, resulting in various degrees of damage. Similarly, birds can get threads from towels used as cage coverings and the like wound around their toes. Sometimes the toes swell so much that the thread becomes embedded and cannot be seen, requiring surgery.

Gastrointestinal Conditions

Pet birds may develop a number of gastrointestinal conditions, including parasites, bacterial overgrowth, cancer, and foreign body ingestion. Cancer and foreign bodies were discussed previously. Intestinal worms are rare in parrots (but common in poultry and pigeons), but *Giardia*, a protozoal parasite, is fairly common. Overgrowth of Gram-negative bacteria (bacteria that are not found in high numbers in healthy birds) is also seen frequently, usually secondary to poor nutrition. These disorders are usually easily treated with antibiotics and anti-*Giardia* medication.

Infectious Diseases

Birds can contract a considerable variety of viruses. The control of viral disease is a very important aspect of poultry farming and pet poultry care, as well as pigeon raising, and vaccines are available to ensure birds remain safe from such infections. Poultry raised as pets or in backyard flocks can also be infected, and the end result can be just as devastating. General good health and nutrition measures and avoidance of the virus are the most important aspects of viral control, especially since at this time there are no approved drugs to kill avian viruses. Treatment is based on supportive care for the bird while the bird's immune system kills the virus.

A partial list of viruses that chickens and turkeys can contract includes adenovirus (affects the liver), influenza (respiratory), Marek's disease and lymphoid leukosis (both cause cancer), pox (skin and mucous membranes), infectious bursal disease (immune system), and infectious laryngotracheitis (respiratory). These conditions are variably mild to fatal diseases, and different individuals can react differently to the same viral strain. Many other viruses can be contracted as well, but this representative group suffices to demonstrate the wide variety of diseases and systems affected.

Because of the hand-raised nature and indoor housing of most pet parrots, viruses are not quite as important or common among this population but can still be fatal. In these cases, the viruses usually come from the pool of breeding birds of various species, some of which are asymptomatic carriers (i.e., they do not show signs of illness but do shed the virus). The most important viral diseases in parrots include PBFD (a coronavirus), polyoma virus, and Pacheco's disease (a herpesvirus). The initial signs of all of these viral infections are generalized lethargy, fluffed feathers, and anorexia, so it is very important to test for all of these pathogens in any sick parrot, especially if they have been exposed to other birds.

As discussed earlier in this chapter, PBFD causes feather abnormalities—curled feathers, cysts, and the like. More importantly, it can cause immune system suppression and destruction in younger birds, which can eventually result in death. Polyoma virus attacks the liver in young birds and usually seems to strike suddenly around weaning, which is the time of greatest stress in young birds. The main sign of advanced polyoma infection is hemorrhage, which may sometimes prove life threatening or even fatal. Pacheco's disease also affects the liver, but is more mild and chronic in adult birds; thus it also can cause many different clinical disorders, including feather picking.

Another common infectious disease is psittacosis, caused by the intracellular bacterium *Chlamydiophila psittaci*. Psittacosis is important because it can be passed to humans and cause pneumonia. The causative bacteria are spread in dust and feces. With very dusty birds such as cockatiels or pigeons, humans are at high risk of breathing the bacteria into their lungs when cleaning their aviaries. In birds, the *C. psittaci* bacterium can cause a range of disorders: in pigeons and some parrots it causes eye and upper respiratory infections, while in some parrots such as cockatiels it can cause fatal liver failure. Clinical signs range from eye discharge, conjunctivitis, and sneezing, to green urates, lethargy, and severe illness. Diagnosis is usually fairly straightforward via testing for bacterial DNA, but can sometimes require multiple tests, biopsies, or special stains. Treatment of psittacosis is also usually fairly straightforward and includes antibiotics, but antibiotics (such as tetracyclines) often need to be given for months because the intracellular nature of the bacteria protects them from the effects of the drugs. Diets for psittacosis that include tetracycline are marketed commercially, reflecting the fact that entire flocks of birds may become infected, and medicated feed is much easier to administer than treating the birds individually.

CONCLUSION

Birds can be very rewarding pets, be they parrots, chickens, pigeons, or some other kind of bird. Conversely, these animals can also be quite difficult and expensive to take care of if they become ill, so it is best to prevent illness and keep pet birds as healthy as possible. Pet bird health depends on suitable diet and correct nutrition, appropriate socialization, protection from toxins and trauma, and timely presentation to the avian veterinarian. Because birds hide illness so well, it is important to bring your pet to the veterinarian for yearly examinations and blood work so that diseases can be caught early, when they are most likely to be treated successfully.

REFERENCES

1. Harrison, G. J., and Lightfoot, T. L., eds. *Clinical Avian Medicine*. Palm Beach, FL: Spix; 2006.

2. Luescher, A. U., ed. *Manual of Parrot Behavior*. Ames, IA: Blackwell; 2006.

3. Bays, T., Lightfoot, T., and Mayer, J., eds. *Exotic Pet Behavior*. St. Louis, MO: Saunders-Elsevier; 2006.

FURTHER READING

Avian nutritional information: http://www.harrisonsbirdfoods.com/learningcenter/
handbook.html

Discussions of various diseases: http://lafebervet.com/clienteducation/

Doane, B. M. *The Parrot in Health and Illness.* New York: Macmillan General Reference
Publishing; 1991.

To find an avian veterinary specialist: http://www.abvp.com/FindDiplomate.aspx

9

Unraveling Animal Behavior

Ellen Lindell, VMD, DACVB, and Sagi Denenberg, DVM, MACVSc (Veterinary Behavior)

CATS

Normal behavior

Cats were once considered to be solitary creatures. This conclusion was drawn because cats typically hunt alone, and they do not wander about in packs. Yet a careful observation of free-running cats has revealed that many cats are quite social. Some cats are solitary, apparently by choice, and most cats are solitary hunters that prey on rodents and other small vermin. Nevertheless, many cats live in social groups, where they form attachments and select preferred associates. Relatives, particularly along matrilineal lines, often remain together. Female cats even care for the offspring of other cats in their social group.

As one would expect of a social animal, cats engage in behaviors that serve communicative functions. When cats travel about, they frequently stop to urinate on vertical surfaces, marking their territory. It is common for a cat to leave many such messages over the course of the day. Similarly, cats frequently use their claws to scratch surfaces such as trees and fence posts. When using these forms of communication, cats select socially significant areas that will be investigated by potential intruders.

Free-running cats within a social group exhibit a behavior known as allogrooming—that is, they groom each other. This behavior serves at least two important functions. First, it helps maintain group health by removing dead hair, debris, and external parasites. Second, it offers an opportunity for the cats to share a common scent. Pheromones, which are chemical compounds that are used for intraspecies communication, are widely distributed over the bodies of the cats as they are groomed. This may be akin to wearing a company logo on a T-shirt.

Housecats are, of course, subjected to constraints. They are not free to choose the size of their home range. Within some households, resident cats form attachments to one another. Other cats share a home but merely tolerate one another. These cats engage in time sharing in an apparent attempt to make the best of living under one roof with a partner that might be less than desirable. Unfortunately, some cats' personalities simply clash—they do not want to share a logo. As discussed later in this chapter, these clashes can create challenges for the humans who share their homes.

Kittens

Kittens are blind and immobile when they come into the world, requiring intensive care at the time of birth. They develop quickly, however, and by six weeks of age kittens are in training. Queens systematically help kittens learn to hunt prey so that even an eight-week-old kitten can be a skilled hunter. Social skills among siblings also develop quickly, and kittens teach one another how to play appropriately. Kittens continue to remain with their queens and littermates for many months. For this reason, singletons and orphans may be at a disadvantage when it comes to interacting appropriately with cats or even humans.

When kittens are adopted from breeders and shelters, they are usually weaned before eight weeks of age. Adopting a kitten at this young age has both advantages and disadvantages. Practically speaking, for reasons related to space and budget, it is difficult for catteries and shelters to continue to offer these active, growing kittens room and board. One considerable benefit of adopting a seven-week-old kitten is that young kittens are still amenable to socialization. The socialization period of cats is much shorter than that of dogs and may begin to wane by seven to nine weeks. Adopting a cat during this sensitive period of development increases the likelihood of peaceful cohabitation with dogs, rabbits, and children. Young kittens more easily accept traveling in the car for family vacations, and they quickly learn to sleep soundly as the neighborhood fire sirens sing.

Management Problems

Whether one adopts a cat or kitten, the newcomer will be a feline. As such, normal feline behaviors should be expected. Normal or not, many behaviors are just not socially acceptable in the human world, so a plan of action to deal with them will be needed. An ideal plan should prevent the cat from engaging in undesirable behavior while offering an opportunity for the cat to engage in a replacement behavior that the household humans will tolerate. In other words, the outcome will be better if, instead of saying, "Stop, stop, stop," the owner says, "Do this instead." Owners must ask themselves, "Are the cat's needs met?" Hunting, sleeping, and exploring are normal daily activities for all felines. Appropriate outlets can easily be provided for housecats. For example, cat food can be placed inside toys that have been hidden about the house so that cats can hunt. Other toys can be used to engage the cat in chasing and pouncing.

Destructive Behavior

It is absolutely normal for a cat to scratch assorted surfaces. As previously discussed, scratching vertical surfaces serves a communicative function. In addition, scratching objects is part of the cat's normal grooming process. Most housecats scratch soon after they wake up from a nap. Some cats select vertical surfaces as their target, while others scratch objects on the ground, and most cats choose one or two favorite substrates to scratch on. Materials that are loosely woven and shred easily are favored—tweed and cardboard, for example—but nothing is off limits. What else is popular? Needlepoint chairs, stereo speaker covers, and, sometimes, the arms of leather couches.

Cats can be taught to scratch appropriate surfaces. It is tempting to simply go to the pet shop and purchase a premade "scratching post"; however, many posts are constructed of tightly woven carpet that is not attractive to all cats. The key to management is to provide the substrate that the cat in question favors *and* to place that material in the appropriate location. If a cat scratches a leather couch arm, then a leather-covered post should be placed directly beside the couch. Rubbing catnip onto the scratching post may provide an additional incentive to use it.

In addition to providing the appropriate material in the appropriate location, it may be necessary to render the original surface less attractive. This can often be accomplished by applying some double-sided sticky tape, available commercially as Sticky Paws, to the object that must not be scratched. Once the cat has accepted the new post, the tape can be removed.

Keep in mind the tried-and-true adage that an ounce of prevention is worth a pound of cure. This philosophy absolutely applies to destructive behavior in our pets. What is the best prevention? Supervision until appropriate habits have been established. As soon as that first kitty claw touches the sofa, distract the kitten. The same rule applies to a newly adopted adult cat. Make an odd sound to attract your cat's attention, and then guide the cat to the appropriate surface, offering quiet praise or even dropping some treats on the ground nearby. In this way, your cat can discover that by scratching a post, snacks appear.

If necessary, cats can wear soft nail caps, called Soft Paws, during the training stages of their entry into the household. Cats that seem refractory to simple environmental modification should visit with a behaviorist, who will be able to offer more detailed guidance. In the past, a surgical procedure, known as declawing, has been used as a remedy for destructive scratching. This procedure is illegal in most countries outside North America and should be the last resort for this problem. Cats can keep their claws and learn to use appropriate surfaces.

A brief note is in order regarding destructive chewing. Occasionally, kittens and cats will chew and ingest objects such as furniture, books, towels, and even sweaters. Oriental cats, such as Siamese and Burmese, are predisposed to chewing and ingesting fabric, particularly wool. The ingestion of nonfood items is known as "pica." Minor chewing by a young kitten generally represents normal exploratory behavior. Excessive chewing, particularly in adult cats, may occur secondary to an underlying medical condition. If no underlying medical condition is present, then the abnormal chewing may be due to a behavioral condition known as "compulsive disorder." The veterinarian or behaviorist can offer a treatment plan to help manage this disruptive and potentially dangerous behavior.

Common Behavior Problems in Cats

House Soiling

Housecats are expected to use their litter boxes consistently. Many cats lose their homes or even their lives because they eliminate in areas that are not socially acceptable. Fortunately, most house-soiling problems can be managed or cured. The key is to investigate all potential reasons for the behavior. A thorough physical examination, some basic laboratory testing, and careful history taking will all be used by the veterinarian to establish a diagnosis. Once the cause is identified, a successful treatment plan can be designed and implemented.

Many cats eliminate in inappropriate locations because of perceived problems with their litter boxes. What could be wrong? First and most simply, the box could be dirty. Litter boxes should be scooped at least once daily. If many cats reside in the home, there must be an adequate number of boxes so that a fastidious cat can find a clean box when needed.

Sometimes cats do not favor the litter that their humans have selected. Before investing in a large bag of novel litter, buy a small sample size. Place two boxes side by side: one with the old litter and one with the new option. If the new litter is boycotted, it is best to donate it to the animal shelter and stick with the tried-and-true original.

Another factor to consider is the size and type of litter box. While some cats like hoods for privacy, if a cat is very large, he might not be very comfortable inside a small, hooded litter box. Cats that have been ambushed by a child or another pet might also prefer an unhooded box that offers a sweeping view.

Not only must the box itself be suitable, but it must also be accessible. A cat with arthritis might not travel up three flights of stairs to her box, and might instead choose another absorbable surface such as a bed or flower pot. A timid cat might not venture past the dog bed or through the playroom just to find a little litter box.

Any unpleasant experience at or near the litter box, such as pain while urinating or a sudden loud sound, can lead a cat to avoid the litter box and seek alternative locations for elimination. A tip-off that the cat is soiling because of concerns with the box itself is that the box will be relatively free of urine and feces. Red flag! Look around the house for evidence.

Marking

Yet another reason for a cat to eliminate in an inappropriate area is to send a message. Remember, urine serves a communicative function. Elimination for the purpose of communication is known as marking. Cats will occasionally mark areas with feces as well.

Urine marks are usually deposited in socially significant areas rather than in hidden corners. Vertical surfaces are usually, but not exclusively, targeted. Multiple deposits may be made on a given day, or the deposits may be very occasional. Meanwhile, the cat that marks about the house will continue to use his litter box on a regular basis.

When the behavioral diagnosis is marking, it is important to search for an underlying trigger. Marking probably serves to soothe a nervous cat; therefore, all potential sources of fear, anxiety, or aggression should be explored. Housecats may mark in response to outdoor cats seen through a window. In multiple-cat homes, the social relationship between household cats should be evaluated. Marking may also occur when there is an unhealthy relationship between the cat and a person, dog, or other animal in the household.

Treatment for marking includes managing underlying medical conditions and reducing stressors as much as possible. Environmental modification may be used to assure that all cats can be safe. For example, multiple safe, comfortable resting surfaces should be provided. Feeding stations and litter boxes can be placed in several areas of the home to assure adequate access for all cats. Commercially available pheromone products such as Feliway can be applied in areas that have been marked, and neutering (males) or spaying (females) intact cats may reduce the frequency of marking, in some cases by as much as 95 percent.

Behavioral modification can also be implemented to reduce marking behavior. For example, cats can be desensitized to some of the triggers that create fear. The intensity of aggression can be reduced as well. In certain cases, veterinarians may prescribe psychotropic medications to further reduce fear and aggression and reduce the tendency to engage in marking.

Fear-Based Behavior

Cats may be naturally suspicious of the unfamiliar, and many cats hide in response to loud sounds. Sometimes, housecats are afraid of certain people, even when those people are members of the household. The degree of the fear response may be affected by individual genetics as well as a lack of early appropriate exposure.

If the fear is mild, the cat may be left to discover on his own, little by little, that no harm will come should he leave his hiding spot.

In some individual animals, the intensity of fear is so great that the cat could refuse to venture out even for food. These cats may even eliminate in their hiding places. Such pets are clearly suffering emotionally. Treatment is available, however. Meanwhile, until treatment has been completed, the cat must be provided with fresh food, water, and a clean litter box. Many cats can be moved to a quiet room, where all of their physical needs can be met.

Behavior modification to reduce fear often involves a process known as desensitization and counter-conditioning. Through desensitization, the cat is gradually and systematically introduced to the trigger of her fear. Counter-conditioning pairs the presence of a frightening trigger with something pleasant, such as play time, brushing, or delicious food. For those cats that are too frightened to even begin behavior modification, the veterinarian may prescribe safe and effective anxiety-reducing medications.

Aggressive Behavior

As discussed earlier, all cats are not equal in regard to social behavior. Some cats simply do not play well with others, while other cats are just not compatible with certain individuals. This type of rejection can be disconcerting when a family adopts a cat, expecting the new pet to simply blend in seamlessly with the other resident felines. A resident cat may behave aggressively toward a newcomer for several reasons. For instance, the resident may be frightened by the unfamiliar cat, and instead of backing off and taking time to observe, she may respond with overt aggression. Were it not for the walls and roof overhead, the new cat in town would almost certainly turn around and find a new place to live.

Unfortunately, a cat that is chased aggressively very often flees. As mentioned in the previous section, he may seek safety under a bed or on a high perch. Whenever there is a chase/flee episode, the chaser is reinforced by the response of the retreating cat. The aggressor learns that aggressive behavior leads to the desired outcome and, satisfied with the results, becomes more likely to repeat this behavior.

Sometimes, cats that have lived together successfully for years suddenly begin to fight. In this situation, a physical examination of both cats is the first step for their owner to take. Either cat might be ill, triggering an aggressive response. If both are deemed healthy, then an environmental trigger should be sought. Often, a cat outside has frightened one of the resident cats, prompting her to redirect her aggression toward her housemate. Another common trigger for the sudden onset of aggression is a visit to the veterinary clinic. In either case, the victim will run, initiating the chase/flee cycle described previously.

When cats clash, it is essential to seek therapy as soon as possible to avoid chronic reinforcement of aggression and fear. The veterinarian or veterinary behaviorist will carefully analyze the interactions between the cats to establish the motivation for the behavior. Then, an appropriate treatment plan can be designed. As with any behavioral treatment plan, the first steps are prevention and safety. The owner should modify the environment to assure safety and access to essential resources for all cats. At that point, behavior modification can be implemented. In many cases, the cats will initially benefit from physical separation except when the treatment sessions are under way.

As challenging as it can be to live with fighting felines, it can be even more disturbing when cats bite household people. Most cats are expected to keep people company—sitting in laps or on desks, purring contentedly when petted. Unfortunately, some cats may bite when petted. They may accept a pet or two, but after a certain number of strokes, they bite and walk away.

It is difficult and not without risk to teach cats to accept unlimited petting. The aggressive behavior in such a case may have a genetic basis, it may be related to inadequate early socialization, or it may occur in response to true physical discomfort. Even so, the cat's owner can live safely by keeping the cat's limitations in mind and paying attention to early warning signs that the cat is becoming tense.

It is more difficult to remain safe with a cat that initiates acts of aggression even when the person is not interacting with it. Some cats lunge at people who move about, while others bite people who are sitting quietly. There can be several reasons for this behavior. Careful analysis of contexts and postures should reveal whether the behavior is related to fear, or whether it represents status-based aggression. In some cases, particularly when visitors are targeted, the apparently offensive aggression may even be due to territorial aggression.

Other forms of aggression by cats toward people include redirected aggression, resource guarding, and inappropriate play behavior. Redirected aggression occurs when a cat is frightened or aroused by something that he cannot reach, and instead attacks the nearby person. Most such bites generate at least a scream, and it seems that the entire event is recorded by the cat as "one big scary experience." Perhaps not surprisingly, the cat responds by becoming fearful. His next encounter with the same person may result in a bite that is now due to fear-based aggression.

Occasionally, cats guard food or people or favorite resting places. These cats can often be managed successfully by teaching them to relax when approached by people in these situations.

Sometimes, cats chase people as they move about the house. These cats stalk and stare and suddenly leap up and bite. Management can include putting a collar bell on the cat so that the people are not caught off guard. Once the person is aware that the cat is approaching, he or she can toss a toy for the cat to chase and grab.

Except in cases of self-defense, it is never appropriate to attempt to exhibit aggressive behavior in response to a cat's aggressive behavior. Similarly, physical punishment is not indicated. A person's aggressive responses will serve to increase fear and, therefore, increase the risk of future attacks. Instead, the underlying motivation for the behavior should be evaluated and changed through behavior modification. If aggressive behavior cannot be predicted with certainty, then the cat should be housed in a separate room except during controlled interactions.

Senior Years

As cats reach their teen years, they may be subject to some age-related behavioral problems. They may also experience anxiety associated with age-related physical changes. Regular physical examinations and laboratory testing by your veterinarian will allow management of the physical contributors to some of these behavior changes, such as the pain of arthritis. Internal organ function declines with age; consequently, cats that produce more urine due to kidney disease or diabetes may need more litter boxes. Cats with arthritis may need lower boxes, or boxes that are on a ground level so that there is no need to climb stairs just to eliminate.

Aging cats can also experience cognitive decline. They may forget what their litter boxes are for or where they are located. They may become less interactive with people, or may spend much time sleeping during the day but pacing in the evening. Nearly one-third of all cats older than 11 years of age may show one or more signs of cognitive decline.

It is important to interact with cats during the day, and even more important to avoid interacting with cats when they are very demanding. If cats are petted or fed whenever they meow, they will almost surely meow with great intensity when their people are sleeping and apparently nonresponsive. It is best that a cat understands that the humans are well aware of his needs and that these attentions are all provided based on the owner's decision rather than the cat's calls.

Summary: Cat Behavior

Cats may seem complicated, but with thoughtful observation, we are learning to understand them, communicate with them, and even teach them new tricks. If cats' desirable behaviors are rewarded, they will be repeated. Undesirable behaviors can be evaluated, and medical conditions that might precipitate unwanted behaviors should be explored. With that understanding, behavior modification can be designed. Some behavioral pathology may be best managed with medication. The outcome of all of these efforts should be a cat that can offer a lifetime of warmth and companionship.

DOGS

Normal Behavior

Free-ranging dogs live in groups that include both males and females of varying ages. Social ranking is determined by age and to some extent by sex, size, and temperament. The dog's social structure has been previously referred to as a pack hierarchy, but this terminology does not properly explain the relationship of dogs with other dogs or with humans.

Given that wolves are ancestors to the domestic dog, it is tempting to compare wolf behavior with dog behavior. New scientific studies of the behavior of wild wolves have established that the wolf pack is a family, with the adult parents guiding the activities of the group. Canine domestication for more than 15,000 years combined with selective breeding, however, has led to extensive variation in morphology in modern-day dogs. With domestication, dogs have lost elements of wolf "body language," and have retained juvenile characteristics. Breeding for traits such as herding, hunting, retrieving, pointing, guarding, and companionship has also led to widespread behavioral differences among breeds. Dogs use visual signaling to communicate, and phenotypic changes (changes in physical appearance) introduced through selective breeding might potentially reduce effective intraspecies communication, particularly between dogs of different breeds. Perhaps early socialization with other dogs (see the discussion of fear prevention later in this section) may help overcome this barrier.

The term "dominance" has become popular in describing all sorts of animals' behavior, and in some cases, a dog might be described as having a "dominant" personality. Although dogs can form dominance relationships, it is not uncommon for their positions in groups to change. Dominance does not describe a relationship between two individuals; rather, it is a relative term that is established by the value of the resource to each individual and the cumulative effects of learning. Thus the term "alpha" is used incorrectly when describing the relationship between two or more dogs, or between dogs and their owners. Hierarchy is neither static nor linear, because the motivation to obtain and retain a specific resource as well as previous learning defines the relationship between two individuals for each encounter. As a consequence, it is possible for one dog to be dominant in one situation and subordinate in a different situation, depending on the context.

Stability is maintained by deference and not by fighting between dogs. Thus "submitting" your dog, attempting an "alpha roll," or pinning your dog may lead to fear, anxiety, and even aggression toward you. Dogs use visual signaling (including body postures, facial expressions, and tail and ear carriage), vocal signaling, pheromones, and scents to communicate with other dogs. By comparison, human-dog relationships are a function of genetics, early handling, and socialization. Such relationships are shaped by learning and consequences, not by dominance or hierarchal relationships.

Canine Development

The first important period of development for dogs is the neonatal period, which extends into the third week of life. Puppies are born with closed eyes and limited physical ability. Therefore, in the first few weeks, care by the bitch is of primary

DID YOU KNOW?

Studies have shown that punishing a pet for undesired behaviors seldom solves the problem. In fact, in most cases it merely serves to increase fear and anxiety, and the pet is likely to show increased aggression toward the owner. Punishment can also weaken the bond between you and your pet, have detrimental effects on the animal's welfare, and lead to the development of other behavior problems.

importance. Grooming and nursing by the mother stimulate the puppies to suckle and eliminate, and helps to keep the puppies in the nest. Good maternal care has been shown to increase the ability to handle stress and facilitate maturation of the nervous system. Similarly, mild stress in the form of gentle human handling during the first two weeks after puppies' birth can improve cardiovascular performance and resistance to disease. Puppies that have been gently handled mature faster, perform better in problem-solving tasks, and are better able to withstand stress as adults.[1] As puppies become more mobile in the second to fourth week after their birth, interactions with littermates help to develop social skills.

The second period of development is a short transition period during which puppies become more mobile and aware of their surroundings. Once their eyes open, at about 14 to 17 days of age, and physical skills develop, puppies begin to explore their environment and refine their social skills. The transition period is followed by the third period, the socialization period, also known as the sensitive period. The sensitive period begins at about 3 weeks after birth, peaks at 12 to 14 weeks of age, and wanes at approximately 16 weeks of age. During this period, the puppy can most readily habituate to people, dogs, other animals, and other novelties in the environment. Inadequate socialization and lack of enrichment during the sensitive period may contribute to fear-based or aggressive responses when presented with certain stimuli. Although heredity plays an important role in the behavior of an individual, positive exposure to a wide range of animate and inanimate stimuli during this period can minimize the development of fear and anxiety.

Spending the first 7 to 8 weeks with her mother and littermates plays an important role in the development of social skills with other dogs. However, by 7 to 8 weeks of age, the puppy should begin her integration into the new home so that exposure to new people and environments can continue before the socialization window begins to close. In addition, weaning is normally completed at 7 weeks of age, and at about 8 weeks of age puppies start developing preferences for elimination location.[2]

The fourth period, known as the juvenile period, extends from about 3 to 12 months of age. Domestic dogs reach sexual maturity at 6 to 9 months (later in some giant breeds) and social maturity at 12 to 26 months of age. Social relationships are established to minimize conflicts within a group.

Prevention of Problem Behaviors

Young puppies routinely exhibit behaviors that are normal but undesirable to their owners. Examples include house soiling, mouthing, and excessive barking. Oral behaviors such as destructive chewing are also common because puppies use their mouths to explore and play.

Management of normal but problematic behaviors is best accomplished by preventing the undesirable behaviors and reinforcing acceptable behaviors. Supervision is the best way to ensure that the puppy does not do something he should not. When the puppy cannot be effectively supervised, he should be housed in an area that has been puppy-proofed. Gates, crates, and exercise pens can all be used to create safe environments for young dogs. Crate training can be easily implemented, but first the owner must view the crate as a positive and comfortable location to leave the puppy when unsupervised. The crate must be large enough for the puppy to stand in and move around, be equipped with a pillow or a blanket, and provide some food and water. The puppy should be placed in the crate for short periods of time initially, with the time spent inside gradually being increased. The crate should become part of the daily routine, such that the puppy spends time inside each day. In addition, the owner should provide favorite chew toys only in the crate, not around the house. Whenever it is time to confine the puppy, the owner must make sure to provide play and exercise, soiling time, and some attention prior to placing the puppy in the create. Lastly, the puppy should never be put in the crate as a form of punishment; the crate should be seen as a positive place, rather than a prison.

To reinforce acceptable behaviors, owners can provide appropriate chew toys, food-stuffed toys, and food-dispensing toys. Acceptable play behavior can be reinforced through structured activities including fetch, tug, walking, and training for rewards.

Following a daily schedule that includes time for exercise, elimination, and socialization helps reduce conflict and provides predictability. A consistent routine combined with environmental enrichment can help keep the puppy on the right track for long-term success and fosters a strong bond between family members and their dog. This daily routine should meet both the social and physical needs of the dog. A puppy can be offered some of his daily ration as rewards during training, and another portion can be offered in food-filled toys. It is more natural for dogs for forage and work for their food rather than eating from a food dish. At the same time, this approach encourages the dog to spend time engaging in desired behaviors.

Puppy Socialization

As discussed earlier, puppies should be exposed to a wide variety of both animate (social) and inanimate stimuli throughout the socialization period. Puppy socialization classes are designed for puppies between 10 and 16 weeks of age. They offer puppies the opportunity to meet other puppies, unfamiliar people, and in many cases other animals, including cats, in a controlled environment. Visits to the veterinarian or groomer, car rides, and meeting visitors in the home provide additional opportunities for exposure. As the puppy matures, exposure to a wide variety of stimuli with positive outcomes should be continued through to adulthood. If a puppy exhibits signs of fear, such as trembling, hiding, or snapping, professional guidance should be sought to assure that the puppy learns appropriate responses. Recent research reveals that taking puppies to socialization classes decreases the chances of relinquishment and euthanasia later in life due to behavior problems.[3]

Obedience Training

Trainers can be recommended to help owners manage normal behaviors that are deemed unacceptable. When such assistance is sought, it is important to select a trainer who uses humane training techniques. Reward-based training methods use gentle shaping to teach and reinforce appropriate behaviors. In contrast, confrontational training styles that are based on punishment are not generally recommended, for several reasons. First, punishment-based techniques often rely on fear and physical discomfort of the dog. Second, punishment is difficult to apply appropriately, as the authority figure's timing and intensity of the rebuke must be precise. Undesirable consequences such as fear and aggression are not uncommon when this type of training is used; in fact, recent studies show that nearly 40 percent of dogs will turn against their owners when confronted.[4]

Behavior Problems

Some dogs exhibit problem behaviors that represent behavioral pathology. Professional behavioral counseling is needed to determine the cause of the behavior, to determine the prognosis, and to design a treatment plan. This treatment will include the implementation of behavior modification, environmental management, and, in some cases. administration of medication.

The process for diagnosing behavior problems should always start with a visit to your veterinarian, as many medical conditions may cause or contribute to the development of abnormal behavior. In fact, a change in behavior may be the first or only sign of an underlying medical problem. Even if a medical problem is resolved, learned behaviors such as house soiling and aggression may persist, necessitating the need for behavior counseling.

Canine Fears and Phobias

Fear is a normal response to an actual or perceived threatening stimulus or situation. Anxiety is a response to fear and agitation, or apprehension when the animal anticipates a threat or fearful situation. The fear response may include panting and drooling, tucking the tail, lowering the ears, gazing away, lowering the body, or vocalizing. Displacement behaviors such as yawning or lip licking may be exhibited. While some dogs use avoidance and escape as their strategy, others employ aggression to remove the fear-evoking stimulus. Some of the more common triggers for fear in dogs include unfamiliar dogs, unfamiliar people, and unfamiliar objects. Sounds that may trigger fear include thunder, fireworks, gunshots, and motor vehicles. Dogs may be afraid of vacuum cleaners, riding in the car, or visiting the veterinary clinic.

Certain dogs may exhibit more generalized anxiety, demonstrating fear or apprehension in a wide range of situations, or in anticipation of a potential trigger. Genetics, insufficient early stimulation and handling, lack of socialization, and unpleasant previous encounters with the stimulus can all contribute to the development of abnormal fear responses.

Phobias are exaggerated fear responses that may be triggered by a single exposure to a particular trigger. Thunderstorms and fireworks commonly trigger phobic responses in susceptible dogs.

Treatment for fears and phobias includes behavior modification. Desensitization and counter-conditioning (DSCC) is one effective technique. Desensitization involves slow and gradual systematic introduction of the pet to the trigger of the fear, while counter-conditioning offers the pet an alternative emotional experience. For instance, dogs can learn to eat, play, or sleep while the trigger is slowly presented.

Separation Anxiety

The term "separation anxiety" is used to describe the anxiety that dogs experience when they are left alone. Signs of separation anxiety may include destructive behavior, vocalization, house soiling, drooling, restlessness, and loss of appetite. These behaviors are exhibited exclusively and consistently when the dog is left alone, often within minutes after the departure. Many dogs begin to exhibit signs just prior to a departure, reacting to cues such as brushing teeth, putting on shoes, and handling keys. Some dogs with separation anxiety seek constant contact or proximity to household people. Exaggerated greeting behaviors such as uncontrolled jumping, excessive barking, and inability to settle are commonly reported as well. There is an association between separation anxiety and noise and thunderstorm phobias, so any dog exhibiting signs of one condition should be screened for the others.

Canine Compulsive Behaviors

A compulsive disorder is diagnosed when a dog exhibits a behavior—typically a repetitive behavior—to an excessive degree such that it interferes with normal function. Some repetitive behaviors may involve grooming or ingestion of inappropriate materials. Other dogs may compulsively chase shadows, imaginary flies, or even their own tails. Compulsive behaviors may first arise as displacement behaviors in dogs that are frustrated, conflicted, or highly aroused. Lack of predictability in the daily routine, alterations in the environment, or lack of sufficient outlets for normal behaviors may be initiating factors. In addition, some breeds may have a genetic predisposition to develop certain compulsive disorders. For example, German shepherds and bull terriers frequently present for spinning or tail chasing.

Because underlying medical conditions may cause any of these signs, a thorough veterinary evaluation is needed prior to establishing a behavioral diagnosis. For example, pain at the root of the tail can lead to spinning, whereas skin irritation can lead to excessive grooming.

Treatment for mild compulsive behaviors may include teaching the dog alternative responses. For example, dogs that spin during greetings can be taught to "sit" instead. Professional guidance should be sought to manage more serious compulsive behaviors. In addition to training to achieve alternative responses, some cases may require behavior modification, environmental changes, and the use of medications. When a dog exhibits a compulsive behavior due to a medical condition, it is important to treat both the medical and behavioral conditions at the same time, as one can trigger and maintain the other.

Aggression

Nearly 70 percent of dogs seen by veterinary behaviorists are treated for aggression. Dog bites are a significant public health concern. In the United States, at least 5 million people are treated for bite wounds each year. Aggression can be defined as distance-increasing behavior—that is, as a behavior that serves to actively increase the distance between the dog and the stimulus. During this process, a dog may exhibit subtle changes in body posture or more overt signs such as barking, growling, or biting. Many types of aggression in dogs are possible, including territorial, redirected, possessive, and pain related. Fear, anxiety, genetics, and learned responses can all play a role in the expression of aggressive behavior in a given dog. Likewise, the effects of early development, socialization, and previous experience can influence the development of aggression. In particular, dogs that are easily aroused are at high risk for aggression.

Before treating a dog that has exhibited aggressive behavior, a physical examination should be performed to check for any medial cause of the behavior. Triggers and contexts for aggression should be identified so that a diagnosis can be established. Initially, the aggression may need to be managed by avoiding these triggers. A combination of behavior management devices, such as head collars and muzzles, can be used to ensure safety. Behavior modification may then be implemented. In addition, some dogs may benefit from the use of medications to reduce anxiety and arousal. The owner must keep in mind that medication will not teach the dog how to behave in similar situations; therefore, psychotropic medications should not be used without behavior modification. A behavioral treatment plan should be devised and supervised by a veterinarian, veterinary behaviorist, or certified applied animal behaviorist.

Fear is a common cause of canine aggression. Aggression that represents a direct response to a challenge or confrontation is sometimes referred to as defensive aggression. Fearful dogs may try to avoid the stimulus, but may become aggressive when they cannot escape or when they are motivated to maintain their place (e.g., on the property, between the owner and the stimulus, near food or a toy), or if they learn that aggression is successful at removing the threat. Genetics, maturity, learning, the stimulus (including its size, the level of threat, and previous experience with it), and the dog's ability to escape the situation are all factors that influence whether a dog is likely to fight or flee. Inadequate socialization, learning, reinforcement of aggressive behavior (e.g., retreat of the stimulus), and punishment can all lead to the development of fear-related aggression.

Possessive aggression is most likely to arise when a person or an animal approaches the dog while she is in possession of something of sufficient value that the dog may use aggression to retain. Although pets that have taken possession of an object and are in the process of ingesting or chewing might be more likely to display aggression, similar behavior might even be seen with dogs that are in the vicinity of the object. Aggression is most commonly displayed when a dog is in possession of highly motivating food, treats, chew toys, or stolen items, but can be related to sleeping places, family members, or another pet. Items that are novel or scarce may increase desirability

Aggressive play is a normal puppy behavior, which may persist into adulthood. When puppies play aggressively with other puppies, they may nip and bite, but will generally resolve the conflicts amongst themselves. If this behavior becomes excessive, owner intervention may be required to redirect a puppy's activities into other forms of play such as toys, or to interrupt the behavior with commands or a leash and head halter. If play with humans escalates to biting, the puppy can be directed to use her mouth in other forms of oral play with toys, such as tug toys, or the interaction should be immediately stopped and resumed when oral play ceases. Tug games will not increase or promote aggression in puppies, but they should be avoided in cases where the puppy may become aggressive over the toy or when the owner is trying to stop the game.

Redirected aggression is directed toward a third party when the dog is prevented or unable to exhibit aggression toward his primary target. This type of aggression is most commonly described when the dog bites the owner as he or she grasps or restrains the dog when trying to prevent or break up a dog fight. Similarly, dogs that might be aggressive toward the veterinarian might bite the person restraining the dog.

Two (or more) dogs in the same household may respond with aggression toward each other as a result of fear, lack of early socialization, or competition over resources (e.g., food, owner's attention, toys, favorite sleeping place). In most households, dogs establish relationships based on deference of one dog to the other, thereby preventing fights. The astute owner must provide sufficient resources to prevent competition and reward appropriate interactions. If the problem persist or escalates, help should be sought.

Ingestive Behavior Problems

Several types of ingestive problems in dogs have been described. Food intake may be excessive, or too little, or the dog may eat too quickly. Some dogs eat non-food items (pica). The ingestion of feces (coprophagia) is not well tolerated by most people. Although coprophagia may be secondary to dietary deficiency, it can be exhibited by dogs that are behaviorally normal. In fact, the bitch normally eats her puppies' stools. Some dogs play with feces and then learn that the taste is appealing, especially the stools of other species.

The ingestion of nonfood objects may reflect the presence of a compulsive disorder. Many dogs, especially puppies, begin to chew and ingest nonfood items as part of investigative and exploratory behavior. Moreover, many feeding problems can be improved through a "work for food" program in which dogs are given food as rewards for training, with the balance placed inside toys that require chewing or manipulation to release the food. This practice encourages exploration; makes feeding an enjoyable, time-consuming, and mentally challenging activity; and can limit the quantity of food eaten and prevent the gorging of food. Feeding and chew toys are best given to the dog when the owner is not around to supervise and provide stimulation. It is important to remember to try the toy several times while the owner is present to ensure safe play time.

When a dog exhibits abnormal ingestive behaviors, a visit with your veterinarian to rule out medical causes such as diabetes, kidney failure, and gastrointestinal disease should be scheduled.

Elimination Behavior Problems

When dogs eliminate indoors on inappropriate surfaces despite adequate attempts at housetraining, or when there are housetraining lapses, a thorough veterinary evaluation is indicated. A variety of medical conditions, including gastrointestinal and urinary tract diseases, can contribute to house soiling. Other causes of inappropriate elimination include marking behavior, separation anxiety and fear, and cognitive dysfunction in senior dogs.

A detailed history is required to determine if the pet has ever been housetrained; if not, a housetraining program should be reviewed. This process generally requires that the owner accompany the pet to her elimination area (e.g., outdoors), reinforce elimination, supervise the pet indoors to prevent or interrupt any attempts at elimination (perhaps with the aid of a leash to ensure continuous supervision), and return the pet to her elimination site when she is again due to eliminate or if there are any signs that the pet is ready to eliminate (e.g., sniffing, heading to the door, sneaking away). Enforcing a daily schedule including elimination opportunities, supervision, and confinement is generally very effective. Pets can either be confined away from those areas where they might eliminate inappropriately or placed in an area where they are not likely to eliminate, such as a pen, or in the room where the dog eats, plays, or sleeps. Providing an indoor soiling area might be an acceptable solution when the owner is gone for long periods of time. Puppies obtained from pet stores or any location where they have been extensively caged are usually much more difficult to housetrain because they have never had to inhibit elimination and may even have learned to play with or eat feces.

Marking through elimination is a form of normal canine communication. Some dogs will mark when they visit unfamiliar households, especially when another dog's odors are present. The dog often assumes a typical posture of a raised or partially raised leg when the surface to be marked is vertical. Stool marking, in contrast, is uncommon. While marking is likely a component of normal communication, it is unacceptable, of course, when it is displayed indoors. Oftentimes, treatment involves addressing the complex social relationships between household dogs, or between dogs and household people. Neutering intact males may reduce the behavior in certain individuals. Treatment will also include supervision and interrupting any attempt at marking with a distraction such as a startling sound.

Dogs may also eliminate when they are overly excited, such as during greetings. Elimination that occurs secondary to fear or anxiety should resolve with treatment of the primary behavioral concern.

Aging

The aging process is associated with progressive and irreversible changes in body systems that could affect the dog's behavior. In most cases, these signs are subtle at first and slow to develop. A detailed behavioral history, physical examination, neurological evaluation, and diagnostic tests may all be required as part of the veterinarian's workup to evaluate potential medical causes of the presenting signs.

Aging dogs may suffer from a decline in cognitive function, which can be manifested as one or more of a group of clinical signs. Recently published data indicate that dogs older than seven years of age already show at least one sign of brain aging. Dogs may become less engaged with family members and other pets, spending more time on their own. They may also exhibit a loss of learned behaviors such as housetraining or ability to recall obedience commands. Their sleep pattern may change, with the dog pacing all night and then sleeping all day. Aging dogs may also exhibit signs of increased anxiety. Some may demonstrate a decreased ability to tolerate being left alone, or an increased response to stimuli that have previously been well tolerated.

While aging is an irreversible process, the development of cognitive decline in canine companions may be slowed or prevented through the use of medications and natural supplements, environmental enrichment, and special diets. Teaching the dog new tasks should be incorporated into the daily routine. Certain older dogs may also benefit from medications to reduce pain or anxiety. Early intervention and balancing physical and behavioral needs can extend the quality of life for senior dogs.

REFERENCES

1. Scott, J. P., and J. L. Fuller. *Dog Behavior: The Genetic Basis*. Chicago: University of Chicago Press; 1974.

2. Overall, K. L. *Clinical Behavioral Medicine for Small Animals*. St. Louis, MO: Mosby; 1997.

3. Duxbury, M. M., J. A. Jackson, and S. W. Line, et al. "Evaluation of the Association Between Retention in the Home and Attendance at Puppy Socialization Classes." *Journal of the American Veterinary Medical Association* 223 (2003): 61–66.

4. Herron, M. E., F. S. Schofer, and I. R. Reisner. "Survey of the Use and Outcome of Confrontational and Non-confrontational Training Methods in Client-Owned Dogs Showing Undesired Behaviors." *Applied Animal Behaviour Science* 117 (2009): 47–54.

FURTHER READING

Miller, P. *The Power of Positive Dog Training*. Hoboken, NJ: Wiley; 2008.

Prior, K. *Don't Shoot the Dog*. Gloucestershire, UK: Ringpress Press Books; 2002.

Serpell, J. ed. *The Domestic Dog: Its Evolution, Behaviour and Interactions with People*. Cambridge, UK: Cambridge University Press; 1996.

Turner, D., and P. Bateson, eds. *The Domestic Cat: The Biology of Its Behaviour*. Cambridge, UK: Cambridge University Press; 2000.

10

Alternative Therapies for Treating Illnesses and Maintaining Health

Nancy Scanlan, DVM, MSFP, CVA

WHAT IS ALTERNATIVE MEDICINE?

The word "alternative" is somewhat unfortunate when it comes to medicine. This term does indicate that nontraditional methods of care can be an alternative to conventional strategies, and in some cases a better alternative, but it tends to set up the idea in many minds that this is an "either-or" situation. In reality, this type of medicine is best used in conjunction with—not instead of—traditional veterinary medicine. However, the use of "alternative" does reflect the fact that sometimes the approach used is a viable alternative to either doing nothing or using a drug with extreme side effects. In addition, some "alternative" methods have become mainstream. For example, a number of nutritional therapies, such as supplementation with glucosamine and lysine, are now part of regular veterinary medicine, and many specialty practices employ acupuncturists as part of their treatments for pain.

Alternative medicine goes by a number of other names: holistic, alternative, complementary, complementary and alternative medicine (CAM). Some also call it "homeopathic," although this terminology is actually wrong—homeopathy is just one aspect of holistic medicine. Each of these names reflects one aspect of holistic medicine.

The word "holistic," sometimes spelled "whole-istic," is intended to convey the idea that this type of medicine tries to take in all aspects of health—body, mind, and spirit. The hospice movement has a much stronger presence in holistic medicine than in conventional veterinary medicine. "Holistic" also reflects the fact that veterinarians who employ these methods also use many parts of conventional medicine, especially surgery, laboratory tests, and emergency care. (Holistic methods, for the most part, are gradual methods, taking weeks to achieve their full effect, so they are not suited for any situation that requires a quick result.) Because they take so long to act, they are also ideal for chronic disease, where conventional medicine has limited answers.

The term "complementary" probably best describes how most holistic veterinarians use this form of medicine: it complements regular veterinary medicine. Some holistic veterinarians use a very small subset of holistic medicine, whereas others use only a very small subset of conventional medicine. Nevertheless, most of these veterinarians consider themselves to be holistic.

"Complementary and alternative veterinary medicine" (CAVM) is the term used by many holistic veterinarians when speaking or writing about holistic veterinary medicine, and it is the term that will be used in the rest of this chapter. It also reflects that these approaches focus their major concentration of effort on the body, some on the mind (with behavioral aspects), and only a very small part on spirit, as opposed to the human holistic movement.

WHAT IS CAVM?

CAVM includes many types of treatments, or modalities. Practitioners of CAVM may use only one of these strategies, or they may incorporate many into their practice. This chapter deals with the modalities that pet owners are most likely to encounter.

Table 10.1 lists some websites where veterinary practitioners with interest or expertise in CAVM may be found. The table also includes website addresses for finding more information about the topics discussed in this chapter, in addition to listing organizations whose membership includes veterinarians and other professionals involved in the many forms of alternative healing discussed in this chapter.

ACUPUNCTURE

The word "acupuncture" comes from *acus*, Latin for "needle," and *pungere*, Latin for "to puncture." Acupuncture is the insertion of very fine needles in specific spots to produce various effects. Acupuncture was the first complementary treatment that was widely incorporated into veterinary practice acts.

General interest in this modality in the United States began in 1971 after reporter James Reston's article in *The New York Times* described how acupuncture was used after his appendectomy in China to relieve pain. The popularity of this practice increased after President Nixon's visit to China in 1972, when pictures of people who were undergoing major surgery with electroacupuncture (stimulation of acupuncture points with very low current) as the only method of pain control were published.

Veterinarians immediately were intrigued by the potential of this therapy for animals, because many painkillers available for animals have severe side effects,

Table 10.1
Useful Websites Related to Complementary and Alternative Veterinary Medicine

Name of Organization	Website	What You Can Find There
Academy of Veterinary Homeopathy	http://www.avhlist.com/avh_index.php	List of veterinarians trained in classical homeopathy
American Academy of Veterinary Acupuncture	http://www.aava.org/php/aava_blog/aava-directory/	List of veterinarians trained in acupuncture
American Herbalist Guild	www.americanherbalistsguild.com	Knowledgeable website about herbal medicine; includes practitioners for both humans and animals
American Holistic Veterinary Medical Association	http://ahvma.org	Information about holistic veterinary medicine, and meetings for holistic veterinarians; link to list of holistic veterinarians
American Veterinary Chiropractic Association	http://www.avcadoctors.com/search_for_avca_certified_doctor.htm	List of veterinarians and chiropractors certified in veterinary chiropractic
Chi Institute	http://www.tcvm.com (lower middle area of the left column)	List of veterinarians trained in acupuncture and Chinese herbal medicine
Institute of Functional Medicine	http://www.functionalmedicine.org/about/whatis.asp	Information on functional medicine and detoxification
International Veterinary Botanical Medicine Association	http://www.vbma.org	List of practitioners (veterinarians and herbalists) with training in herbal medicine
International Veterinary Acupuncture Society	http://ivas.org/Members/VetSearch/tabid/124/Default.aspx	List of veterinarians trained in acupuncture and Chinese herbal medicine
Prolotherapy website	http://www.getprolo.com	Information on prolotherapy and list of doctors who perform it on humans
Tellington TTouch website	http://www.ttouch.com/pracDirectory.shtml.	Information on TTouch and list of practitioners
Veterinary Orthopedic Manipulation site	www.vomtech.com/practitioners.htm	General information about veterinary orthopedic manipulation (VOM) and list of VOM practitioners
List of holistic veterinarians	http://www.holisticvetlist.com	You can search for a veterinarian by type of CAVN

including diarrhea, gastrointestinal ulcers, kidney damage, and liver damage. A group of California veterinarians formed the North American Veterinary Acupuncture Association, which eventually was replaced by the International Veterinary Acupuncture Society (IVAS) and the American Academy of Veterinary Acupuncture (AAVA), later joined by the Chi Institute. A course was developed to train veterinarians in acupuncture; later, a course on Chinese herbs was created as well.

Currently, veterinarians can become certified in veterinary acupuncture either through IVAS training or at the Chi Institute in Florida. When looking for a veterinarian who is properly trained in acupuncture, you should look for the designation "CVA," "OMD," or "LAc" after the person's name. The letters "CVA" after a veterinarian's name indicate that he or she is a Certified Veterinary Acupuncturist and has completed a veterinary certification program. The letters "OMD" or "LAc" indicate that the individual has a degree in Chinese medicine (including acupuncture) for humans.

Acupuncture is most commonly practiced by inserting needles into specific acupuncture points. There are two groups of points in animals: the traditional points identified in ancient Chinese literature and "transposed" points, which are adaptations of points on human charts applied to animals. The traditional points reflect the ancient uses of animals for food, to reproduce, and for labor (hence, points for lameness). Transposed points reflect the role that pets have today as members of the family. We are trying to do the same things for them as for humans, so a chart of transposed points for animals has many more points than a traditional chart and lets us treat chronic disease better.

Most veterinarians use the form of acupuncture based on traditional Chinese medicine (TCM) theory. TCM states that acupuncture points are points along lines, or meridians, that travel up and down the body. Acupuncture maps show anatomical positions of points and their locations along the meridians. Regardless of whether one believes in the meridians, there is a great deal of research showing that acupuncture points do exist. Many acupuncture points correspond to areas of lower electric resistance on the body[1]; thus an instrument measuring this resistance (it is called a pointfinder, but is actually a very sensitive ohmmeter) can be used to find the points. In addition, points often correspond to areas where nerves penetrate fascial sheaths (a sheet of connective tissue surrounding tissues, especially muscles) and where bundles of nerve endings, arteries, and veins are found together. Although it is possible to decrease pain perception somewhat by inserting acupuncture needles in many different places, by far the biggest effect is obtained when needles are placed at the acupuncture points best suited for them.

In addition, some effects, such as a release of epinephrine, occur only when specific points are stimulated.[2] Thus, as Chinese practitioners have long said, different points do have different functions, and you cannot just go around blindly inserting needles and expecting special effects.

The number of points used depends on the practitioner and the problems that are specifically addressed. Some acupuncturists use the same points at each visit, as long as they are working. Others change each time. If many problems are being addressed, some points might be used at one visit, with different points being targeted at another visit. Needles may be left in for a period ranging from 5 to 30 minutes, although 15 to 20 minutes is the most common length of time.

Needles may be simply left in place, or they may be twirled or otherwise manipulated. Heat may be applied to the needles, using a lit cylinder of a dried, compressed herb called moxa. An electrical current may be applied (electroacupuncture) either briefly or for the whole session. Acupuncture points may be injected with any liquid substance (aquapuncture), with vitamin B12 or B complex most commonly used, but homeopathic preparations too may be used, among other liquids (though usually not water). Low-level lasers ("cold" lasers) are used by some practitioners to stimulate acupuncture points. (Cold lasers can also be used as an array of beams, in a pad placed over an area, which stimulates blood flow and speeds healing. This method, though valid, is not acupuncture.) Some veterinarians use only the non-needle method (e.g., only injecting points, or only applying an electric current directly to points), but most incorporate needles as part of the treatment. There is no one, single correct way to perform acupuncture, and veterinarians develop the method that works best for them and their patients.

One special kind of electroacupuncture is known as EAV (electroacupuncture according to Voll). In this method, electrical resistance is measured at the ends of the acupuncture meridians (at the nail beds of all the toes). If the measurement is higher or lower than expected, a small current is applied, until the level returns to normal. One problem with this method is that most dogs have no dewclaws on their back feet, so the meridians that end in the big toe of humans are not represented. Also, if dogs have had the dewclaws on their front feet removed, there is no way to access the points we see on the thumbs of humans. EAV is not a widely used procedure, but there are some veterinarians who practice it.

Another subset of acupuncture is called medical acupuncture. This type of acupuncture claims that the Chinese theory of medicine is simply superstition and that only acupuncture based on research is valid. The problem with this perspective is that most Western research has focused on the use of acupuncture for pain relief, so medical acupuncture emphasizes this aspect. In addition, by rejecting the Chinese theory of medicine, it ignores the fact that, to be licensed to perform acupuncture on humans, or to use Chinese herbs for them, a practitioner must pass a lengthy test in which the majority of questions concern Chinese theory.

The most common use for acupuncture is to relieve pain, but it can be employed for many other purposes, such as stimulating the colon (for pets suffering from megacolon) or helping paralyzed animals regain function of their limbs. Acupuncture stimulates the nervous system. Endorphins and enkephalins (the body's own version of morphine-like substances) are released at the area where the needle is inserted, and at the corresponding areas in the spinal cord and brain. In addition, serotonin (a neurotransmitter that represents a different part of the pain relief system) is released. For all these reasons, acupuncture can be more effective than a shot of morphine: its effect is more local and specific, and the release of serotonin, a body-wide pain reliever, is an added benefit.

In addition, placement of acupuncture needles at some spots specifically releases other chemicals. Two locations may be targeted to stimulate the release of epinephrine: one is just below the nose pad, and the other is on the hind foot just under the hind foot pad. Stimulation of these spots can be helpful when an animal is in shock, or if she suffers from cardiac arrest. This is an exception to the general rule that most holistic methods take a long time to achieve their full effect. Other areas can be targeted to stimulate labor in animals that are having problems whelping by releasing oxytocin. In addition, placement of needles in some areas will release other hormones, which can help increase the number of eggs ovulated and released.

Owners whose pets have never had acupuncture often ask how the practitioner keeps the animal still during the session. An acupuncture needle is far thinner than the thinnest hypodermic needle, so it is much less irritating or painful when inserted. When it is placed in an acupuncture point, an animal may not feel the needle at all, or may just feel when it is inserted, and then not after that. Once an animal has experienced the pain-relieving effect of acupuncture, the acupuncturist is usually her friend for life. It takes only one to two sessions for animals to figure out that the practitioner actually makes them feel better, not worse.

As long as there is some nerve function remaining, acupuncture can also help with weak or paralyzed animals. The one exception is animals such as dachshunds that become suddenly paralyzed and do not have any perception of pain. (This condition is referred to as having no deep pain reflex.) In my own practice, I have done acupuncture on animals that have been unable to stand for months, but that still had deep pain reflexes, and they were able to stand and walk again. Sometimes this effect can be quite dramatic: they may be carried in and after a treatment go walking out.

In addition, acupuncture can help with nerve damage. I once saw a cat whose leg had been severely injured; her leg looked normal, but the cat kept trying to chew her foot off. Her veterinarian had recommended amputation, and the owner declined. The foot had to stay bandaged, and the cat had to wear an e-collar (one of those collars that looks like a lampshade) whenever she was not with the owner. I performed acupuncture, inserting needles into the foot (the cat never appreciated this act). After one treatment, while the owner still had to keep the foot bandaged, the cat no longer had to keep the e-collar on. With multiple treatments, the bandage was finally removed, never to be used again. In humans, nerve damage often produces a pins-and-needles feeling. This cat was likely feeling the same effect, and acupuncture decreased the worst part of these feelings.

Acupuncture can also make an animal with kidney failure feel better. A cat was once brought to me that had extremely severe kidney failure and had stopped eating. The cat was also extremely fractious. The animal refused a special diet, so acupuncture was her only hope. After a single treatment, during which the cat would allow placement of only five needles, she went home and started eating and drinking again.

Acupuncture can even help some behavior problems. A dog was brought to me because her owner thought she had no interest in life any more. After a life of play, exploring everywhere, ruling the backyard, and generally having a good time, the dog suddenly did not want to leave her owner's side. She did not even want to go outside, and her owner had to push the dog out to urinate and defecate. A physical examination and lab tests did not show anything unusual, except for arthritis in one hip. The arthritis was treated, but it made no change in the dog's behavior. Acupuncture was performed to treat points that would increase the "yang" in the pet's body. (Yang is the strong, masculine, outgoing part, while yin is the quiet, contemplative, internal part of a body.) At the time, I was new to acupuncture and overdid it. The dog came back the next week in the opposite state of mind. She did not want to stay inside, wolfed her food, barked at everything, and was generally obnoxious. Chinese medicine emphasizes bringing things back in balance, so I used points to balance the animal. The dog went back to being her normal, less obnoxious self, and never had another problem.

Chinese theory also tells us about some other things Western medicine ignores, such as "wind," "heat," and "cold" as "pathogens." Some people think this is silly superstition, but experience with old dogs that have arthritis shows that they feel worse on a windy day than they do on a still day. Some acupuncture points and Chinese herbs specifically address this particular problem of wind. A wind condition is characterized as things that come and go, such as spasms and epilepsy. Interestingly, the acupuncture points and Chinese herbs that work for arthritis can also affect spasms and seizures. Veterinarians who do not understand TCM theory will not be able to use Chinese herbs as well as those who do.

Finally, Chinese medicine emphasizes balance, and the idea that we are all made up of opposites (the yin/yang theory mentioned earlier). TCM theory emphasizes bringing everything back into balance, rather than just beating down whatever is excessive. This means treating deficiencies both by trying to help the body be less deficient and by decreasing excesses.

CHINESE HERBS

In the United States, a veterinarian can learn acupuncture without using Chinese herbs; however, the two are meant to be used together. In China, veterinarians learn about both. In the United States, anyone who is licensed to perform acupuncture on humans must take a course that teaches about both. Such education is important because there are a number of conditions that respond better to herbs than to acupuncture, or to a combination of herbs and acupuncture rather than to either one alone.

Some people are alarmed at the idea of using Chinese herbs because of past problems with contamination of items such as dog food ingredients imported from China. They also have heard stories about Chinese herbs adulterated by antibiotics or heavy metals, and those that contain items such as bear bile. A number of companies manufacture their products in the United States, and these companies are careful to avoid contamination, using laboratory tests on the raw ingredients as well as the finished product to make sure there are no problems. These companies also do not use ingredients that harm animals, and they omit herbs that can have dangerous side effects. By using products from these companies, a holistic veterinarian ensures that only safe ingredients are used for your pet. The safest companies are the ones that sell only to veterinarians; their owners are very knowledgeable about Chinese medicine and give lectures regularly on the subject, thereby ensuring that veterinarians understand how to use their herbs properly and effectively.

Most Chinese herbal formulas are derived from formulas listed in several hundred Chinese texts. A Chinese formula usually has four parts:

- The main (emperor or chief) herb, which has the primary action of interest
- The deputy herb, which reinforces actions of the main herb, but may also treat secondary problems in the disease
- Assistant herbs, which can act in a similar way as deputy herbs, but also decrease the toxic effects of other herbs
- Envoy (directing) herbs, which direct the action of the formula to a specific place (e.g., a formula that treats arthritis in the lower back rather than the whole body)

Many people think that because most bottles of herbs do not list specific amounts of each herb on the bottles, the formulas are secret. Instead, if you look up the ancient formula, you can see the exact proportions of each herb. Some Chinese herbal formulas can be used without understanding TCM theory. For example, most cases of severe arthritis in dogs correspond to a single Chinese syndrome known as "bony bi." If you use Chinese herbal formulas for bony bi syndrome, you are treating all the things related to arthritis that we see in these cases. In contrast, if a pet has a problem such as inflammatory bowel disease, which can be associated with different symptoms and respond to different things in Western medicine, you will see a similar range of options in Chinese herbal medicine: there are lots of possible treatments. To use the correct formula, a veterinarian must characterize many of the animal's symptoms to determine a Chinese pattern before recommending a formula.

Although humans usually take Chinese herbs three times per day, animals are typically treated at intervals of twice per day. Chinese herbs come in many forms: teas, tinctures, large pills, tea pills (small pills), and powders. Most pets will not drink Chinese herbal teas, although some are claimed to do so. Chinese herbal teas are usually strong, are often bitter, and have a pronounced herbal taste. Tinctures can work, especially if you set them in a pan of hot water when first opening the bottle, to drive off excess alcohol. (If you follow this approach, make sure the final dose you give is not too strong, because the herbal part of the tincture is now more concentrated.) Tinctures are usually administered directly into the mouth. Powders, by comparison, are usually mixed in the food. This approach works well if the pet is a real chow-hound, but otherwise is more difficult. Tablets or small round tea pills are the form most often used to give Chinese herbs to animals. Your veterinarian will let you know the correct dose for your pet's size.

You can find practitioners who use Chinese herbs in Table 10.1. Unfortunately, there are a number of veterinarians who practice Chinese medicine who are not on the various lists identified in the table. The list at the Chi Institute indicates those who have completed herbal training and certification through this organization. The IVAS list is currently a little difficult to use to find a Chinese veterinary herbalist, and the AAVA list does not have this information. The best way to find someone who uses Chinese herbs is to identify the veterinary acupuncturists in your area and then call and ask them.

OTHER HERBS FOR VETERINARY PRACTICE

There are two other general groups of herbs that holistic veterinarians may use: Ayurvedic herbs (from India) and Western herbs, which include European, North American, and some South American herbs. Ayurvedic medicine bears some resemblance to Chinese medicine: the system is thousands of years old, patterns of disease are recognized, and herbs are recommended according to patterns rather than named disease. Recently, research on a number of Indian herbs has sought to verify that they have the specific properties attributed to them in Ayurvedic medicine.

Ayurvedic Medicine

Like Chinese medicine, Ayurvedic medicine is based on the idea of balance. Ayurveda says the body is made of three doshas: vatta, pitta, and kapha. Vatta controls the mind and basic body functions (such as heartbeat and breathing). Pitta is responsible for the digestive system and for hormonal control. Kapha controls strength, immunity, and growth. Herbs are prescribed on the basis of the balance of these three doshas. For humans, treatment may also include recommendations for diet and lifestyle changes.

Western Herbs

Most Western herbs are used either as individual herbs or as combinations of herbs doing the same thing. Most pet owners are much more familiar with these products, and they are easier to find at herb stores than Chinese or Ayurvedic herbs. Echinacea is an excellent example of this type of herb.

The quality of information about herbs and the actual quality of the herbal products themselves vary widely. The Veterinary Botanical Medical Association (VBMA) is an association made up of veterinarians interested in herbal medicine and knowledgeable herbalists who have things to contribute about herbs for animals. Many of the VBMA members use Western herbs.

The American Botanical Council supplies expert-reviewed information on herbs and has published the German Commission E papers on these products. In Germany, the government must approve any herbs that are sold; the governmental body handles this task is called Commission E. The Commission E monographs cover more than 300 herbs and include information on the uses, indications, side effects, contraindications, and pharmacological actions of each herb. This organization does not simply rubber stamp each herb; rather, it rejects those that fail to meet the German standards. When an application is rejected, the corresponding monograph states the side effects and pharmacological actions of the herb.

In the United States, the path to use of Western herbs typically begins with a Western diagnosis, thorough physical examination, lab tests, and sometimes x-rays. A good veterinarian may combine Western herbs with standard medicine, or even use Western herbs to counteract the side effects of drugs or to decrease the amount of a dangerous drug that may be needed. These herbs are most often used in a way similar to U.S. drugs, so often the particulars of their administration can be easier to learn. However, to use them to best effect, a veterinarian should be familiar with all of these herbs' actions, including their potential interactions and side effects.

CHIROPRACTIC

Chiropractic is the manipulation of joints to improve musculoskeletal health. In most states, chiropractic on animals can be performed only by a veterinarian, or by a chiropractor under the direct supervision of a veterinarian. Because of some differences between animals and humans, before an animal is treated by a chiropractor it should be examined and x-rayed by a veterinarian. Chiropractors should be aware of the applicable anatomical and physiological differences, especially between dogs and humans. The best way for them to do so, and for veterinarians to receive training in chiropractic, is to become certified by the American Veterinary Chiropractic Association (AVCA). This certification ensures that practitioners are aware of differences in the curve of the cervical spine, the dangers of adjusting a back in dogs with ruptured intervertebral discs, and the need to x-ray dogs that have been hit by a car.

Once the veterinary exam has been done, animals that are in pain—especially those with rigidity, decreased range of motion, or muscle spasms—often benefit from a chiropractic adjustment. Likewise, for animals that improve with acupuncture or massage, but not on a long-term basis, sometimes chiropractic is a better answer.

You can find AVCA-certified practitioners by visiting the organization website (see Table 10.1).

VETERINARY ORTHOPEDIC MANIPULATION

Another way of manipulating the spine is by using someone trained veterinary orthopedic manipulation (VOM). By using equipment similar to some that is used by chiropractors, VOM practitioners treat fixations in spinal joints and release trigger points. VOM training is available only to veterinarians, and to chiropractors and other professionals who work directly with veterinarians. See Table 10.1 for information on finding a practitioner with VOM training.

OSTEOPATHY

Osteopathy, which is relatively new to the veterinary world, also aims to correct problems with a malfunctioning neuromuscular system and can be used for the same type of problems that chiropractic addresses. Osteopathic manipulations are performed a little differently than chiropractic adjustments, so any person performing this therapy must be trained in its use. There is a certification course in osteopathy available for veterinarians, but currently it emphasizes horses only, and many more non-veterinarians have been trained than veterinarians.

PROLOTHERAPY

Prolotherapy consists of the injection of high concentrations of dextrose mixed with a local anesthetic and often with vitamin B_{12} to create scar tissue. This treatment is used in pets with unstable joints, especially in the back or knees. If a pet has a tendon or ligament problem and is not yet ready for surgery, or if you dislike the idea of surgery, prolotherapy may be helpful.

Prolotherapy should be performed only by a veterinarian who has experience with this modality. Also, good knowledge of animal anatomy is required, so you should avoid non-veterinarians who offer this service. Prolotherapy is a relatively new therapy, and even for humans the number of practitioners is not very large.

NATURAL NUTRITION

Natural nutrition is based on the idea that pets should eat only natural ingredients. This approach to pet care emphasizes that pet foods should be free of artificial flavors, colors, and preservatives, as well as plant or animal derivatives such as gluten or by-products. In addition, food should be as fresh as possible. Most holistic veterinarians agree with these precepts. One group advocates feeding pets

DID YOU KNOW?

- Holistic veterinarians were using many supplements before they became accepted as part of regular veterinary practice.
- Prebiotics (fiber in foods) and probiotics (such as acidophilus) have been studied recently in conventional veterinary medicine as being important for general intestinal health.
- Pet owners are using an increasing amount of holistic treatments for themselves and their pets. In 2009, 38 percent of U.S. adults reported using some form of holistic treatment for themselves, and pet owners bought $1.4 billion worth of animal supplements.

(primarily dogs and cats) only raw meat with slightly cooked vegetables. Some recommend that they eat bones as their only source of calcium.

The problem with diets that are too extreme is that not all animals do well on them. Some do not have enough stomach acid to fully digest bones. Others do better with lightly cooked meats. All, however, do better when they eat foods without artificial flavors, colors, and preservatives. Also, the addition of gluten (usually in the form of corn gluten meal) to many pet foods is one factor that has contributed to many animals' chronic gastrointestinal diseases.[3] Feeding a homemade diet, or one based on whole foods, can help many of these pets recover. Unfortunately, many of the published homemade diets are unbalanced. To obtain a balanced diet, you can submit a request for such a plan, with the ingredients you wish to use, to board-certified veterinary nutritionists. They will recommend diets with the proper proportions and specific vitamin-mineral mixes to balance the diet.

Many natural diets are marketed today. Several are now sold by the "big box" pet stores, but you can also find them at smaller pet stores that specialize in natural diets and supplements. Some other diets are labeled as "natural," but actually just add some natural ingredients to a diet containing food derivatives. A truly natural diet does not have corn gluten meal, meat or poultry by-products, or artificial flavors, colors, or preservatives. Ideally, meat will be used instead of meat meal (although it can be difficult to properly make a dry food without meat meal). Meat meal has been pressure cooked until all the liquid has boiled off, then ground into a meal. Some amino acids (the building blocks of protein) evaporate with the liquid during this process, and cross-linkage of amino acids may occur so that the resulting components cannot be as easily digested.

There is one type of natural diet that may not be as good as it sounds: dehydrated meat. This product is crunchy like a dry food, but made of pure meat. At least some animals have problems with it. Many pets tend to swallow food whole, or in large chunks. Since dehydrated meat does not always rehydrate well inside animals, it can prevent them from getting the full benefit of their meal.

The best diet is one that contains meat and some vegetables and possibly some grain. Some pets do best on a grain-free diet, whereas others always have problems unless they eat a little grain. Some do best on a low-fiber diet (no vegetables), whereas others do better on a high-fiber diet. One way to determine which is best for your pet is to try a diet. If your pet's elimination consists of soft stools on this diet, slowly switch to one that uses different groups of ingredients. For example, if you feed a product containing meat, vegetables, fruits, and grains, and your pet does not do well, first try a diet based on meat and grains or meat and potatoes. If this approach does not work, you may want to try fish or poultry instead of meat. If you are feeding canned food to your pet, you might try a homemade diet. If you are feeding raw food and your pet does not do well, try cooking the food. In general, pets do better on natural diets than on cheaper commercial diets, but you may have to experiment to find the form of natural diet that works the best for your companion animal.

NUTRACEUTICALS

Nutraceuticals are nutritional substances that are used for disease prevention and control. They include vitamins (e.g., vitamin E), minerals (e.g., zinc), amino acids (e.g., DLPA [DL-phenylalanine]), co-factors for chemical reactions in the body (e.g., CoQ 10), and basic building blocks (such as glucosamine). Of all the methods used by holistic veterinarians, administration of nutraceuticals is the one that has been most rapidly integrated into "regular" veterinary practice. This approach is particularly likely to be used in dermatology practices, and more recently in pet foods and supplements for arthritis.

Nutraceuticals are used for many reasons. The most common reasons are to improve an animal's skin and coat and to help the joints of older pets. Some products, such as fish oil, have many benefits and so can be used for many purposes. Fish oil helps skin and joints by suppressing PGE_2, a molecule that promotes inflammation.[4] Fish oil also helps animals with cancer by increasing survival time, increasing time in remission, decreasing side effects of radiation therapy, and decreasing cancer cachexia (weight loss and wasting away from cancer).[5]

A broad group of nutraceuticals are antioxidants, which include vitamins A, C, and E, among others. When giving vitamins, it is best to give all factors involved with those vitamins, to get the best results. For example, when giving vitamin C, include bioflavonoids; when giving vitamin A, include carotenoids (all of them, not just beta carotene). Also give antioxidants as a group: vitamin E works best, with a decrease in side effects associated with higher doses, when given with vitamin C.

Be sure you know the potential side effects or drug interactions of any supplements you are giving. Some side effects, such as the diarrhea that comes from excess vitamin C, are relatively harmless. Others, such as the serotonin syndrome seen when you combine the amino acid DLPA with the painkiller Tramadol, can be fatal.

Supplements that can help skin include fish oil, vitamin E (be sure to use it with vitamin C), vitamin A (be careful of toxic overdose), and zinc. Supplements that help bad joints include glucosamine, chondroitin, methylsulfonylmethane (MSM), fish oil, the amino acid DLPA (not if you are using Tramadol) and vitamins C and E.

HOMEOPATHY

Homeopathy is based on the philosophy that "like cures like." It assumes that if a substance causes certain signs in large doses (such as digitalis poisoning causing heart problems), use of the same substance in extremely small doses will help that problem. Another tenet of homeopathy is that as you are being cured of one disease, you will temporarily see signs of previous illnesses.

The recommendation of a homeopathic substance depends on a complex analysis of symptoms; it is not as simple as saying "arnica is good for bruises." If you look at any book on homeopathy, you will see that more than one remedy can work for a specific problem. However, the way a homeopath chooses a particular remedy is to see which of all those remedies matches all other signs seen in the patient, even if they do not seem to have anything to do with the main problem. (This is similar to the Chinese method of looking at the whole body, and choosing from general herbs the one which best matches the Chinese pattern of symptoms.)

Classical homeopathy can achieve some amazing results, but it can take a long time (months), and results may be only partial if the remedy is not the correct one. For Americans used to a quick fix, it can be hard to be patient, but remember this when working with a homeopath.

The Academy of Veterinary Homeopathy (AVH) is the organization that certifies veterinarians in homeopathy. You can find a list of certified veterinary homeopaths, as well as veterinarians with a special interest in homeopathy, by accessing the websites given in Table 10.1.

HOMOTOXICOLOGY

Homotoxicology was developed in the 1950s by a German physician, Dr. Reckeweg. He correlated Western diagnoses of disease with various homeopathic items and created combination remedies using multiple ingredients of various dilutions. In addition, he developed the idea that disease is caused by toxins that invade the interstitial spaces (the spaces between body cells, which Reckeweg called the matrix). Thus, to cure a disease, you need to remove the toxins from the matrix. This idea has been confirmed more recently by research in humans, and there is an organization, the Institute for Functional Medicine, that has a yearly meeting highlighting the role these toxins play in chronic disease.

Homotoxicology uses remedies both to get rid of these toxins and to address the diseases themselves. There is no certification program at this time for homotoxicology, but you can search for veterinarians with a special interest in homotoxicology at the American Holistic Veterinary Medical Association's website.

MASSAGE THERAPY

A number of forms of massage therapy exist, not all of which are suited for animals. Many massage therapists are unaware of this fact, so if you take your pet to a massage therapist, be sure he or she has worked with animals or is associated with a veterinarian. Training in massage therapy is available to veterinarians, physical therapists, and technicians as part of physical therapy certification programs.

Massage therapy is especially helpful for muscular problems, for senior animals, and for pets recovering from surgery. Pain from muscle spasms is often misdiagnosed as joint pain or intervertebral disc disease. While pain can be difficult to diagnose for a veterinarian without training, its source is much easier to pick up for a good massage therapist. Massage, including trigger point therapy, can have amazing results; for example, relief of a muscle spasm can result in an instant 30 percent increase in muscle strength.

Trigger point therapy is the release of spasms caused by a "trigger point" in a muscle. These points consist of hyperreflexive areas in the muscle that easily go into spasm after exposure to cold, wind, or even sudden movement.[6] If the point stays in spasm long enough, it will recruit neighboring fibers until whole muscles or muscle regions will be one big, tight mass. If the spasm is not released in the trigger point, the main spasm will never release. A good massage therapist will be able to find and release these points and help you learn to release them yourself.

Massage therapists may be associated with a specific practice, or they may be part of a physical therapy group. Massage therapy works best when integrated with at least one other form of physical therapy, such as acupuncture, chiropractic, swim therapy, or underwater treadmill use.

TTOUCH

TTouch is a special kind of touch therapy, derived from work done by Feldenkreis for humans. By touching animals in specific ways and by helping them to move in special ways (through mazes, over bridges, and so on), animals are "reintroduced" to their bodies. The result can be a reduction in long-term chronic pain and some amazing behavioral changes. Some veterinarians are trained in TTouch, but most practitioners of this modality are not veterinarians. If your pet is suffering and other methods are not working, it can be worthwhile to look into this therapy. If your veterinarian does not know any TTouch practitioner, you can look for one online.

REIKI

Reiki is a special kind of energy work developed in Japan, where hands are placed above—not on—the patient. It is especially good at calming pets, and some veterinarians employ Reiki practitioners in their practices for this purpose. A practitioner is not taught Reiki—instead, he or she is "attuned" in a few sessions with a Reiki master. Some holistic veterinarians practice Reiki or, if they do not, can refer you to a Reiki practitioner.

DETOXIFICATION

The idea of fasting is to decrease the amount of toxins to which an animal is exposed so as to let the body process toxins that are already in the body. Pets are constantly exposed to toxins in the form of insecticides, deworming products, disinfectants, and other items that are processed by the liver. Insecticides and dewormers are not 100 percent benign: if your pet is overdosed on them, he will get sick. With a large enough exposure, an animal may die. The reason these products may be used successfully is that the amount administered is typically small enough for the pet's liver to process it to a benign form, but large enough to kill fleas, ticks, and worms. If a pet is exposed to too many toxins at once, or if he has a liver that functions more slowly than the average liver, these toxins will build up in the animal's body.

The body creates some toxins of its own. You can see evidence of this process in certain diseases. For example, urea is created from waste products of protein metabolism. When the kidneys are not functioning properly, the amount of urea in the blood increases, and an animal becomes toxic. Other chemicals are also created as part of normal liver function; if the liver is not functioning properly or if it is overloaded, these chemicals can build up in the animal's system. At first, they will be stored in the fat. When fat depots are full, however, the toxins will circulate more widely and build up in the interstitial spaces (spaces between cells). This effect can cause chronic inflammation, chronic pain, and increased susceptibility to infections.

While homotoxicology addresses this problem, another way of removing the toxins, or detoxifying, is to use a modified fast. A body needs certain substances every day, including a small amount of protein, to function properly. If these materials are not provided, the body will tear down muscle to get protein, raid other sources for whatever it can find, or suffer from decreased or lower functioning of the processes that manage toxins. For these reasons, a complete fast is counterproductive. In contrast, a partial fast, in which the body still receives enough of these items, plus everything the liver needs to process the toxins and protect itself, is a quicker way to get rid of the toxins.

Sometimes even a partial fast works a little too quickly. Cats especially can have problems with fasting and, if done for too long, may develop hepatic lipidosis (fatty liver, where a large part of the liver is replaced by fat), a potentially fatal disease. This effect can happen in as little as three days, especially in obese cats. It is best not to fast cats for longer than one day. Dogs that are already weak, sick, or toxic may also have adverse reactions to fasting. Thus, when subjecting any animal to a fast, it is best to do so under the supervision of a veterinarian who is familiar with the concept.

You may also hear the term "detox" (detoxification) as a description of the process in which an animal naturally eliminates toxins from the body without fasting. This reaction, which occurs when the body gets rid of toxins, may appear as vomiting, diarrhea, excess urination, or just greasy, dandruffy skin until the toxins are gone. When switched to a better diet, sometimes the animal will react this way.

BACH FLOWER REMEDIES (OR ESSENCES)

Bach (pronounced "batch," not like the name of the composer Bach, although very few people pronounce it correctly) was a British physician who noted the relationship between unhealthy emotional states and disease. He created 38 remedies to help cure these problems, and classified them based on 7 primary mental states: fear, uncertainty, insufficient interest in present circumstances, loneliness, oversensitivity to influences and ideas, despondency or despair, and over-care for the welfare of others (Table 10.2).

Table 10.2
Bach Flower Remedies

Mental State	Subtype of Mental State	Remedy
Fear	Terror or panic	Rock rose
	Ordinary everyday fears	Mimulus
	Vague fear that something dreadful is going to happen	Aspen
	Fear of stress	Cherry plum
	Fear for others	Red chestnut blossom
Uncertainty	No confidence in oneself	Cerato
	Inability to decide between two things	Scleranthus
	Easily discouraged	Gentian
	Unable to believe anything more can be done	Gorse
	Fear the one does not have enough strength to carry on	Hornbeam
	Want to do something great but no great calling	Wild oat

(Continued)

Table 10.2 (Continued)

Mental State	Subtype of Mental State	Remedy
Insufficient interest in present circumstances	Not happy in one's present circumstances	Clematis
	Living in the past	Honeysuckle
	Gliding resignedly through life	Wild rose
	Suffered so much he or she gave up	Olive
	Obsession	White chestnut
	Clinical depression	Mustard
	Cannot learn from the past experience	Chestnut bud
Loneliness	Independent types	Water violet
	Want everything done faster	Impatiens
	Always need to be with others	Heather
Over-sensitivity to influences and ideas	Agree with others just to keep the peace	Agrimony
	Serve others and neglect oneself	Centaury
	Swayed from own ideals by others	Walnut
	Jealousy, envy, revenge, or suspicion when there is no need	Holly
Despondency or despair	Think one is never as good as others	Larch
	Always blame oneself	Pine
	Think everything one tries is too hard to achieve	Elm
	Feel life is unbearable	Sweet chestnut
	Sudden misfortune brings great unhappiness	Star of Bethlehem
	Resent misfortune	Willow
	Fighting strongly to get well	Oak
	Must get rid of something dirty in one's body	Crab apple
Over-care for welfare of others	Worried about one's family	Chicory
	Want everyone to do things one's own way	Vervain
	Believe others would benefit from doing things the way one does	Grapevine
	See good in all people and all that surrounds them	Beech
	Deny oneself pleasure because it will interfere with one's work	Rock water

You may already be familiar with the most popular of the Bach flower remedies: Rescue Remedy, which is a mix of 5 of the original 38 remedies (rock rose, impatiens, clematis, star of Bethlehem, and cherry plum), and is especially good for anxiety. Most holistic practitioners are aware of this remedy and may recommend it for use in animals before going on car rides (for pets who get car sick) or before visiting the veterinarian. Specific Bach remedies are used for specific subtypes of anxiety or other emotional problems.

The 38 Bach remedies are prepared somewhat like homeopathic preparations, but are almost all derived from flowers. They are diluted in a homeopathic manner, but are more robust—for example, they can be put in hot drinks, whereas this preparation is not recommended for homeopathic remedies.

Several companies make similar preparations, and some others go beyond the original 38 that Bach created. Purists believe that only the original ones are valid, whereas other practitioners believe the newer ones can also have some great effects.

AROMATHERAPY

Aromatherapy is another plant-based method, albeit one that is based on essential oils that are steam-distilled from various plants. Most of the plants used for this purpose are flowers or herbs, but any aromatic plant may have some benefit. The biggest mistake that people make is to use excess amounts of aromatherapy oils for therapeutic purposes. Any natural treatment, in a high enough concentration, can have a toxic effect on humans—and on their pets as well. Dogs and cats have a much more sensitive sense of smell than humans, so aromatherapy products in high concentration can cause skin irritation, headaches, and even seizures. High concentrations can even be toxic to an animal's liver, so you should not use aromatherapy unless you know what you are doing. This is especially true of their use in cats, as items that may be safe for dogs and humans may not be safe for cats.

Aromatherapy oils are diluted in carrier oils before use. All such oils should be natural and plant derived. After proper dilution, a drop or two may be placed on the top of the animal's head or on the collar to help with various problems. Some uses, such as application of lavender oil to fight infections,[7] have been verified by research. Aromatherapy products can be found in candles, incense, some herbal collars, shampoos, and sprays. Before you use any of these products, be sure to consult a holistic veterinarian who is familiar with aromatherapy to be sure you will not harm your pet.

ANIMAL COMMUNICATORS

Many people claim to be able to talk to animals. Some of them are very crafty at extracting information from you in general conversation and presenting it back to you later as what your pet told them. Perhaps they really believe they are accomplishing something, but the ones who really are doing what they say they can do generally do not want a big history from the pet's owner. (Too many facts can interfere with what they are doing, so that they cannot tell if their findings reflect what you said or what the pet said.)

Communicators are best at communicating what animals are feeling and may give you insight into specific behavior problems. A good communicator may start by describing an incident or a specific toy that you did not tell them about, and then going on from there. The best way to judge a communicator is by the results: Did the person pick up on the problem? Did he or she give you new insight? Did the communicator confirm something you were wondering about, or maybe your veterinarian's recommendations? It is always good to have two professionals who agree with each other. This makes their opinions even more valid.

CONCLUSION

Holistic veterinary medicine, or CAVM, is especially good at treating chronic conditions and can complement conventional treatments, making them more effective. It may even have a solution for a problem that Western medicine has no answer for. CAVM may be the answer you need for problems you have been unable to resolve using other ways or means. Finally, some other forms of holistic therapy are less widely used, but you may run across a holistic veterinarian who performs them.

REFERENCES

1. Colbert, A. P., A. Larsen, and S. Chamberlin, et al. "A Multichannel System for Continuous Measurements of Skin Resistance and Capacitance at Acupuncture Points." *Journal of Acupuncture Meridian Studies* 2, no. 4 (2009): 259–68.

2. Smith, F. W. K. "The Neurophysiological Basis of Acupuncture." In *Veterinary Acupuncture*, edited by A. M. Schoen. St. Louis, MO: Mosby; 1994: 33–53.

3. Gaschen, F. P. "Is It Time to Revisit Adverse Reactions to Food in Dogs and Cats?" In *Proceedings*. American College of Veterinary Internal Medicine; 2008. Available at: http://www.vin.com/Members/Proceedings/Proceedings.plx?CID=acvim2008&PID=pr22982&O=VIN

4. Gueck, T., et al. "Alterations of Mast Cell Mediator Production and Release by Gamma-Linolenic and Docosahexaenoic Acid." *Veterinary Dermatology* 15 (2004): 309–314.

5. Davenport, D. J. "Use of Nutraceuticals in Cancer Therapy. In *Proceedings*. Western Veterinary Conference; 2006. Available at: http://www.vin.com/Members/Proceedings/Proceedings.plx?CID=wvc2006&PID=pr11859&O=VIN

6. Niel-Asher, S. *The Concise Book of Trigger Points*, rev. ed. Berkeley, CA: North Atlantic Books; 2008: 26.

7. Cavanagh, H. M., and J. M. Wilkinson. "Biological Activities of Lavender Essential Oil." *Phytotherapy Research* 16, no. 4 (2002): 301–8.

FURTHER READING

Bland J. *The 20-Day Rejuvenation Diet Program.* Lincolnwood, IL: McGraw-Hill; 1999. (For a more complete discussion of detoxification)

Blumenthal, M., ed. *The Complete German Commission E Monographs.* Austin, TX: American Botanical Council; 1998. (Translation of the German studies on Western herbs, with references)

Pitcairn, R., and S. Pitcairn. *Dr. Pitcairn's New Complete Guide to Natural Health for Dogs and Cats.* Emmaus, PA: Rodale; 2006.

Schwartz, C. *Four Paws Five Directions.* Berkeley, CA: Celestial Arts Publishing; 1996. (Good discussion of Chinese medicine, acupuncture, and Chinese herbs)

11

Pet Nutrition

Mark B. Taylor, MA, DVM

Nutrition is loosely defined by some as a science where the interactions of "nutrients" such as vitamins, minerals, proteins, fats, carbohydrates, and water are tested and studied in organisms. Nonscientists refer to nutrition as a process of assimilating the right combination of foodstuffs needed to grow or maintain bodily functions. Malnutrition, in contrast, can be defined as under- or over-supplementation of one or more nutrients. For example, in underdeveloped and impoverished countries, humans commonly suffer from protein malnutrition. In the United States, a significant proportion of the entire population suffers from over-nutrition (excess fat levels in daily diets). Over-nutrition can also be considered a form of malnutrition.

In companion animals, such as dogs and cats, the interactions of nutrients have been studied extensively, through the work of organizations such as the National Research Council (NRC) and the Association of American Feed Control Officials (AAFCO). Both NRC and AAFCO have been essential to both pet food manufacturers and veterinarians in developing safe and nutritious food for domestic dogs and cats by helping to formulate balanced commercial diets in domestic dogs and cats through all life stages (except geriatric stages).[1] A commercial "balanced" diet does not mean that the diet's weight is balanced with anything for comparison. Rather, a diet that is "balanced" contains the correct amount of all known essential nutrients (vitamins, minerals, fat, protein, and carbohydrates) necessary to sustain a particular life function such as growth, lactation, gestation, or maintenance.

HISTORY AND STANDARDS IN ANIMAL NUTRITION

Commercialized pet food has origins dating back to 1860, when James Spratt developed and manufactured a kibble that he sold for many years in England and eventually in the United States.[2] Through the decades, other manufacturers of such products appeared, such as Clarence Gaines of Gaines Dog Meal, and eventually the Ralston Purina Company. The first therapeutic diet designed for the treatment of renal disease was formulated by Mark Morris, Sr., in 1948.[2]

Due to the increased need for regulating and standardizing what domesticated dogs and cats were eating, AAFCO was officially formed in 1909.[1] This agency currently comprises government officials, but is not directly under government control or management. AAFCO creates guidelines that manufacturers can use in formulating pet foods. Because AAFCO is not under government control, states are not required to adhere to this organization's guidelines and recommendations; however, approximately 66 percent of all states have adopted AAFCO standards.[2] Those states that have not adopted AAFCO guidelines can potentially sell and distribute within their borders commercialized or privately manufactured diets that are unbalanced (under- or over-fortified with various nutrients).

The NRC is a nonprofit group that evaluates and compiles scientific literature pertaining to nutrients and their effects in domestic animals. Formed in 1916, the latest publication from the NRC relating to dogs and cats (*Nutrient Requirements of Dogs and Cats*, 2006) nicely summarizes all available literature on nutrients, including, in most cases, which effects excesses or deficiencies of a particular nutrient have on growing, gestating, lactating, and adult dogs and cats.[2] For each researched nutrient, the NRC has developed daily nutrient intake recommendations.

Every type of pet food or treat commercially sold in the United States must provide guaranteed analysis (GA) information on its label. The GA ensures that minimums and maximums of certain nutrients are contained in every package. Protein, fat, moisture, ash, and carbohydrates are typically listed. A GA, however, does not mean that the product is complete and balanced for a pet in a particular life stage. Thus, when marketing a product as a complete and balanced diet, pet food manufacturers must disclose on the product label the method used to validate the claim. Most commercial manufacturers in the United States use AAFCO standards and testing methods, which must be described using either of the following statements:

1. [Diet name] is formulated to meet nutritional levels established by AAFCO dog/cat food nutrient profiles for (gestation and lactation, growth, maintenance, or all life stages).
2. Animal feeding tests using AAFCO procedures substantiate that [diet name] provides complete and balanced nutrition for puppies/kittens for [life stage].[1, 2]

Any deviation from either of these statements is considered "misbranding" and a violation of the U.S. Code of Federal Regulations.

For the first statement to be used, a food formulated to meet nutritional levels established by AAFCO must be chemically analyzed by either a private or commercial laboratory. If the final analysis determines the diet contains a deficiency or an excess of a particular nutrient, the recipe must be altered until the product complies with AAFCO allowances.

For the second statement to be used, a feeding trial must be conducted. A feeding trial is a 6-month study in which 8 dogs or cats are fed exclusively the diet in question.[3] Prior to conducting the feeding trial, basic blood profiles and chemistry are performed; they are repeated at the conclusion of the 26-week period.[1] Body weights are also compared before and after the feeding trial. A growth feeding trial is conducted similarly, but only for 10 weeks during the most active growth phase of the puppy or kitten.[1]

NUTRIENTS OF CONCERN

It is beyond the scope of this chapter to explain in detail how nutrients (water, protein, fat, carbohydrates, vitamins, and minerals) are fully utilized biologically by the animal host, but a general coverage of these essential nutritional components is necessary to better understand the needs of your pet and how to meet them.

Water

Water is essential for life. From providing turgor pressure in plants to blood pressure in animals, water is the medium through which nutrients are carried from cell to cell. Water provides cellular support, allowing for diffusion of ions (charged atoms or molecules) and molecules from blood vessels (arteries and veins) to cells, or from cells to cells. Many biochemical reactions form water as the final product or use water as an intermediary substrate. Water, a component of blood, can be placed under pressure, allowing vessels to remain open. Distended vessels allow for nutrients, ions, hormones, zenobiotics (chemicals not found naturally in the body), and toxins to travel from various places in the body.[3] Water in sweat and saliva is also used to cool surfaces due to its evaporative properties.

Given its many critical roles, water must be the central focus of a pet's daily intake. Providing clean and plentiful water is important in keeping body systems regulated.

Protein

Proteins are polymers (chains) of amino acids (the most basic subunit of a protein) of varying lengths. "Essential" amino acids are those amino acids that cannot be synthesized by the host and must be supplied in the diet.[3] Nonessential amino acids are those amino acids that can be synthesized by the host and, therefore, are not required in the diet.[3] Both animal tissue and plant tissue contain protein; however, the types and amounts of nonessential and essential amino acid content of each tissue type vary substantially. Plant-based proteins contain more nonessential amino acids than animal protein—an important factor when considering what to feed growing kittens and puppies or animals with various types of disease such as liver failure.

Protein is used by the body in the synthesis or accretion of skeletal, cardiac, or smooth muscle, and for the synthesis of blood proteins that transport minerals or act as cellular messengers. Proteins can also be used in the synthesis of cellular membrane "gates" (channels or cell wall openings through which ions or nutrients move into or out of the cell). Finally, proteins are used as an energy source in the process of gluconeogenesis—the formation of glucose from the amino acid. In animals with impaired liver or kidney functioning, gluconeogenesis can lead to excessive circulating blood levels of ammonia, which can cause deleterious clinical signs such as (but not limited to) feeling unwell, vomiting, and anorexia.[3]

Fats

All mammals require fats (lipids) for synthesis of hormones, vitamins, cell membranes, and various intracellular and intercellular signaling events, and as a storage form of energy. Some types of fats can be synthesized within cells, whereas other types of fats must be consumed in the diet (essential fatty acids). As an energy source, fat provides twice the amount of energy as protein or carbohydrates (glucose). Thus, when thinking about feeding companion animals, it is important to understand how much dietary fat is consumed on a daily basis. Pet obesity is not only a syndrome, but is also considered to be a disease.

In terms of cholesterol, less consideration is paid to the effects of dietary fats on blood cholesterol levels in companion animals than in humans. Atherosclerosis (plaque formation in arteries) occurs with much less frequency in our pets than in humans. Many theories exist regarding the resistance of development of arteriole plaque in small animals, but are outside the scope of this discussion. In general, dietary fat levels are not restricted in pet feeding unless the pet is predisposed to pancreatitis or has problems processing dietary fat (with occurs in certain breeds of dogs, and in animals with liver disease, diabetes, or endocrine dysfunction).

Some types of fats have beneficial effects on the coat and skin of animals and have been shown to prevent or inhibit inflammation. Omega-3 fatty acids are a type of fatty acid (fat) that is found in plants, fish, and algae. Although several types of omega-3 fatty acids exist, only two types have been the focus of clinical research: docosahexaenoic acid (DHA) and eicosapentaoenoic acid (EPA). DHA and EPA are found in algae and cold-water fish such as salmon and herring. Other types of omega-3 fatty acids derived from plants such as linseed (flax) are commonly used in pet foods as a principal source of omega-3 fatty acids. Flax seed oil, however, is less than one-eighth as effective at preventing inflammation as DHA and EPA because mammals cannot convert the types of omega-3 fatty acids found in flax seed to DHA or EPA very efficiently. Recommended dosages of EPA and DHA for small animals range from 20 to 100 milligrams per kilogram of body weight per day.

Fish oil and other types of oil capsules rich in DHA and EPA are commonly sold to pet owners as supplements. Unfortunately, most of these supplements contain only fractions of the total amount of DHA that is currently recommended. In addition, supplementing an average-size dog with DHA can increase the daily feeding costs by more than 10 times, and may unbalance the diet through the addition of excessive fat (DHA is a type of fat that can be used as an energy source). Interestingly, therapeutic diets (prescription diets) formulated for skin or joint management contain the higher recommended dosages of EPA and DHA, making any fatty acid supplementation unnecessary.

Carbohydrates

Dietary carbohydrates are polymers (chains) of glucose and/or fructose, two types of sugars. Commercial forms of carbohydrates come from corn, rice, potato, barley, and wheat. Furthermore, carbohydrates can be used as a dietary source of fiber (fermentable or nonfermentable). Fermentable fiber sources promote colonic health, whereas nonfermentable fiber sources are used to add fecal bulk and help with elimination of waste.

Simple sugars are commonly classified as monosaccharides (one sugar unit), disaccharides (two sugar units), and trisaccharides (three sugar units).[3, 4] Examples of disaccharides include sucrose, lactose, and maltose. Simple sugars are readily absorbed through the process of digestion.

Complex carbohydrates are typically defined as four or more units of glucose and/or fructose linked together. A polymer of glucose can be digestible or indigestible, depending on how the glucose units are linked together. For example, cellulose (wood pulp) is a simple polymer of glucose, yet the way in which the glucose units are linked makes it indigestible. In commercial and therapeutic pet foods, cellulose may be added to help with gut motility and to facilitate elimination of feces. Added dietary cellulose can help with satiety because it adds bulk, leading to the sensation of feeling full.

Fermentable fiber sources contain polymers of fructose. They are utilized by bacteria in the colon, which in turn make useful and essential by-products for

DID YOU KNOW?

Pet allergies to corns and grains are often reported, but are actually a myth. In reality, the most common food allergens in dogs are beef, dairy, chicken, lamb, and egg. Wheat can be an allergen, but less than 15 percent of all dogs in a recent study were allergic to wheat, and fewer than 6 percent of all dogs were allergic to corn. For cats, beef, dairy, fish, lamb, and poultry were the top offending allergens.

the host. Examples of fermentable fiber sources include juice pulp, pectin, beets, and whole fruits.

Vitamins

Many vitamins are essential for maintenance and growth. For a molecule to be considered a vitamin, it must meet the following criteria:

- It must be essential such that without it clinical signs of deficiency will be seen.
- It must be derived from the diet and not able to be synthesized by the host.
- It cannot be a protein, fatty acid, or carbohydrate.[5]

It is important to note that vitamins have been defined in more stringent terms in other sources and that different hosts (e.g., dog, cat, pig, sheep, primate, and human) have different vitamin requirements. For example, dogs and cats synthesize vitamin C, so it is not required in their diet. Thus vitamin C for the dog and cat is not essential and technically not considered to be a vitamin.

Vitamins can be classified into two basic categories: water soluble and fat soluble. Fat-soluble vitamins (vitamin A, D, E, and K) are vitamins that dissolve readily in fat; thus they are easily assimilated and stored by the host. In fact, overzealous supplementation of fat-soluble vitamins can cause toxicity.

Vitamin A (retinol) is derived from a group of compounds called carotenoids, which are found in yellow and orange fruits, vegetables, and tubers. This vitamin is essential for growth and reproduction, vision, and maintenance of healthy skin, and it is involved with protein synthesis.[5, 6]

Vitamin D is essential for blood calcium regulation through intestinal absorption, is required for bone development, and has been recently been implicated as being significant in a properly functioning immune system.[6] Unlike humans and other species, dogs and cats cannot convert a vitamin D precursor, dehydrocholesterol, in the skin to a more active form of vitamin D. While we humans can create vitamin D while basking in the sun, dogs and cats do not have this adaptation.

Vitamin E acts as a free-radical (a molecule with an unpaired electron) scavenger and has the ability to donate an electron to those molecules that are acting as free radicals.[4] If left as free radicals, these molecules would have the potential to denature or alter proteins and damage DNA. Vitamin C molecules would then replace the electrons that the vitamin E molecules donated. Fats in pet food are particularly susceptible to spontaneously forming free radicals as a result of exposure to addition of light, heat, or air, so vitamin E is a common additive in pets foods to prevent free-radical events that cause rancidity.

Last among the fat-soluble vitamins, vitamin K is important in bone development and essential in the blood clotting process. For example, common rodenticides interfere with the major action of vitamin K, rendering the host's blood unable to clot, and ultimately leading to the animal's death.

Water-soluble vitamins can be divided into the B vitamins and vitamin C. These nutrients are more difficult to absorb than the fat-soluble vitamins.

The B vitamins include thiamin, riboflavin, niacin, pantothenic acid, pyridoxine, cobalamin, folic acid, choline, and biotin. Whole grains, liver, vegetables, poultry, and yeast are excellent sources of many of these vitamins. Specific functions of B vitamins are well known, and these vitamins are known to be involved in almost every step of cellular metabolism. In fact, adding B vitamins to the diet can actually increase the metabolism and stimulate the appetite.

Vitamin C (ascorbic acid) is essential for bone and collagen development, functioning of the immune system, and prevention of periodontal disease.[5, 6] As mentioned earlier, it also helps prevent the formation of free radicals by regenerating vitamin E. Unlike the B vitamins, vitamin C is found in citrus fruits and many vegetables. Cats and dogs do not technically have a requirement for vitamin C because they can synthesize it within their bodies. Humans, primates, guinea pigs, and some species of birds and bats, however, do require vitamin C.

Minerals

Minerals are required for (but their use is not limited to) cellular functioning, nerve conduction, regulation of various cellular channels (openings in the cell membrane), regulation of blood pressure, and blood acid-base status. Minerals can be classified into three categories based on the relative amounts that are required by the body: macro, micro, and trace. Macro minerals include calcium, phosphorus, magnesium, sodium, potassium, and chloride. Micro minerals include iron, zinc, copper, manganese, iodine, and selenium. Trace minerals include chromium and boron. With the exception of the trace minerals, AAFCO has determined the maximum and minimum safe levels of the various minerals to be supplied in pet food.

SPECIAL CONSIDERATIONS FOR CATS

When it comes to the formulation of pet food, certain unique factors must be considered in developing diets for cats. For example, cats are unable to synthesize taurine (an amino acid), cannot utilize carotene as a vitamin A source, and are unable to synthesize vitamin D in the skin.[7]

Taurine is a sulfur-containing amino acid that is used in the development of the retina and is necessary for the prevention of dilated cardiomyopathy (thinning of the walls of the heart). It also combines with bile acids to form bile salts, which are used in the digestion process to emulsify fatty acids. Without emulsification (dispersing or breaking up fat), little fat from the diet would be absorbed. Unlike dogs, cats cannot synthesize taurine from various precursors due to the low activity of two necessary enzymes within their system. Including taurine supplementation in commercial diets has proved problematic due to the formation of various types of sugars during the heating process that is employed in manufacturing these foods.[7] When unusual sugars are present, they become available to the bacterial population of the cat's colon, causing these organisms to grow in large numbers. The increased bacterial population then metabolizes the taurine intended for the host.[2, 7] To prevent taurine from being depleted by the colonic bacteria, manufacturers have made changes in the cooking and canning process to reduce the amount of sugars formed.[2]

Cats also are dependent on arginine (an amino acid found in meat) and arachidonic acid (a type of fat in animal flesh) to ensure their good health. A diet without these nutrients can have serious consequences. For example, feeding kittens an arginine-free diet can result in the development of neurological signs, weight loss, coma, and even death.[7] Researchers have determined that cats need arginine in their diet to convert ammonia to urea (the urea cycle), which is then excreted by the kidneys and eliminated from the body. Without a functioning urea cycle, ammonia levels rapidly build in the bloodstream and cause severe neurological symptoms. Arginine is found in skeletal meats and organs, which is why cats should not be fed a vegetarian diet.

All mammals except cats can convert dietary linoleic acid (a type of fat) to arachidonic acid.[7] Arachidonic acid is used for the production of eicosanoids, which are essential for growth, reproduction, neuronal cell signaling, and the inflammation response.[3] Sources rich in arachidonic acid include animal fat, muscle, and organ tissue.

Vitamin A is derived from carotene in all mammals except felines. Carotene is a molecule that, when cleaved in the middle, yields two molecules of vitamin A (retinol).[4] Vitamin A is essential in the development of the retina, genetic transcription, immune functioning, embryonic metabolism, and many other functions.[5, 6] In cats, the enzyme necessary for cleaving carotene into two retinols is lacking. Animal tissue such as organ and skeletal meats, however, contain abundant levels of retinol.

Nicotinic acid (NAD, also known as vitamin B_3) is essential in cellular metabolism and can be synthesized from tryptophan, an essential amino acid found in meats, grains, vegetables, and fruit.[6] Two metabolic pathways exist in dogs and cats to form NAD; however, in cats, one of two pathways is dominating, preventing the other pathway from forming NAD. Thus NAD must be added to commercial diets for cats to prevent deficiencies.

Cats either lack or have limited quantities of enzymes necessary for digesting or assimilating carbohydrates, yet—remarkably—they have been shown to be rather efficient at assimilating carbohydrates.[3, 7] In the majority of commercial diets, a significant proportion of calories stem from carbohydrates, leading to an ongoing and rather heated debate as to whether carbohydrates should even be fed to cats.

One last unique trait regarding the nutrition of cats: cats are unable to process dietary sugars efficiently because they lack two enzymes, hexokinase and fructokinase.[7]

FEEDING LARGE-BREED DOGS

A large-breed dog is commonly defined as a puppy that will have a final adult weight of more than 50 pounds. Some sources further classify large-breed dogs such as Great Danes and mastiffs as giant-breed dogs. Regardless of the classification, certain nutrient requirements must be considered when feeding the large-breed puppy, particularly in regard to calcium and fat. Early research demonstrated that feeding large-breed puppies large amounts of calcium and/or fat through their most active growth phase (3 to 6 months) causes a range of developmental orthopedic diseases (DOD). The most common DODs seen include, but are not limited to, hip and elbow dysplasia. Even if the diet is corrected shortly after the active growth phase is finished, DODs can manifest long after growth has stopped.

Large-breed growth diets have been formulated to be less energy dense (less fat) and to contain reduced amounts of calcium and other nutrients relative to regular growth diets. This modification is necessary due to the enormous differences in stomach volumes between large, small, and toy breeds. Regular and small-breed puppy growth diets are higher in energy and nutrient density relative to large-breed growth diets—a difference meant to ensure the small or toy puppy will be able to satisfy her energy and nutrient requirements when her stomach is full. Because such dogs have a smaller stomach, their food must be more energy dense to meet their needs. Conversely, a mastiff puppy eating a small-breed or regular puppy chow may consume too much energy and nutrients before feeling satiated, resulting in excessive energy (fat) and calcium intake, and making DOD much more likely.[8] Maintaining optimal body condition through the transition into adulthood is extremely important in the large breed and is easier to achieve by feeding these pets a large-breed growth diet. Current recommendations suggest feeding these animals a large-breed puppy diet until they reach 12 to 16 months of age.

FEEDING PUPPIES AND KITTENS

Puppies and kittens have dietary requirements that are different from those of adults. In particular, their overall nutritional requirements are greater. As such, commercial growth diets are formulated to be higher in fat to accommodate these youngsters' needs for growth as well as their higher activity levels. Adding more dietary fat also increases the energy density of the diet. By increasing the energy density, the kitten or puppy is able to consume enough calories despite having a much smaller stomach than his adult counterpart.

Protein requirements for growing puppies and kittens are also higher than those for adults on maintenance diets. Protein is used not only for muscle tissue synthesis but also for bone and organ development. In puppy/kitten products, protein levels are typically several percentage points higher on a dry matter basis than those in adult commercial diets.

In general terms, puppies should be fed a commercial diet formulated for growth at least three times daily. Small-breed dogs should be fed a growth diet for 7 to 12 months and large-breed dogs for 12 to 16 months. Both small-breed and large-breed commercial growth diets are available, with each formulation containing different nutrients and nutrient densities. It is important to follow the manufacturer's guidelines for feeding.

Kittens should also be fed a commercial growth diet several times daily for the first year of life. Free-choice feeding is generally not an acceptable method of feeding and has been associated with juvenile obesity.

FEEDING SENIOR CATS AND DOGS

Senior animals can be defined as cats and medium-breed dogs older than seven years. In large- and giant-breed dogs, the classification of "senior" is often cut to five or six years to reflect these animals' generally shortened life span.

Currently, there are no AAFCO nutrient requirements for senior cats and dogs. However, senior diets typically have reduced sodium levels, are easier to chew and digest, and may or may not have higher protein levels to counteract the reduced ability to assimilate dietary protein. Thus commercial diets formulated for seniors are recommended by most veterinary clinical nutritionists. Large-breed senior diets include ingredients geared toward counteracting arthritis. To date, and with the exception of omega-3 fatty acids, the effectiveness of additives thought to slow arthritis has not been supported in research studies.

FEEDING RAW DIETS

Thanks to information spread on the Internet and in other lay publications, raw diets have gained much popularity. The American College of Veterinary Nutrition (ACVN) frowns on the practice of feeding raw diets to pets for safety reasons and because of the many unfounded and unproven claims propagated through various venues touting the benefits of such diets. One commonly held belief is that feeding fresh meats and vegetables enables the body to absorb the many delicate and undiscovered nutrients that are destroyed in the cooking or retorting process. Whether these undiscovered nutrients actually exist has yet to be determined.

Because domesticated pets have a life span more than twice as long as that of their feral counterparts, the necessity of feeding them a raw diet is arguable. Other sources claim that cats and dogs evolved to digest and process raw ingredients (not cooked); consequently, raw ingredients must be digested more efficiently than cooked ingredients. Numerous studies have determined that raw ingredients such as potatoes are actually more than 60 percent indigestible. Cooking helps break down the potato starch and other plant starches into forms that are more readily available and utilized by the body. With regard to meat, cooking helps to break down indigestible connective tissue surrounding muscle tissue, allowing for more efficient utilization of its nutrients. Granted, cooking destroys or reduces the activity of many vitamins and minerals. Manufacturers and food scientists account for this factor in the final commercial product by adding stabilizers that enable these nutrients to survive the cooking process.

In terms of safety, many raw-diet enthusiasts believe that dogs or cats have a natural ability to fend off pathogens. No studies exist demonstrating that dogs or cats are more resistant to pathogens than humans. Furthermore, no studies have shown that wild animals are more adept than domesticated animals in fending off food-borne pathogenic bacteria and parasites. Numerous case reports have documented that dogs and cats fed raw diets are highly susceptible to pathogenic bacteria such as *Salmonella* and *E. coli*. Often overlooked parasites such as tapeworms and roundworms, which may cause serious, life-threatening damage in animals and humans. For example, some forms of beef tapeworms can lead to the formation of giant cysts in the lungs and brains of humans. While U.S. Department of Agriculture (USDA) meat inspectors are veterinarians with advanced training in the recognition of parasites and pathogens, not every piece of meat sold can physically be inspected or otherwise tested for the presence of pathogenic bacteria and parasites, which is why cooking meat is strongly recommended.

A concern that most veterinarians and members of the ACVN have is that raw diets are generally unbalanced. Most raw diets are predominately meat based, and whole bones are added. Bones, by themselves, yield little calcium through digestion. Because meat is high in phosphorus and low in calcium, raw diets are generally calcium deficient. To offset this deficit, the body demineralizes the skeleton to liberate calcium, leaving a frail and brittle skeletal frame. Meat-based raw diets generally lack minerals, water-soluble vitamins, and fat-soluble vitamins. Thus, after a few months of being fed a raw diet, the most predominant clinical signs among cats and dogs are a poor and scruffy haircoat, skin lesions and hair loss, a weakened immune system, and poor muscle tone.[9] To date, a commercial vitamin "premix" has yet to be developed that offsets the vitamin and mineral deficiency that is observed with raw diets.

The content of raw diets is generally high in fat but contains only moderate to low amounts of protein. Raw meats generally have a high fat content, evident by excessive marbling—a function of consumer preference. The fat content in raw diets or pure fat (e.g., vegetable oils) feeding in general will support a "glossy" haircoat, which many raw feeders erroneously conclude is an indicator of health.

Some raw diet recipes include organ meats as a source of vitamins and minerals. It is true that organ meats such as liver and hearts have high mineral and vitamin content, but if animals are fed this items too frequently, toxicities can result. For example, liver has high concentrations of iron, copper, and fat-soluble vitamins. Feeding excessive amounts can cause serious clinical signs such as skin lesions, lethargy and collapse, black and tarry stools, and kidney failure.[6, 8]

Table 11.1
Dietary Resources for Pets

Manufacturer (Location of Headquarters)	Website	Types of Products
Freshpet (Secaucus, New Jersey)	www.freshpet.com	Fresh, pasteurized, shipped-frozen diets
Rayne Clinical Nutrition (Kansas City, Missouri)	http://raynenutrition.com	Fresh, high-tech, low-temperature-processed diets
General Mills (Minneapolis, Minnesota)	www.generalmills.com	Cereals and product information

Some commercial manufacturers have successfully developed and formulated raw diets that meet AAFCO allowances for maintenance. While such products can greatly reduce the incidence of nutrient toxicity or deficiency, the danger of communicating pathogenic bacteria and parasites to the pet and/or to the humans handling the final product persists. Some manufacturers attempt to address this issue by freezing the product in hopes of killing off the harmful bacteria. The reality is that many bacterial pathogens survive freezing.

The closest alternative to feeding your pet a raw diet is feeding it a pasteurized product. Freshpet and Rayne Clinical Nutrition (Table 11.1) offer balanced, pasteurized diets that not only are formulated to meet AAFCO allowances for all life stages, but also have passed AAFCO feeding trials. The products are flash pasteurized, cooled rapidly, and then refrigerated, or they have used technology that enables lower processing temperatures to be used than are required with conventional food-manufacturing methods. Ingredients such as green tea extract and lemon juice have been added to control microbial growth. Pasteurization uses one-third of the cooking temperatures compared to commercial canning or extruding process, while still effectively killing bacterial pathogens and parasites.

HOMEMADE DIETS

Since the pet food toxicity scandal of 2006, in which the addition of melamine to various pet foods resulted in thousands of pet deaths, many consumers have become mistrustful of commercial diets. Capitalizing on this fear, the number of homemade diet recipes exploded on the Internet, in magazines, and in other publications. The majority of these recipes, however, are unbalanced and propagate the same problems found with feeding raw diets in terms of nutrient toxicity or nutrient deficiency. A common belief is that adding vegetables to a recipe somehow balances the diet. In reality, adding vegetables of any combination to a generic homemade diet results in a diet deficient in many essential vitamins and minerals.

Another misconception is that a published diet can be tailored to a dog or cat of any size. In reality, nutrient requirements are different for the small dog relative to the large dog. Cats, for example, differ vastly in their energy requirements (obese versus thin). Thus a "one size fits all" recipe can potentially be dangerous, causing excessive weight gain or weight loss as well as vitamin and mineral deficiencies or excesses.

Several lay nutritionists have created well-developed and easy-to-use websites, offering nutrition consulting, ration-balancing services, and informative literature. It is important to thoroughly research these websites to determine what training (if any) these nutritionists actually have. The result may be surprising, despite the polished and professional appearance of the website. It is best if the nutritionist is a veterinarian with an in-depth knowledge of veterinary medicine and has also been trained in clinical nutrition so that he or she can identify the nutrients of concern according to what the pet needs. For example, the animal with an inflamed pancreas (pancreatitis) will have much different nutritional requirements than the healthy pet. While a lay nutritionist can only guess at the requirements, a clinical nutritionist has extensive knowledge of the requirements and is familiar with the latest research studies. The ACVN website (see the Further Reading section at the end of this chapter) has a list of approved and recommended clinical veterinary nutrition consulting services, which can help formulate a custom homemade diet for any pet with any normal or abnormal clinical condition.

OBESITY

Prevalent in humans, obesity is one of the leading health concerns for veterinarians as well, who also see this condition all too frequently in their animal patients. An estimated 24 to 42 percent of all cats and dogs in the United States are overweight or obese. The advent of commercial balanced diets has eliminated the worry of feeding unbalanced diets. Nevertheless, because these diets are very energy dense, it is easy for the pet owner to fill a bowl without understanding how many calories the animal will consume relative to the pet's actual energy needs. Feeding guidelines are often written on the product label; however, pet owners often mistake a "cup" to be a regular 16-ounce cup, scoop, handful, or tumbler, instead of an 8-ounce baking cup. Commercial pet food may also seem less appetizing, monotonous, or boring to the pet owner, resulting in the feeding of numerous, energy-dense table scraps such as cheese, bacon, turkey, steak, and chicken.

Adding to the obesity syndrome are commercial treats that are designed to be highly palatable rather than nutritious. Two of the key nutrients driving palatability for the dog include sodium and fat; in other words, increasing either or both in treats adds to palatability. As a result, many more calories and sodium can be added to the pet's diet, similar to the phenomenon found in human fast food. Commercial treats are not marketed as a complete diet, so they do not have to be balanced or nutritious.

Obesity is now considered to be a multifaceted disease rather than a simple problem. Numerous studies have documented the effects of being overweight on life span, incidence of cancer, immune function, wound healing, joints, and chronic load stress, and the presence of other comorbidities such as diabetes in the cat and pancreatitis in the dog. In fact, the list of diseases exacerbated by obesity is enormous. Given these relationships, fat is no longer considered to be a benign storage of energy in the body. A host of inflammatory molecules are produced by the breakdown of fat, and these molecules have an additive effect on organs such as the pancreas, liver, heart, urinary tract, skin, and immune system. With increasing amounts of fat, it makes sense to assume that increasing amounts of inflammatory molecules will be produced.

Embarking on a weight-loss program for the pet can be a rather enjoyable experience for both the pet owner and the veterinarian. Prior to initiating such a program, the thyroid status of the pet (in dogs) must be evaluated and corrected if necessary, regardless of the animal's age. The most accepted and safe way in which to promote weight loss is to feed a diet that has been formulated for weight loss. Commercial over-the-counter (OTC) diets intended for weight management are not formulated for weight loss. The most successful strategy in weight reduction in the obese animal includes feeding a diet high in protein and restricted in fat. If the amount of food fed to the pet is simply restricted using a regular commercial diet or a weight-management OTC diet, the pet will lose both fat and lean muscle tissue; moreover, she will not receive the optimal amounts of nutrients. In therapeutic diets, protein levels and other nutrients have been enhanced to help maintain lean muscle tissue through the transition of weight loss. Therapeutic diets intended for weight loss are also restricted in fat, and some offer enhanced fiber content to promote satiety. Because fat is easily assimilated and stored in the body, it is very difficult to promote weight loss without restricting fat.

Many veterinarians have sophisticated weight-management software. These software programs calculate energy needs for weight loss based on more optimal body weights and then determine how much of a particular diet to feed the animal based on those needs. The results can be displayed graphically at every visit. In this author's experience, these programs are sorely underused.

Regardless of availability of software, the most essential component of a weight-loss program is continual and regular rechecks. In this author's experience, more than 90 percent of pets achieved successful weight loss when rechecks were scheduled for every 2 weeks. Beyond 2 weeks, successful weight loss was more difficult to achieve. Pet owners need to see that what is being fed is working or not working. If the pet has not lost weight over a period of two to three visits, it becomes essential to determine whether any confounding variables—such as leftover food, children, family members, outside food sources, or treats—are at play. If no confounding variables are present, the energy needs need to be reduced by 10 to 20 percent and body weight reevaluated in 2 weeks. The process of digestion is an energy-consuming event. Thus feeding the same amount of food three times daily versus twice daily allows for more calorie consumption.

It is important to emphasize that OTC treats often are a hidden source of calories, with a large percentage of their calories being derived from fat. Very few low-calorie OTC treats exist. The palatability of OTC treats creates moments of perceived satisfaction for both the pet and the owner; consequently, pets are often given too many treats per day despite being fed a correct amount of therapeutic food formulated for weight loss. Some widely available alternative low-calorie palatable treats include Cheerios and Kix cereals, popcorn, green beans, and therapeutic treats formulated to be fat and calorie restricted. For some dogs, simply removing a portion of kibble from the daily amount of kibble to be fed and placing it in a treat jar is sufficient to create the effect of a treat.

Exercising and altering the feeding method can enhance weight loss. It is difficult to make cats exercise, yet some pet owners have been successful in using laser lights and various toys to stimulate movement. For cats that are unwilling to move, it is essential to recheck them frequently to determine if their energy needs should be reassessed. In dogs, exercise is much more practical, although caution should be emphasized in grossly obese pets. Grossly obese dogs are susceptible to heat exhaustion, circulatory and pulmonary failure, and limb injury during exercise.

In multiple-pet households, obesity management can be extremely difficult. In the multiple-cat household, the therapeutic diet may be placed within reach of all cats and the regular diet on higher surfaces. If the obese cat has no limitations on jumping, then placing the regular diet in a box with a hole small enough to exclude the obese cat is sometimes sufficient. In the multiple-dog household, it is important to meal-feed all members. It is best to feed the obese dog away from the other pen mates. When all are finished, the bowls should be removed before the obese dog is allowed to interact with his non-obese counterparts.

If weight-loss software is not available, the veterinarian can calculate energy needs for weight loss by determining the pet's resting energy requirements (RER) at ideal body weight. Many formulas to calculate RER exist, but tables are often displayed in pet food product guides. The amount of calculated calories can then be divided by energy density (kilocalories per cup) of the food being used. It is important to not overly restrict the amount of calories in dogs and cats. In cats, aggressive restriction of calories results in excessive fat mobilization, which causes liver dysfunction; known as hepatic lipidosis, this condition can be a serious medical condition. In dogs, aggressive restriction of calories results in excessive weight loss, making the dog more susceptible to rebound weight gain. Thus, for both species, 1 to 2 percent weight loss per week is considered safe.

FEEDING YOUR PET

When feeding puppies and kittens, meal feeding several times daily (two to three times daily) is considered the best schedule. Pouring out kibble once daily (free choice) has been associated with obesity and digestive disorders. Feeding instructions are provided on every bag or can of pet food. The amount recommended of dry diet per day is based on a measured 8-ounce cup. Often, pet owners mistake a glass or tumbler as a cup, which in turn provides the pet with three to five times her daily energy need.

DOES YOUR PET NEED SUPPLEMENTS?

Hundreds of supplements exist on the veterinary market. If you are feeding your pet a high-quality commercial diet, then supplements are generally unnecessary. If you believe that a supplement is needed, then the amount of nutrients in each supplement must be added to the nutrients already provided by diet. This sum (nutrients in the diet plus nutrients in the supplement) must be compared to the AAFCO or NRC guidelines to ensure that toxic amounts are not reached. Some supplements contain ingredients that have not been studied in small animals and can actually be toxic. As a general rule, avoid using supplements unless you are specifically directed to do so by a licensed veterinarian.

HOW TO BUY THE RIGHT PET FOOD

With more than 500 types of commercial diets on the market, choosing a diet can be a daunting task. When choosing a diet the following issues should be considered:

- Has the diet been through AAFCO feeding trials, and where does the manufacturer get its commodities (ingredients)?
- Who provides the company's scientific direction, and does it employ veterinary clinical nutritionists to help guide its formulations?
- Does the company have a toll-free number that you can call for technical help?
- If a toll-free helpline is available, what are the qualifications of the person who answers the calls? Is he or she a veterinarian? Where did the person get his or her nutrition training?
- Does the company promote more than just its name? Is it involved in other programs designed to promote animal health and welfare?
- How many times has the company had quality-control issues such as bacterial contamination recalls?

These are some of the questions that you should ask versus being cowed by fancy packaging and misleading labeling statements.

REFERENCES

1. Association of American Feed Control Officials (AAFCO). *Association of American Feed Control Officials: Official Publication*. Oxford, IN: AAFCO; 2008.

2. Crane, S. W., E. A. Moser, C. S. Cowell, et al. "Commercial Pet Foods." In *Small Animal Clinical Nutrition*, 5th ed., edited by M. S. Hand, C. D. Thatcher, R. L. Remillard, et al. Topeka, KS: Mark Morris Institute; 2010: 157–90.

3. Gross, K. L., R. M. Yamka, C. Khoo, et al. "Macronutrients "In *Small Animal Clinical Nutrition*, 5th ed., edited by M. S. Hand, C. D. Thatcher, R. L. Remillard, et al. Topeka, KS: Mark Morris Institute; 2010: 49–105.

4. Garrett, R. H., and C. M. Grisham. *Biochemistry*, 3rd ed. Boston, MA: Thomson Brooks/Cole; 2005.

5. Wedekind, K. J., L. Kats, S. Yu, et al. "Micronutrients: Minerals and Vitamins." In *Small Animal Clinical Nutrition*, 5th ed., edited by M. S. Hand, C. D. Thatcher, R. L. Remillard, et al. Topeka, KS: Mark Morris Institute; 2010: 107–148.

6. National Research Council (NRC). "Vitamins." In *Nutrient Requirements of Dogs and Cats*. Washington, DC: National Academy Press; 2006:193–245.

7. Morris, J. G., and Q. R. Rogers. "Comparative Aspects of Nutrition and Metabolism of Dogs and Cats." *Waltham Symposium* 7 (1989): 35–66.

8. National Research Council (NRC). "Minerals." *Nutrient Requirements of Dogs and Cats*. Washington, DC: National Academy Press; 2006: 145–92.

9. Taylor, M. B., D. A. Geiger, K. E. Saker, et al. "Diffuse Osteopenia and Myelopathy in a Puppy Fed a Diet Composed of an Organic Premix and Raw Ground Beef." *Journal of the American Veterinary Medical Association* 234 (2009): 1041–48.

FURTHER READING

M. S. Hand, C. D. Thatcher, R. L. Remillard, et al., eds. *Small Animal Clinical Nutrition*, 5th ed. Topeka, KS: Mark Morris Institute; 2010.

Nutrient Requirements of Dogs and Cats

American Academy of Veterinary Nutrition: www.aavn.org
Association of American Feed Control Officials: www.aafco.org

12

Pets and Disasters

Garry G. Goemann, DVM, MPH

A disaster is defined as "a calamitous event, especially one occurring suddenly and causing great loss of life, damage, or hardship, such as a flood, airplane crash, or business failure."[1] The loss of a family pet may not be as dramatic an event as the great loss of human life that occurs in disasters of the magnitude of Hurricane Katrina or the Haitian earthquake (the latter considered the largest humanitarian loss in the history of the world to date), but even the loss of one pet can greatly affect our lives. While few of us will ever encounter large-scale disasters, the loss of a single pet in a house fire or through an open fence gate leading to permanent loss of that beloved pet are forms of animal disasters that can be just as devastating to an individual or family as a large-scale natural disaster.

Disaster responders know that disaster victims will most likely be on their own for the first 72 hours following an incident. While help may arrive before then, especially when response teams have been pre-deployed to a disaster area, such as in the case of an approaching hurricane, the standard suggestion is to be prepared to be on your own for a minimum of 72 hours. Initial response efforts must be directed toward injured victims. This chapter focuses on both the human and animal victims who have survived the disaster and must maintain themselves until help arrives, or who have evacuated the disaster area and must support themselves during this initial period.

The greatest percentage of disasters likely encountered by pets are those occurring in and around the home, including human-made disasters related to such things as rat poison, snail bait, and confrontation with automobiles. While the discussion in this chapter is directed toward animal planning and preparation for a major disaster, the same steps will enable a pet owner to prevent or survive an emergency or disaster of lesser proportions.

Two basic types of disasters are distinguished: natural disasters and human-made or human-origin disasters. Natural disasters include events such as hurricanes, tornadoes, earthquakes, and wildfires started by lightning. These types of disasters may or may not be preceded by warning signs and a period of time to plan, prepare, or react. Certain natural disasters occur with little to no warning, such as earthquakes, and allow no time for planning or preparation.

Human-made disasters include events such as terrorism attacks, dam ruptures, structure failures, and wildfires started by human acts. With disasters of this type, individuals may or may not have time to prepare for or react to them. A disaster such as a collapsing dam may be preceded by structural signs of impending failure, providing some form of warning prior to the actual dam failure, or the dam collapse may occur immediately due to structural failure. An act of terrorism such as the attack on the World Trade Center provides no warning at all. Given that both natural and human-made disasters may not be preceded by any warning, it is important to plan ahead for either.

WHY INCLUDE ANIMALS IN DISASTER PLANNING?

The psychological effect of the human-animal bond, or human-animal interdependent relationship, has been well documented. It has been shown to have a profound effect on children, adults, seniors, and families.[2] This relationship between humans and their pets has tremendous implications in disasters and disaster response. A Canadian study showed that dog owners with high levels of human social support were significantly less lonely than non-pet owners with high levels of human social support.[3] Grief counselors have documented that the grief from separation or from not knowing the fate a lost pet can be equal to or greater than that experienced when a human loved one dies.[4] Sebastian Heath, in his book *Managing Animals in Disasters*, noted that 8.7 percent of people failed to evacuate in the 1997 Arboga Flood (Marysville, California), either because they were unable to evacuate to shelters with their animals or because they lacked proper equipment to evacuate their animals out of the flood zone. This equated to nearly 10,000 people.[5]

Such research emphasizes the profound influence that the relationship between people and pets can have on disaster evacuation and response. This relationship between human and animal has not only been shown to affect the evacuation of people before and immediately after a disaster, but is also a factor in people returning to a disaster site, often before the area has been approved for their return, to search for their pets or to retrieve, feed, and water those animals they left behind.

The importance of planning and preparation for animal care in case of a disaster cannot be overstated. Disaster response failures are generally a failure of planning or of failure to follow the operational plan. This chapter discusses the full range of planning—from the most common, least complex disasters to the largest and most complex disasters.

ASSESSMENT

Assessment is the basis upon which a disaster plan is developed and the first step in disaster planning. Assessment is the act of evaluating the surrounding environment and determining the conditions and items that are likely to either cause a disaster situation or affect the ability to evacuate or respond to the effects of a disaster. Risk assessment includes considering the likelihood of what can happen and where. It determines which disasters are the most important to plan and prepare for. Although it might seem obvious which large disasters might affect a community or state, often there are potential disasters, or risks, lurking daily in the immediate environment that are less conspicuous as risks or threats or possible hazards.

Assessment begins by dividing the environment into segments and determining their components, considering the possible threats within each. These various environments range from micro-environments, such as a dog run, a laundry room, or other place in the home where a pet is kept in a tightly isolated space, to the environment of communities, resident states, and potentially the entire country.

It is important not to overlook the home micro-environment where the family and pets spend the greatest percentage of time, as it is the site where the chance of a disaster occurring is greatest. Chemicals and toxins that may reside in garages or laundry rooms and yards may prove to be the cause of a disaster when encountered and possibly ingested by pets. The illness or loss of a family pet initiated by ingestion of these potentially dangerous items would be a devastating disaster to an individual or a family. Maintenance of fences or electronic fence systems is another critical consideration in disaster planning and preparation involving animals. Gate locks can prevent the accidental release of a pet.

The neighborhood or community is the next larger segment of the environment. Assessing the risks of the neighborhood or local community is an important part of a disaster plan. For a person living within the community, it is likely that the disaster potential existing on a daily basis will go unrecognized. A good primary resource for community assessment is local and state emergency management agencies. Risk assessments are part of these agencies' planning process, and much of the information sought on an individual level may be already available from these sources. This information can serve as an excellent foundation for developing an assessment for home and family.

It is usual to accept the environment for what it is and to not aggressively search out the potential risks that businesses and industries within the community pose. Nuclear and gas-fired power plants, for example, pose inherent hazardous risks to their local communities. Other potential risks in the community include chemical plants, processing plants (even something that may appear as innocuous as a grain elevator), fertilizer manufacturing plants, and fertilizer distribution facilities.

The geographic demographics of the community play a great role in the type of disaster that can occur in a community. The area of the country where one resides will predicate the kind of major disasters that are likely to occur. For example, Great Plains communities have little likelihood of being directly affected by a hurricane, although they could experience increased rainfall and flooding in the aftermath of such a storm. Coastal areas are less likely to be affected by forest fires, although some areas of Florida are routinely involved with wildfires spreading across the landscape. These examples show how the diversity of the geographical landscape can affect the type of disaster that might occur in an area.

Physical demographics of a region are also important. Air routes, landing approaches, and take-off patterns to an airport, with planes passing overhead at decreased altitudes, will increase certain risks to the community. These air traffic patterns can also produce loud noises that can frighten pets, especially new pets, provoking them to run and possibly escape.

Railroads running through the community and the environment surrounding the railroad tracks present additional factors to be considered in risk assessment. Train routes often border streams and rivers, which can increase the environmental impact on a community should an accident or toxic spill occur. A toxic spill into a waterway could extend the impact to a downstream community. Transport of toxins, chemicals, nuclear waste, and explosives through a community can affect large numbers of people should an accident or intentional release occur. In addition, interstate highways and local highways with heavy truck traffic present threats to communities. All of these routes of transportation bring potential hazardous risks through communities on a daily basis, which can make assessment much more difficult.

Pipelines and large power lines crossing the community can present additional risks. These structures may also influence the routes by which one might leave a community in the event that evacuation becomes necessary. Such structures can be damaged by earthquakes, tornadoes, and hurricanes, or even terrorist attacks—just a few of the many potential disaster scenarios.

While assessing the community, it is important to pay attention to the travel routes of ingress and egress, especially those that contain bridges crossing streams or rivers, those that traverse adverse environments such as steep canyons that could become impassable as a result of torrential rains or an earthquake, and those that could be affected in other ways, such as by fallen power lines or large fires. Assessing the evacuation routes to determine safe options is important in case evacuation become necessary, as well is identifying refuge destinations such as safe shelters or lodging for family and pets. The disaster kit or cache—a supply of items needed at the time of evacuation or a disaster—is discussed later in this chapter; it should include a list of shelters options and available lodgings.

An additional component of assessment is having a discussion with the family veterinarian during the pet's annual visit. Any special needs for pets or special medications necessary for transport should be determined with the veterinarian's assistance. These items should be included in a pet first-aid kit, which would also be a part of the disaster kit.

PLANNING

After the assessment of the home, community, and state has been completed, it is time to start developing a plan. The best response to any disaster occurs when one has a plan, and the best plan for dealing with pets in any disaster is for owners to take the pets with them when evacuating or to keep their pets with them and under control if sheltering in place and not evacuating. Evacuating with one's pets should be done whether the departure is anticipated to last for only a few hours or several days. Do not leave pets behind unless it is the only possibility. Leaving food and water down for the animals will not suffice, and doing so puts the animals at great risk because the conditions in any disaster may change. An animal should not be left behind while chained up or locked in a cage. A hurricane may intensify or weaken, wildfires may switch directions, and earthquakes will typically have aftershocks that can cause additional damage. It is too late to plan in the midst of a disaster, and people put themselves and their pets in harm's way when they try to do so. A common mantra among first responders and disaster responders is that "the scene of the disaster is not the time to exchange business cards."

In the face of a disaster, people may make different decisions than they would normally make under less stressful situations. What seems an obvious choice to one family member during an event may not be so obvious a choice to another family member. At the time of a disaster or a pre-disaster evacuation, the stress level is very high, such that people may respond reactively and less rationally. Taking action is the proper response in a disaster rather than coming from a state of reaction. The same is also true of pet disaster responses. Pets are able to sense the anxiety of their owners and the situation, and they may also react with abnormal behaviors, such as biting at a familiar pet when stressed. Caution should always be exercised when dealing with animals during the time of an emergency or disaster; the environmental conditions have changed for them, just as they have changed for their humans.

The disaster plan should be dynamic and flexible, and should address all of the possible scenarios that were discovered while doing the assessment. For example, living in the Sacramento River Valley presents many possible scenarios. Winter and spring flooding occur with some regularity. In such events, residents are likely to evacuate to higher elevations in the Sierra foothills or up into the mountains. Earthquakes are also a common phenomenon in this area; depending on the epicenter, one might evacuate in a multitude of directions. Summer wildfires in the Sacramento River Valley, Sierra foothills, and the Sierra Mountains may preclude evacuation up into the hills. Each of these scenarios addresses a different possible disaster affecting the same location, yet the evacuation plan needs to be different for each, addressing any obstacles that may be presented by different disasters.

A planned evacuation should include the shortest route to the safest destination. Traffic, obstacles, and risks need to be considered when planning routes to the safest or declared location. For example, fuel must be considered, as supplies may not be readily available during an actual disaster. The plan should include primary and alternate evacuation routes. Knowing ahead of time where a place of refuge can be found will help to reduce stress. Thus arrangements with friends or relatives who are willing to shelter you and your pets are best made in advance. Given that multiple families may be evacuating to a safe relative's location, issues such as animal allergies and fear of pets must be considered for all parties concerned. Often local veterinarians will be familiar with the lodging chains that allow pets. Online searches can be made for pet-friendly hotel and motel chains, and many facilities that usually do not allow pets will alter their policies during disaster situations. (The Resources list at the end of this chapter includes some websites where you can find the locations of pet-friendly motels and hotels.) Consider the types of disasters you need to plan for, and then make plans for several safe, distant evacuation sites.

It is important that the plan not only address the possible disaster hazards, but also incorporate the daily activities of the family. The time and date when a disaster may strike are not predictable in most cases; therefore, the plan needs to address the whereabouts of all family members as well as their animals. Family members may be out of the house or out of the area when a disaster occurs. For instance, the hamster's location in the cage in a bedroom will not change, but the family hunting dog may be out with the father and children in the field when an incident occurs, making communication difficult.

Alternative evacuation plans for pets should be made for those situations when the owners are not home or are unable to evacuate their own pets; thus a neighbor or animal caretaker who is familiar with the pets should be included in the plan. Reciprocal agreements between neighbors may save the lives of the pets when the family is not home. Include a designated spot for notification when evacuating a neighbor's animal. It might consist of a note on a family bulletin board or a note taped on the most common entrance door. The selection of a designated phone number is discussed in the next section.

Be aware that the person evacuating or rescuing the pets may not be a family member or designated caretaker. The caretakers may not be able to reach the animals in an emergency, either. While it is advisable to evacuate with one's pets, some situations will not allow for that plan to be realized. In the case where someone unfamiliar is rescuing the pets, having a pet disaster kit and clear and complete instructions about the pets' care available can be very important. It may be days before owners are reunited with their pets, and it can be life threatening for pets to be without their medications or to be fed ingredients that might cause medical problems.

OUT-OF-AREA PHONE NUMBER

No matter what the plan is, it is recommended that a contact number be identified that all family members can call at the time of an emergency or disaster.

The number should have a different area code belonging to a close family member or friend. Choose a person who is more likely to be at home and able to be reached, rather than a young active family member who often is absent. Grandparents, aunts, and uncles are often good choices. This contact point should be someone who is accountable and will not become so stressed as to become nonfunctional at the thought of the loss of a family member or pet.

All members of the family should be familiar with the designated phone number, and young children who might not remember it should carry it with them or have it stored either in their personal emergency cell phone or in some secure place at their school or day care. There is a greater likelihood that a cell phone will be able to successfully call out of an area than a local number following a disaster. Also, if phones are down in the disaster area and the phone number is a local number, it is less likely that family members will be able to reach a common local number. Temporary cellular phone towers are available and can be quickly brought into service in a disaster area. A simple message posted to the common contact number that a family member is safe and a way to locate or contact that person will be a great comfort to other family members.

A common contact phone number is important when considering the pets of the family as well, and should be provided to any pet caretaker or friend who might care for them. Having such a number available also provides any caretaker or rescuer with information needed to assist them in reuniting the pet with the family. The contact number should be included as a secondary number on the pet's tags or collar. An inexpensive engraver, like that used to identify private property with driver's license numbers, can be used to inscribe contact phone numbers on the reverse side of an ID or rabies tag. If the animal is lost and later found, rescue organizations could use the number to notify the owner that the pet is safe and where to claim it. Planning ahead will alleviate situations where people have to search for their pets in multiple animal shelters because the owners were unable to get to their homes at the time of a disaster or their animal caretaker was unable to evacuate the pets for them.

Newly developed technology has created websites where individuals in a disaster can post information about their whereabouts. This technology also allows for searches for friends and relatives. Similar technology developed by www.petfinder.com was used after Hurricane Katrina to aid in reuniting pets with their owners.

If you reside in a multiple-family dwelling, notify the landlord and the other tenants of the existence of pets. Ideally, pet owners will have a relationship with someone nearby who could care for pets in the event of an emergency or disaster.

While some sources recommend placing stickers in an obvious place notifying emergency responders and disaster responders that there are animals in the house, the value of this practice is often disputed by first responders. Their reasoning is based on the fact that a sticker does not positively identify the pets in the household or let responders know that the pets are actually home. A first responder should never be asked to enter a dangerous situation to save an animal, yet most are also animal lovers and would do so if they were confident that an animal was involved in the event and at risk. Window stickers do not identify where the animals are in the house, or explain that the animals in the fenced backyard are not the animals that are listed on the sticker. The confusion surrounding placement of animal identification stickers on homes could result in injury to a first responder. In lieu of relying solely on such stickers, the best solution is to be a responsible pet owner and develop the best plan that results in the best possible outcome for the pet. Contact your local emergency responders to determine their preference regarding window stickers.

If evacuation is advised, it is always best to evacuate with pets and be safe rather than to risk injury by remaining in the disaster area. If evacuation is not possible because there is insufficient time to evacuate or no safe evacuation route is available, sheltering in place may be the only option. This strategy requires creating the safest environment possible. Sheltering in place is defined as remaining inside one's residence with the doors and windows sealed and the heating, air conditioning, and ventilation systems turned off, so as to avoid the introduction of smoke or toxic fumes when residents are unable to evacuate from a toxic environment.

Three important items helpful for sheltering in place are plastic sheeting or large plastic trash bags, towels or sheets, and duct tape. When sheltering in place, the duct tape can be used to tape over glass windows to prevent or minimize shattering and to seal windows and doorways with plastic sheeting to prevent the introduction of toxic elements from the outside environment. Towels and sheets should be packed into any frame or opening in the shelter structure. This strategy is used when toxic components in the environment preclude leaving the premises safely and it is not safe for rescuers to penetrate the environment. An overturned tanker car or semi-truck that has off-gassed and contaminated the air in a neighborhood is one example when sheltering in place may be required.

Of course, when the disaster has subsided, new dilemmas may be confronted. Regardless of the reason for the inability to evacuate, it may be necessary to survive for an extended period without normal services such as electricity, water, other energy sources, and communication resources. Food sources may not be available due to rushes on grocery outlets prior to, during, or immediately following a disaster, damage to the stores or sources, or supply transportation issues.

If a generator is available to provide temporary power, the preparedness planning should include storing sufficient fuel to run the generator for several days, whether it is run continuously or intermittently. Because most disasters are unpredictable, with insufficient time to gather fuel, food, and other provisions, it is necessary to maintain a constant backup supply. Ideally, this fuel supply should be rotated on a regular basis so that the fuel stays fresh. Additives may be used to extend the storage time for the fuel, but a rotational system would better ensure positive results.

DID YOU KNOW?

- Every environment contains the risk for several types of disaster threats, so disaster plans must be flexible.
- As many as 25 percent of human deaths in large disasters have been attributed to owners placing the care and safety of their pets above their own welfare.
- Your veterinarian is a great source of information about caring for your pet during a disaster.

Disaster plans should include a minimum of a seven-day food and water supply that is sustainable for both family and pets. If electrical power is lost, refrigeration is lost and freezer storage will be unavailable. Therefore, a food supply that will survive austere conditions and that can be prepared for consumption with available resources becomes necessary. The same considerations apply to pet food. The stress of a disaster, with or without evacuation, affects pets, and minimizing the effects on pets by doing whatever possible is important to keep animals comfortable and eating appropriately. Alternative food supplies should be considered. Be aware that open canned food will not store for normal periods without refrigeration. Greens and other fresh foods for pocket pets present similar problems, so having sustainable food, and having pets trained to eat a variety of foods so that they continue to eat even under abnormal conditions, is recommended. Testing different foods on pets preceding an event might help ensure that pets continue to eat and will reduce their stress level. This point is probably most important for cats and the exotic pets, but may also apply to some finicky dogs. Check with the pet's veterinarian before experimenting with different diets.

If evacuating to a public shelter, information regarding the location of pet-friendly shelters and co-sheltering sites can be obtained in advance from local or state emergency managers. The passage of the Pets Evacuation and Transportation Act of 2006 modified the Stafford Act so that state and local governments are now required to plan for household pets in a disaster. With proper plans enacted, the local government emergency management agency can be reimbursed for the cost of evacuation, sheltering, and veterinary care during a disaster that has received a Presidential declaration.[6] This law has encouraged states and local emergency management agencies to include pet evacuation and sheltering in their disaster plans. Supplies that are recommended to prepare for a disaster are discussed in the next section.

PREPARATION FOR A DISASTER

Once the plan has been developed, it is time to get prepared. Preparation means first reviewing the plan that has been developed and then determining what is needed when facing a disaster. A successful emergency plan requires gathering and organizing information, knowing where that information is stored and can be quickly accessed, obtaining the supplies necessary to maintain family and pets through the initial disaster period, and then being able to gather all of that information and the supplies in a very short period of time when faced with a disaster. This section outlines some of the things that need to be done to help ensure the survival of the family and pets during a disaster.

Develop and organize a list of entities that are important in planning for a disaster or evacuation so that when an impending disaster or threat looms, a list of contact phone numbers, email addresses, and physical addresses is easily accessible to assist you in your response to the disaster. This list should include any contact that could potentially assist in protecting the family and its pets, such as radio stations, emergency management agencies, hotels or motels on the evacuation route, the out-of-area phone number, and family and friend contact lists. The family list should include cell phone numbers and work phone numbers. It is important to have this contact information available so that in times of high stress you do not have to worry about remembering or gathering numbers. Keep a copy of these contacts in an easily accessible place, with additional copies placed with the disaster supply cache. It is also advisable to keep copies of the contact list and rabies certificates in each family vehicle.

Information regarding the identification of family pets should also be kept handy with the contact list. All family pets need to carry identification, and two forms of identification are best. One form should be a permanent form of identification, whereas the other may consist of a collar with identifying tags including contact information. The permanent identification should be one of two types: microchip or permanent tattoo. Microchips are available through most veterinary clinics and may be registered through the manufacturer or sponsor to identify the pet and provide contact information on a national level. The most current addresses and phone numbers should be updated with these sources. Most animal disaster response groups have microchip readers to identify animals and positively link the animal to an owner if information is current. Although the circumstances are often too hectic to scan each animal during initial triage, animals are usually scanned for a microchip when time allows, with workers then doing everything possible to reunite pets with their owners. It is important to be sure that the microchip number is clearly identified on all medical records and vaccination certificates. Tattoo identification can permanently identify a pet but may not be as readily traceable as the microchip in terms of reuniting the pet with the owner. Photos of the pet, including family members, should be included with the kit.

A copy of the pet's medical records may be obtained from the veterinarian and can be updated annually or at each visit. While the vaccination and laboratory record that is generally supplied by veterinarians for each pet gives basic information, it is advantageous to have a complete medical record available in case the pet develops any problems. Availability of a complete record is especially important for pets that have any medical problems and for senior pets. In Hurricane Katrina, several veterinary hospitals were completely destroyed and owners were unable to retrieve their pets' records. As most of the clients for these hospitals were affected by the disaster, if they did not have duplicate records they were forced into a situation of starting over with a new veterinarian to get the proper medications for their pets. While this situation was an extreme example of what could happen, it emphasizes the importance of keeping copies of records for pets. Failure to do so means not only a time delay in obtaining care for pets, but also additional costs. Records will expedite medication refills if necessary and make it easier to get the proper medication.

A signed letter authorizing treatment by a veterinarian or veterinary hospital should be kept with the pet disaster kit, and a copy given to any animal caretakers or neighbor who is designated to evacuate pets when an owner is not or cannot get home. This document should also contain a liability release for any caretakers, which can help eliminate any roadblocks for necessary treatment. Although reasonable treatment is certainly provided by veterinary responders to rescued or sheltered animals, knowledge that a pet is an owned animal and has paperwork including a release would provide the documentation needed to carry out advanced treatment when necessary and desired.

A minimum 14-day supply of any medications should be available at all times, along with a written copy of a pet's prescription. Allowing the prescription level to fall below a 14-day supply may mean that a pet may be off needed medications for a period of time if it is not possible to obtain a refill immediately. This cache of medications should also include a minimum of one or two doses of heartworm preventive medication and two doses of flea and tick preventive agents. Additional bathing may be required due to the disaster conditions or the evacuation site; thus additional flea and tick preventive applications may be required. If a pet is near the date when the next dose of medication is required, lack of a sufficient backup supply could mean that the pet goes through an unprotected period. In the case of the Gulf Coast, where hurricanes are the most likely disaster and the weather conditions predispose pets to exposure, preventive medications are even more important due to the exposure risk. Keeping current on vaccinations and prophylactic medications will further protect the pet if it becomes necessary to place the animal in a kennel or if the pet is housed in a sheltering situation where he is exposed to other animals with backgrounds of varying medical care.

Pets should be maintained in comfortable carriers or kept on a leash while evacuating or sheltering. Control of any pet is important, because companion animals may be exposed to other animals in stressful situations; fights and bites are not uncommon when many animals are sheltered in unfamiliar circumstances. Whenever possible, keeping animals under control with leashes or carriers will minimize confrontations. For this reason, leashes, collars, muzzles, and carriers should be part of the disaster cache. A properly fitting muzzle for each pet is recommended, as pets may bite when they are evacuated or rescued by someone with whom they are not familiar or when they are kept in a stressful, austere environment. Given this concern, you may also want to discuss with the pet's veterinarian the need for tranquilizing medication to reduce stress if necessary and to ensure such medications are part of the pet disaster kit.

THE PET EVACUATION KIT (CACHE)

The pet evacuation kit, or cache, should include a minimum of 7 days—and preferably 14 days—of food and water. Canned food should be of a size that does not provide more than one day's supply or even one meal's supply per can in case proper refrigeration is not available after the can is opened. A can opener for any canned foods is a must. A flashlight and a radio, with spare batteries for each, should be included as well. Chemical light sticks represent an alternative light source.

An emergency flashlight and emergency radio should also be part of the kit. These devices come in many configurations with multiple power sources including internal dynamo/crank power generators. (Many also have the capability to charge cell phones.) Such radios enable individuals to stay in touch with news sources that can provide information of human evacuee shelters, pet shelters, safe travel routes, and other disaster-related information. Sheltering organizations will typically broadcast the location of animal shelters through the media so that owners can be reunited with their pets as soon as possible.

Inexpensive inverters that safely convert direct current (DC) power from automobile batteries to alternating current (AC) power are now available and can be used to charge cellular phones, flashlights, and power computers. Sufficient fuel for a vehicle to recharge the car batteries must be available.

Personal items for the pet, such as familiar toys or blankets, will aid in reducing the animal's stress. Using the evacuation carriers as the pet's bed or shelter in the home prior to any event will familiarize the pet with it and decrease the stress.

Large-scale disasters can impose major financial problems on those in the disaster area. For this reason, it is recommended to keep some cash on hand for an emergency situation. This need was particularly evident following Hurricane Katrina, as many financial institutions were damaged or destroyed in the hurricane. Bank accounts were sealed until the institutions could get their computers and bookkeeping departments operational. People who had accounts in these institutions were also unable to use automated teller machines (ATMs) at any location because their bank's computer systems were offline and account information could not be accessed. This proved a great inconvenience and highlights the importance of having cash funds available at the time of an emergency or disaster. Cash might also be required to purchase pet supplies and care.

PREPARATION AND ISSUES FOR OTHER TYPES OF PETS

Exotic and pocket pets require special attention when preparing for and dealing with a disaster. Special attention must be paid to transportation and minimizing stress for the types of pets described in this section.

Birds

Minimizing stress and maintaining temperature control are the two most important points when evacuating or sheltering birds. Birds are best transported in small covered cages. Caution must be exercised to ensure that the bird has sufficient air flow and does not become overheated. In addition, steps must be taken to prevent the bird being exposed to cold weather and chilling drafts. Vehicles should be preheated prior to transport of birds in cold conditions. Birds should be returned to their normal-size cage in a quiet location after transport, but keeping the cage covered will help reduce stress. In large-scale disaster responses, avian rescue groups who are well experienced with handling and caring for birds often establish bird-friendly shelters to assist evacuees.

Sprinkler systems with backup power source are recommended for aviaries to minimize smoke and cool the environment. The best care can be given by the bird's owner, who knows the traits and habits of the bird; therefore, every effort should be made to evacuate the bird with the family. Medical records are important, because a negative test for psittacosis and tuberculosis may be required before a bird is allowed into a shelter, as these diseases may be transmissible to humans.[7]

Reptiles

Transport of reptiles may be accomplished in either a cloth bag or a small carrier, with the pet being returned to a cage after transport. The cage should be secure and, as with all exotic pets, planning for possible escape should be a consideration.

Encouraging elimination (defecation) prior to placing the animal in the transport container may be done by allowing the pet to soak in water. This should be done—but only if time allows—for snakes, lizards, and tortoises. Feeding reptiles may not be necessary during most evacuation time frames due to the normal eating habits of these pets. Food should be included in the pet evacuation kit, but reptiles should be fed only as necessary because feeding can increase stress and cause contamination of the pet's environment. The evacuation site environment should be as tightly controlled as possible, as well as quiet and free of traffic as possible.

Amphibians

Amphibians can be transported in plastic containers or watertight plastic bags. It is best to transport only one pet in each container. Amphibian pets are classified into aquatic (frogs) and semi-aquatic (salamanders) species. Aquatic pets can be easily transported in sealed plastic bags, provided these containers are opened occasionally to exchange the air in the bag. Semi-aquatic pets may be transported more easily in plastic containers, with a minimum of moisture provided via moistened paper towels or moss to prevent spillage. Fresh air exchange is accomplished by perforating the container around the upper surface, being careful not to create sharp edges on the interior surface of the container. The evacuation environment should be maintained as close to the pet's normal environment for temperature and humidity. As with all pets placed into a strange environment, keeping the pet in a quiet area with minimal traffic is advantageous.

Feeding amphibians may increase their stress level and contaminate the environment of the pet. Feeding should be minimized or eliminated for a reasonably short period, and a clean environment maintained to the extent possible.

Pocket Pets

One of the more important aspects of evacuating with pocket pets (e.g., rats, mice, hamsters, gerbils, ferrets, sugar gliders, hedgehogs) is ensuring that they are evacuated in a carrier that closes securely and that they are unable to open or chew through it. Because these animals are natural burrowers and chewers, there is an increased likelihood that pocket pets will attempt to escape when traveling or placed into an unfamiliar environment. As with all exotic pets, sufficient amounts of their normal food and supplements are required during the evacuation period. An additional need for most pocket pets is exercise equipment and toys to make their environment a little more like home.

PRACTICING THE PLAN

With the assessment completed, the plans written, and the preparation completed, it is now time to practice the plan. This is a very important step in the disaster management process, and the overall success or failure of the efforts can depend greatly on the practice of the plan.

Families can initiate the practicing of the plan by discussing some of the possible large- or small-scale scenarios that might exist in the home and community. Start by considering the threats in the home. Discuss simple mitigation techniques for both humans and pets. Teaching children what to do in case of an emergency can mean the difference between life and death. Knowing when to call 911, how to scale a rope ladder from a second-story window in case of a house fire, and how and when to "drop and roll" are essential to preserving life. It is also important to discuss these emergencies in relation to family pets. Repetition is important to thoroughly ingrain safety practices in all family members.

Human life should always take precedence over animal life, yet most individuals would probably do something careless and dangerous to rescue pets in an emergency or disaster situation. Rushing into a burning building to rescue a pet, venturing out onto thin ice to rescue a dog or deer that has broken through, and failing to evacuate a disaster situation because an owner either is unable to take the animals to a shelter or lacks equipment and methods to evacuate the animals are all frequently encountered examples of this tendency.

Practice is the hallmark of disciplined first responders. Indeed, it is this repetition of routine procedures that allows these individuals to respond to an event and perform these acts in the safest way they possibly can. Response must come from action, not reaction. When reacting to a situation, a knee-jerk or initial response does not always consider the best plan or the safest plan available. If the plan has been practiced, it is more likely to be followed and to be safe.

Discussing the plan at a family meeting is a starting point. Short and concise meetings are best. All members should have a copy of the family contact list and have memorized or have on their person the out-of-area contact phone number. The contact list should be carried in written form by each family member. Include the topic of pets in the discussion of the plan, and ensure that each person knows what he or she should do if that individual is the only family member home at the time of notification or occurrence of a disaster. Make family members aware of the location of both family and pet disaster kits and important papers for evacuation, at all times emphasizing that no risk should be taken to rescue family items or the pets in the case of imminent threat or danger.

The next step is to walk through an emergency or disaster event. Teach children how to dial 911 or how to use a feature that automatically dials this number. Point out the location of important papers, family and pet evacuation kits, gas and electrical shut-off, and other important locations in the residence. Small children should be shown important information and locations, and may require more repetition. Schedule "special" sessions for them to review procedures pertinent to them. Have sessions that deal with pet exclusive issues.

Table-top exercises can be used to review plans that address various situations. Using maps of the residence and maps of the area, the family can "walk through" various scenarios. This sort of practice allows for all family members to participate and give input or have questions answered regarding the plans. It should be recognized that *all* plans are dynamic, because changes in the environment may affect the plan in innumerable ways. Practicing the plan allows for recognition of these changes and identifies which elements need to be changed to keep a plan relevant. As the family ages, pets change, and the community changes, so will the plan.

Disasters large and small occur every day. This chapter is not meant to emphasize the dangers faced by families with pets in everyday life, but rather to celebrate the gift of pets and to help their owners minimize the effects of these disasters on families and pets alike. Whatever part of the outline is completed will make a difference. Moreover, the difference made by planning and practicing a plan ahead of time will minimize the detrimental effects of an incident and decrease the stress for both families and pets, whether evacuating or experiencing the force of the disaster.

DISASTER KIT (CACHE) FOR PETS

- Identification (collar with tags and tattoo or microchip)
- Documents
  - Medical and vaccination records
  - Proof of ownership
  - Contact list
  - Authorization for treatment for veterinarian
  - Liability release for animal caretaker
  - Instructions
    - Feeding
    - Medications
  - Evacuation route maps with pet-friendly shelters, motels, and hotels indicated
  - Current photos, ideally with family members
- Food, 14-day supply (manual can opener, can covers, utensils)
- Water, 14-day supply (gallon jugs, one gallon per day average)
- Food and water dishes, individual, non-spill preferred
- Blanket or mat
- Tie-out stakes, running lines
- Cages for each animal
  - Mandatory for cats, recommended for dogs (especially small dogs)
- Flashlights
  - Battery powered with spare batteries
  - Alternative-power emergency flashlight
- Radios
  - Battery powered with spare radios
  - Alternative-power emergency radio
- First-aid kit
- Litter box or disposable litter trays and litter for cat
- Personal items for pet
  - Collars, harness, leashes
  - Toys
  - Handling equipment
  - Muzzles as needed (for rescuers' use)
  - Heavy leather gloves for cats
- Cleaning supplies
  - Paper towels
  - Trash bags

Bird Addendum

- Proper diet and necessary supplements
- Temperature-control items
  - Hot-water bottles or bottles to fill with warm water when needed and available
  - Misters
- Cage covers
- Toys
- Perches and scratching items

Reptile Addendum

- Misters (spray bottle)
- Water container for soaking and cooling
- Heat source
  - Heating pad or battery-operated heat source

Amphibian Addendum

- Additional carrier for cleaning and in case of broken or leaking carrier
- Food as required

Pocket Pet Addendum

- Bedding materials
- Exercise equipment and toys

REFERENCES

1. Dictionary.com. Available at: http://dictionary.reference.com/browse/disaster

2. Delta Society. "Improving Lives Through Service and Therapy Animals." Available at: http://www.deltasociety.org/Page.aspx?pid=3153)

3. Duvall, A. "An Examination of the Potential Role of Pet Ownership in the Psychological Health of Individuals Living Alone." *Anthrozoos* 23 (2010): 37–54.

4. Schaffer, C. *Human Animal Bond Considerations During Disasters* [Lecture]. Integrated Medical, Public Health, Preparedness and Response Training from the Department of Health and Human Services, Dallas, TX, April 15, 2009.

5. Heath, S. E., S. Voeks, and L. Glickman. "A Study of Pet Rescues in Two Disasters." *International Journal of Mass Emergencies and Disasters* 18 (2000): 361–81.

6. United States Congress. Law 109-308, Pet Evacuation and Transportation Standards Act (PETS Act). *Congressional Record* 2006: 152. http://www.mwcog.org/security/security/otherplans/stafford.pdf

7. "Taking Care of Pets in Disasters." The City of Lewes: The First Town in the First State. Available at: http://www.ci.lewes.de.us/Taking-Care-of-Pets-in-Disasters

RESOURCES

Pet-Friendly Motels and Hotels

www.OfficialPetHotels.com
www.petswelcome.com

Animals in Disasters

American Veterinary Medical Association, "Saving the Whole Family": www.avma
.org/disaster/
Federal Emergency Management Agency: www.fema.gov/plan/prepare/
animals.shtm

Reptiles and Amphibians as Pets

http://animal-world.com/encyclo/reptiles/reptiles.htm

Tornado Safety

http://www.quakekare.com/emergency-preparedness/tornado- preparedness.html
?gclid=CMHf4LCH8J8CFQQNDQodlxn-XQ

Federal Emergency Management Agency (FEMA) Disaster Preparedness All-Hazards Preparedness Information

http://www.fema.gov/plan/index.shtm

Delta Society Human Animal Bond Resource Center

http://www.deltasociety.org/Page.aspx?pid=315

Index

About the Editor and Contributors

Editor

RADFORD G. DAVIS, DVM, MPH, DACVPM, has been a veterinarian for more than 20 years, practicing in small animal emergency medicine before taking a position at Iowa State University, College of Veterinary Medicine. Since 1998, Dr. Davis has taught and trained veterinary students, state and federal workers, and others in the fields of public health, zoonoses, bioterrorism, and One Health, with many publications in these same areas. Currently, he is active in improving animal and human health, alleviating hunger, and reducing poverty in developing countries around the world through the application of One Health concepts.

Contributors

KRISTINA D. AUGUST, DVM, graduated from Colorado State University, College of Veterinary Medicine, in 1991. She now owns a small-animal housecall practice in Iowa specializing in well care, preventive medicine, in-home treatment of chronic disease, and end-of-life care.

MELISSA CIPRICH, DVM, is a faculty member at the College of Veterinary Medicine at Iowa State University. Her focus is in spay/neuter education, clinical veterinary public health endeavors in the community, and public health in Native American communities.

CRAIG DATZ, DVM, MS, DABVP, DACVN, is an assistant professor and a clinical nutritionist at the College of Veterinary Medicine, University of Missouri in Columbia, Missouri. He has many years' experience in private practice, and currently teaches veterinary students about the art and science of veterinary medicine and surgery. He has written a number of articles, textbook chapters, and scientific papers.

SAGI DENENBERG, DVM, MACVSc (Veterinary Behavior), provides behavior referrals at the North Toronto Animal clinic in Thornhill, Ontario. Dr. Denenberg is a frequent lecturer in veterinary behavior and has many publications and book chapters in this field. Dr. Denenberg is a recipient of the American Veterinary Society of Animal Behavior Award for Excellence in Research of Animal Behavior.

GARRY G. GOEMANN, DVM, MPH, has been a veterinarian for more than 35 years and has been involved in disaster medicine and response for more than 15 years. He is currently the Team Commander of National Veterinary Response Team (NVRT) 5 and Regional Coordinator for the American Veterinary Medical Association's Veterinary Medical Assistance Team program. Dr. Goemann teaches bioterrorism, foreign animal disease, and veterinary disaster response training classes throughout the United States and has assisted in the development of several federal and state courses for veterinary responders. He has responded to more than major national disasters and events and received various rewards for disaster response, including the National Disaster Response System Team Member of the Year.

REBECCA A. JOHNSON, PhD, RN, FAAN, is the Director, Research Center for Human-Animal Interaction in the College of Veterinary Medicine, and the Millsap Professor of Gerontological Nursing and Public Policy in the Sinclair School of Nursing at the University of Missouri. She is also President of the International Association of Human Animal Interaction Organizations (IAHAIO). Dr. Johnson presents her research internationally on the subject of dog walking for health of humans and dogs, is the author of more than 30 peer-reviewed publications, and is the author and editor of two books (*Walk a Hound, Lose a Pound* and *The Health Benefits of Dog Walking*).

ELLEN LINDELL, VMD, DACVB, owns a private specialty practice in the New York area. She has published chapters in veterinary textbooks and lectured nationwide in the field of veterinary behavior.

ELISA M. MAZZAFERRO, MS, DVM, PhD, DACVECC, is the Director of Emergency Services at Wheat Ridge Veterinary Specialists in Wheat Ridge, Colorado. Her publications include "Emergency and Critical Care Procedures" in Kirk and Bistner's *Handbook of Emergency Treatment* and "Emergency and Critical Care" in *Clinical Companion to the Five Minute Consult*.

JEFFREY L. RHODY, DVM, is owner and chief veterinarian of the Lakeside Veterinary Center in Laurel, Maryland. His caseload includes many small-mammal patients, including rabbits, ferrets, rodents, sugar gliders, and hedgehogs. He is an active member of the Association of Exotic Mammal Veterinarians.

NANCY SCANLAN, DVM, MSFP, CVA, is past president of the Veterinary Botanical Medical Association, past president and current full-time executive director of the American Holistic Veterinary Medical Association (AHVMA), and editor of the AHVMA's *Journal*. The author of *Complementary Medicine for Veterinary Technicians and Nurses,* Dr. Scanlan is a certified veterinary acupuncturist.

MARK B. TAYLOR, MA, DVM, is a botanist and veterinary ultrasonographer who is soon to be board certified in the field of veterinary nutrition. Dr. Taylor has publications in both botany and veterinary medicine and currently works as a mobile veterinary ultrasonographer in south Florida.

NIKLOS WEBER, DVM, DABVP (Avian, Canine, and Feline), is the owner of a specialty veterinary hospital in Northern California and has been a small-animal and exotic pet veterinarian since 1995. Dr. Weber is the author of numerous articles in peer-reviewed veterinary journals and also researches homing pigeon exercise physiology.

DANIELLA R. YAAKOV, DVM, is head of the pet exotics medicine department at the Koret School of Veterinary Medicine, Hebrew University, Israel.